The Collapse of Communist Power in Poland

The collapse of communist power in Poland in 1989 was unforeseen and unexpectedly sudden. Based on extensive original research, including interviews with key participants, this book examines the process whereby the Communist Party lost power. It sets out the sequence of events and examines the strategies of various Communist Party players both before and during the Round Table negotiations with Solidarity in the spring of 1989.

This volume argues that the specific negotiating strategies and institutional arrangements agreed by the communist party representatives in the Round Table discussions before the partially free elections in June were key factors in communism's collapse. In tracing the gap between what the PZPR (Communist Party) expected in each bargaining scenario and the actual outcome, Hayden assesses the evidence to determine whether the party members were far-sighted strategists attempting to control and shape the process of democratic transition in Poland, or whether they were caught up in a set of dynamic circumstances where strategic mistakes produced unexpected political results.

This book shows that on many occasions, PZPR decision-makers ignored expert advice, and many Round Table bargains went against the party's best interests. Using in-depth interviews with key party players, including General Jaruzelski, General Kiszczak and Mieczysław Rakowski, as well as Solidarity advisors such as Adam Michnik, *The Collapse of Communist Power in Poland* provides a unique source of first-hand accounts by key players in Poland's revolutionary drama.

Jacqueline Hayden is a lecturer in politics at the Department of Political Science, Trinity College, Dublin. She worked as a current affairs journalist and radio producer for 15 years before completing her PhD in 2002. Her previous books include *Poles Apart: Solidarity and the New Poland* (Dublin: Irish Academic Press, 1994) and *Lady G: A Biography of the Honourable Lady Valerie Goulding LLD* (Dublin: Townhouse Press, 1994).

The Collapse of Communist Power in Poland

Strategic misperceptions and unanticipated outcomes

Jacqueline Hayden

Routledge
Taylor & Francis Group

LONDON AND NEW YORK

First published 2006
by Routledge
2 Park Square, Milton Park, Abingdon, Oxon OX14 4RN

Simultaneously published in the USA and Canada
by Routledge
270 Madison Ave, New York, NY 10016

Routledge is an imprint of the Taylor & Francis Group

© 2006 Jacqueline Hayden

Typeset in Times New Roman by
Newgen Imaging Systems (P) Ltd, Chennai, India
Printed and bound in Great Britain by
Biddles Ltd, King's Lynn

British Library Cataloguing in Publication Data
A catalogue record for this book is available
from the British Library

Library of Congress Cataloging in Publication Data
A catalog record for this book has been requested

ISBN 0–415–36805–7

Contents

Preface

Why did the Polish communist party (PZPR) lose power over the summer of 1989? The starting point of this volume is the fact that, heretofore, there has been no satisfactory answer to this question. It is an important question which goes beyond the specific context of the collapse of communism in Poland to the underlying causes of regime change as a phenomenon. Understanding what caused the Polish communist party to collapse is not only challenging in the context of theories of stability and change but it is also challenging because of the effect of the Polish collapse on the process of change in the rest of Eastern and Central Europe in 1989.

This volume is the product of a 25-year association with Poland which began when I was lucky enough to be sent to Poland in July 1980 by an Irish newspaper, *The Irish Press*, which wanted copy on the new Polish Pope and on the impact of his pontificate on his native country. On my arrival in Warsaw, I made my way to the homes of a list of dissident contacts and was lucky enough to be generously welcomed by Jan Lityński and Krystyna Lityńska. Jan was a prominent dissident, editor of *Robotnik* (*The Worker*), an underground newspaper published by KOR (Workers' Defence Committee). Over the course of the next month, I travelled all over Poland with Jan as strikes started in various factories, and was eventually invited to a planning meeting of the Free Trade Unions of the Coast in the company of Lech Wałęsa and the rest of the committee on the eve of the start of the Gdańsk shipyard strike that was to launch the Solidarity trade union, Solidarność.

I stayed in touch with the Polish story and with my Polish friends throughout the 1980s. In 1989, by then working for Irish radio, I covered the semi-free elections in June and began gathering the in-depth interviews with key players from both the PZPR and the Solidarność-led opposition that would form the basis of this current volume. However, the primary source on which the analysis is based derives from a series of interviews conducted with key communist party actors. The interviews were mainly conducted in Poland during 1999 and 2000. Several key figures were interviewed on more than one occasion. The analysis is also based on an examination of Politburo records, contemporary documents as well as the research of other scholars.

Given the fact that neither the PZPR nor the opposition Solidarity trade union, Solidarność, anticipated the fall of communism at the outset of the Round Table process in February 1989, the big question is what explains the collapse of the party's hegemony so shortly after its negotiators had concluded a deal with Solidarność that they thought would enable the communist government to continue business as usual and carry out its economic reform programme. It is an important question because even a cursory examination of the deals agreed at the Round Table indicates that PZPR negotiators appeared to have adopted positions and strategies during the negotiating process that resulted in far from optimal institutional arrangements and outcomes for the party. So, if it is assumed that the PZPR were rational and strategic actors and did not deliberately decide to hand power over to the Solidarność-led opposition, the question is what explains the behaviour and strategic choices that brought about the collapse of the party's power?

This volume examines a range of Round Table bargaining scenarios in order to track the gap between the communist party's strategic intention and the actual institutional outcome. Adam Przeworski[1] and Josep Colomer[2] have offered conflicting accounts of the motivation of regime liberalizers during the periods of political crisis. Przeworski emphasizes the role of strategic mistakes and chaos in facilitating regime change, while Colomer argues that regime liberalizers may behave non-myopically, in other words, may look forward to long-term political and other goals, especially at the outset of the process of change. This volume focuses on the Round Table process and adopts an analytic narrative[3] approach which allows for a tractable and explicit analysis of the intentions and strategic behaviour of PZPR negotiators. Crucially, it separates intention from actual behaviour and, by applying a rigorous standard of rationality, makes it possible to identify where the outcome was not the one intended by actors.

The application of a theoretically driven analysis has shown conclusively that Polish party reformers were rational and strategic in intent when they initiated the consultation process with the Solidarność-led opposition. The evidence shows that negotiators did not perceive themselves to be relinquishing power. It is also clear that this rational intent predisposed party reformers to prefer a 'broadened dictatorship', as outlined by Przeworski, or an 'intermediate regime', as specified by Colomer, but not an immediate transition to democracy. While it is evident that some PZPR players anticipated that the process of democratic change might be faster than the competitive elections planned for 1993, the dominant view was that the deal represented a breathing space in which the party could prepare itself for competitive politics in the future. Solidarność's weakness in the period prior to the Round Table was the communist party's opportunity to reach an agreement that would retain maximum incumbent power.

In the context of whether PZPR negotiators were non-myopic and far-sighted in their strategic behaviour before and during the Round Table, though the analysis confirms the fact they were rational in intent prior to the start of the process, it has also conclusively been shown that party negotiators made mistakes in the conduct of the bargaining over institutions. Their consistent failure to ensure that they had reliable information about the institutional choices they were making tends to confirm Przeworski's contention that democratic transition follows from the mistakes of regime liberalizers who seek 'broadened dictatorship'.

This process-driven account relies on a thin or minimal conception of rationality to track the gap between ideal, formally rational behaviour and the historical reality of the PZPR's actual behaviour during the course of its Round Table negotiations. It has proved a useful heuristic in the analysis of a complex set of events where elite actors engaged in a round of bargaining over institutions such as the proposed electoral system that created its own dynamic. The analysis has conclusively shown that over a range of bargains and scenarios, the PZPR's strategies produced unanticipated outcomes. These outcomes could have been anticipated had party negotiators sought out up-to-date information in relation to a range of institutional choices and had they listened to the advice of sympathetic advisers.

Not only is it the case that the PZPR's misperceived strategies produced an unanticipated outcome, but it is also arguable that the failure to update information is the key to any explanation of the collapse of communist power in Poland in 1989. It is plausible to conclude that rationally intentioned PZPR actors with up-to-date information would not have negotiated the suboptimal institutional bargains agreed at the Round Table and may not, as a consequence, have lost power in the dramatic way they did following the June elections. Clearly, perfect information had the potential to change the course of the history of both Poland and the rest of Eastern Europe.

Notes

1 A. Przeworski, *Democracy and the Market*, Cambridge: Cambridge University Press, 1991.
2 J. M. Colomer, *Strategic Transitions: Game Theory and Democratization*, Baltimore, MD and London: The Johns Hopkins University Press, 2000.
3 R. H. Bates, A. Greif, M. Levi, J. L. Rosenthal and B. R. Weingast, *Analytic Narratives*, Princeton, NJ: Princeton University Press, 1998.

Acknowledgements

This book would not have been possible without the advice and support of Krystyna Lityńska and Jan Lityński. In July 1980 they offered both hospitality and the opportunity to meet their fellow dissidents, trade unionists and future Solidarność leaders. Later on, with their help, I began to meet senior communist leaders and subsequently the leaders of the post-communist SdRP (now the SLD).

The most important influence on this book has been the seminal work of Adam Przeworski and Josep Colomer who lead the field in the analysis of regime change and transition. I am indebted to Michael Laver for pointing me in a fruitful theoretical direction; his advice, in relation to both methodology and theory building, has been most productive. I am also grateful to him for his careful reading and comments on the first draft of this text. R. J. Hill has been a constant source of knowledge and advice and has been generous with his time. Kenneth Benoit read a number of early drafts and offered sound advice on methodological matters. Michael Marsh read the first draft and gave useful advice.

Jerzy Wiatr has been extremely generous with his time. Since 1989, he has provided lengthy interviews on a number of occasions and read the first draft of this volume. His comments and suggestions were all helpful. I am particularly grateful to him for his encouragement over the years. Stanisław Gebethner, Piotr Winczorek and Jacek Raciborski were enormously knowledgeable in relation to the institutional bargaining at the Round Table.

The main source for this volume is a series of interviews with former members of the PZPR. In particular, I would like to thank the following: General W. Jaruzelski, General C. Kiszczak, Stanisław Ciosek, Mieczysław Rakowski, Janusz Reykowski, Jan Bisztyga, Andrzej Werblan and Sławomir Wiatr. However, while the focus here is on the PZPR, the analysis would not have been possible without the insights of opposition dissidents, Solidarność activists and Polish scholars. I would like to thank all of them for their time, insights and advice. In particular, I would like to thank the following: Lech Wałęsa, Adam Michnik, Bronisław Geremek, Janusz Onyszkiewicz, Lech Kaczyński, Jarosław Kaczyński, Bogdan Borusewicz, Alina Pieńkowska, Ludka Wujec and Grażyna Staniszewska.

The late Fr Józef Tischner provided invaluable insights into the motivation of players on both sides of the Round Table.

I would also like to sincerely thank Anna Gwiazda for her generous help with translation and proofing. Jane O'Mahony has been a constant support. I would also like to thank Frank, Ben and Charlotte Clarke for their wholehearted support and patience while I pursued this research.

I would also like to thank Ms Nina Smolar of Aneks for permission to include documents published in Tajne dokumentry Biura Politycznego.

Abbreviations

KC	Komitet Centralny (Central Committee)
KC PZPR	Komitet Centralny Polskiej Zjednoczonej Partii Robotniczej (Polish United Workers' Party Central Committee)
KOR	Komitet Obrony Robotników (Worker's Defence Committee)
NSZZ Solidarność	Niezależne Samorządne Związki Zawodowe Solidarność (Independent Self-Governing Trades Union Solidarity)
OPZZ	Ogólnopolskie Porozumienie Związków Zawodowych (All Poland Trade Union Alliance)
PAN	Polska Akademia Nauk (Polish Academy of Science)
PiS	Prawo i Sprawiedliwość (Law and Justice)
PRL	Polska Rzeczpospolita Ludowa (Polish People's Republic)
PRON	Patriotyczny Ruch Odrodzenia Narodowego (Patriotic Movement for National Rebirth)
PZPR	Polska Zjednoczona Partia Robotnicza (Polish United Workers' Party)
SD	Stronnictwo Demokratyczne (Democratic Party)
SLD	Sojusz Lewicy Demokratycznej (Democratic Left Alliance)
ZSL	Zjednoczone Stronnictwo Ludowe (Peasant Party)

1 Introduction

Neither the communist party (PZPR) nor Solidarność foresaw the fall of communism at the outset of the Round Table[1] process in Poland in February 1989.[2] Shrewd participants on both sides understood that the balance of power or Poland's political equilibrium was about to undergo some form of change. However, neither communist party negotiators nor their Solidarność counterparts expected that the PZPR would lose power in the dramatic way it did following the Round Table process and the first semi-free elections on 4 June 1989.

The puzzle addressed here is how to explain the speed and timing of the collapse of communism in Poland. If certain assumptions[3] are made about the rationality of the behaviour of communist party negotiators, the central question is why rationally, self-interested individuals adopted positions and strategies during the Round Table process that led to suboptimal outcomes for the communist party on a range of vital issues and institutional choices. In simple terms, the question to be addressed is why communist party actors adopted strategies and negotiated institutional arrangements in the course of the Round Table process that precipitated the collapse of the party's hegemony in Poland.

This book explores the hypothesis that the speed and timing of the collapse of communism in Poland can be explained by the strategic behaviour of PZPR leaders and negotiators involved in the Round Table. In the context of this hypothesis, it is postulated in game theoretic terms that dynamic change was precipitated because both communist party and opposition actors were playing the political game in conditions of uncertainty without full informational resources. The idea is a simple one. It is underpinned by the notion that misperception and false expectations by actors about their best choices or optimal strategies, at one point in a game or round of negotiations, may compromise their ability to behave optimally at the next round. It follows that such misperceptions about the outcomes of strategies may have led to outcomes that were not expected by PZPR players at the Round Table. Specifically, the PZPR's strategic misperception precipitated electoral defeat and the eventual dissolution of the communist party!

There has been no comprehensive, theoretically driven analysis of the PZPR's role in the process that led to its loss of power. The absence of a PZPR-centred account of the process of change in Poland in 1989 is not just an unfortunate lacuna in the literature; it is the underlying reason why there has been no satisfactory explanation of why and how the PZPR's political hegemony collapsed so dramatically in the aftermath of the partially free June elections. By analysing the PZPR's strategic choices both before and during the Round Table process, this study will redress the lacuna in the literature and explain how and why communism collapsed so speedily in Poland in the summer of 1989. The analysis of the collapse of communism in Eastern and Central Europe is situated in a range of academic discourse and approaches to the explanation of political change, revolution and democratic transition that are, in turn, underpinned by several theoretical perspectives. Leaving aside for now the question of whether the events of 1989 should be described as a revolution or as some other conceptual phenomenon, these events have been subjected to structural, agent- or elite-driven explanations as well as being analysed in the context of a vast case study literature.[4] Exclusively top-down or bottom-up explanations have not adequately explained why communism collapsed when it did, nor have they brought much light to bear on how it collapsed, that is, they have not provided an explanation of the underlying process of change that occurred.

There have, however, been a number of accounts that have tracked the background or structural conditions that precipitated the endgame of communism in Eastern Europe. George Sanford[5] notes Zbigniew Brzeziński's[6] argument in *The Grand Failure: The Birth and Death of Communism in the Twentieth Century* that communism entered into a 'General Crisis' in the late 1980s. Andrzej Rychard, amongst other authors, has referred to 'systemic exhaustion'.[7] What is generally meant by this terminology is that, by the mid-1980s, the time had arrived when the system, in part or whole, was no longer susceptible to reform.[8] There are several constituent parts in this set of background preconditions of collapse.

A number of writers have noted the central role played by economic decline.[9] In the post-1970 period, the command economy began to fail, to varying degrees throughout the Soviet bloc. Economic growth slowed or stopped and plants and enterprises were not efficient and there were massive consumer shortages. People's lives were hugely affected by arbitrary distribution of goods because of queuing and shortages. Corruption, both small scale and large scale, was prevalent. The Black Market was robust and inflation grew, as did the size of the hard currency debts and borrowings.

This economic picture was briefly interrupted by attempted cyclical reforms. While the reform efforts were often revolutionary, they were also often destabilizing. Partial marketization created social divisions:

> The Yugoslav and Hungarian experiences confirm that it was especially dangerous in its introductory and transitional phases by causing elite division and social discontent which often curtailed reform before it could get into full swing and produce any benefits.[10]

In the Polish context, it was the various efforts towards economic reform – mainly in the form of price rises – that led to the social explosions of 1970, 1976, 1980 and 1988. Virtually all of the Polish communist party leaders spoken to in the course of research for this volume argue that the main motivation behind the initiation of talks with Solidarność and the opposition in 1988 was the realization that its attempts at economic reform had failed. The same was true of Hungary and Yugoslavia, where various attempts and varieties of party reform ended in different degrees of failure. In the Polish case the 'net effect of the regime's alternate toying with partial corporatist and pluralist solutions only built up the pressure for full democratization'.[11] Also, in the context of the perceived battle between communism and Western capitalism, there were a number of areas in which capitalism appeared to be winning. In the late 1970s and early 1980s, the Soviet bloc's economic problems became more obvious to its own citizens particularly to those who had access to West European, mainly German, television. It was becoming increasingly difficult for Eastern European party leaders to camouflage the disparity between living conditions under communism and those in the West.

Another important contextual factor was the clash between the Leninist system of monocentric political power and the pressures of a modern differentiated society. Modernization, albeit spotty in the Soviet bloc, created demands that could not be dealt with in the context of monocentric politics. Sanford remarks that deStalinizing regimes paid a heavy price for being associated with the system of terror, which, by the 1960s, they rejected.[12] In fact, in the Polish case, the repeated attempts at reform spearheaded by reformist elements within the party further weakened its hold on society.

Adam Przeworski has noted the impact of the collapse of ideological belief in the communist system amongst party cadre.[13] This collapse was not, of course, confined to the party alone. Society also became accustomed to a sort of double-speak. There was a clash between official discourse, where the official line was parroted, and reality or everyday family and social language.[14] Apart from the cognitive dissonance generated across society, the collapse of belief in communist ideology had far-reaching consequences. As Adam Przeworski has remarked:

> By 1989, party bureaucrats did not believe in their speech. And to shoot, one must believe in something. When those who hold the trigger have absolutely nothing to say, they have no force to pull it.[15]

Another factor with mixed degrees of importance across the Soviet bloc was the decomposition of communist elites. This was a particular problem in Poland where factionalism had always been rife. However, after 1980, when General Jaruzelski suppressed Solidarność with the introduction of martial law, the party membership became highly differentiated over issues relating to ideological, economic and political direction. Solidarność's challenge and the party's initial response to it showed that even within the party there were those who accepted pluralism.[16] In simple terms, the conflict between hardliners and party reformers became more open and public.

Communist regimes were also badly exposed after the signing of the Helsinki Accords.[17] After 1975, Eastern European regimes were increasingly vulnerable to Western pressure in the context of explicit standards of human and civil rights agreed in the Accords. Failures, abuses and nonconformity in this area provided support for internal dissident groups such as Charter 77 in Czechoslovakia and KOR (Workers' Defence Committee) in Poland who were able to exploit the fact that the People's Democracies were not adhering to their commitments.

The fatal blow to communism was undoubtedly Gorbachev's abandonment of the Brezhnev Doctrine. In retrospect, it is clear that Gorbachev's announcement that the Soviet Union would not invade or crush Eastern European governments who initiated change or reform, fatally undermined the USSR's hegemony in the region. In *The Rise and Fall of State Socialism*, David Lane argues that the effects of Gorbachev's *perestroika* and *glasnost* policies had a profound impact on political stability in Eastern Europe. Gorbachev believed that *perestroika*, technically meaning restructuring, would lead to reform within the parameters of Soviet socialism.[18] However, in Eastern Europe where communist governments were less securely grounded and where there was opposition and dissidence, Gorbachev's reforms and policies had more profound consequences for the integrity of the regimes.

Gorbachev had endorsed a critique of state socialism, *perestroika*, which demanded reform not only in economics but also in politics. It was not possible to simply start an efficiency drive, which is arguably what Gorbachev wanted because the economy was so bound up with local government. As a result of the linkage between the economy and local government, Lane argues that *perestroika* also involved democratization of local government. As some of the governments of Eastern Europe began to adopt Gorbachev's other policy of *glasnost*, which came to mean opening up or a freeing up of the constraints on expression in the media and public arena more generally, this atmosphere of pluralism or acceptance of democratization and pluralism spread. Lane argues that the effects of Gorbachev's policies were twofold: first, the political elites were confused, less confident and began to split.[19] Arguably, it was a time of almost palpable disequilibrium. Many party leaders and apparatchiks pondered over what would happen if Gorbachev were to be toppled and the status quo returned. While the Gorbachev reforms may have suited the party reformers, many in the old guard feared such changes. The second impact, identified by Lane, was the growth of a public disquiet.[20] Across Eastern Europe two processes were occurring: some members of the political elites were withdrawing their support for the system and initiating processes of change, and at the same time popular movements of change were gaining support and social recognition.

Gorbachev's revision of Soviet doctrine had a profound impact on foreign policy decisions. The primacy under Marxist–Leninist theory of the class interest was used by Soviet leaders to justify their defence of the unity and identity of the whole bloc. In the past, attempts to weaken the links between Moscow and Eastern European governments had been met with intervention and invasion by the USSR. Hungary in 1956 and Czechoslovakia in 1968 are both examples of the USSR not tolerating deviance. But the Soviets did not always adopt the military option and invade. The Polish leadership crushed Solidarność in 1981 with the mere threat of Soviet intervention. Earlier in Poland, in 1956 and in 1970, and later in the mid-1970s, food riots or wage demands had been met with violent repression; however, these were before Gorbachev's abandonment of the Brezhnev Doctrine which stipulated that communist governments were not only responsible to their own people but also responsible for the maintenance of the integrity of Marxism–Leninism in all socialist states. Gorbachev had this to say about his view of the Soviet Union's responsibilities to its satellite neighbours:

> Immediately after the funeral of my predecessor, Chernenko, I called a conference of political leaders of the Warsaw Pact countries and told them clearly that now we were actually going to do what we had for a long time been declaring: we would adhere strictly to the principle of equality and independence, which also included the responsibility of each party for the development of its own country ... This meant that we would not commit acts of intervention or interference in their internal affairs. My counterparts at that conference, as I came to understand later, did not take what I said seriously. But I did adhere to this principle and never departed from it.[21]

It is far from clear at what point Gorbachev's counterparts in Eastern Europe did begin to take seriously what he was saying. In fact, trying to pinpoint when the realization of the abandonment of the Brezhnev Doctrine had truly sunk into the minds of the party leaders in Eastern Europe is a crucial question for scholars trying to assess the impact of the new Sinatra Doctrine on the calculus of party reformers. While the question of how much party leaders actually understood the significance of Gorbachev's commitment to non-intervention is problematical, it is clear that for those who did understand, there was a massive change in the cost–benefit ratio of initiating change. Simply put, Gorbachev's abandonment of the Brezhnev Doctrine lessened the potential costs to reformers or those wishing to challenge communist orthodoxy. There was no longer a single ideology. It was now possible for national, anti-communist or pro-reform groups of any shade or colour to challenge the one-party command economy. The system was in disequilibrium.

There was an international and externally controlled economic dimension to this disequilibrium. Gorbachev wanted to disengage from the Cold War but Western leaders throughout the 1980s raised the stakes of successful disengagement. Germany, under Helmut Kohl, pressed the cause of East Germany. Kohl wanted a united Germany as the price for USSR's entry into what he called the 'European home'. As mentioned earlier, the command economies of Eastern Europe were collapsing and so was the USSR's ability to offer support to its client states. Once Gorbachev made it clear that Eastern European states had to refloat their own economies alone, they began to look to the West for economic development. The West, in the form of Ronald Reagan, Margaret Thatcher and Helmut Kohl, made the conditions of aid consequent on political and economic pluralism. Thatcher, for her part, demanded competitive elections and a multi-party system in the USSR.[22]

In essence, Gorbachev had effectively put in motion a situation where the West was able to make certain demands on behalf of the citizens of Eastern Europe which linked the satisfaction of a range of Gorbachev's goals with the satisfaction of the West's demands for the liberalization of the personal rights and freedom of the people of the region. David Lane successfully argues that it was this factor that led to the downfall of communism in Eastern Europe:

> Perestroika undermined state socialism economically, ideologically, and politically: the organizing principles of the centrally managed and controlled economy were cast in doubt; Marxism–Leninism was subverted; the party as the dominant political institution was destroyed.[23]

In the USSR, this impulse came from top-down, from the elite around Gorbachev, but in Eastern Europe, the thrust was both from below and 'from already established counter-elites vying for power'.[24] The communist leaderships in Eastern Europe were simply weakened and undermined by Gorbachev. Or, as was the case with the Polish reformers, the Gorbachev initiative reduced the costs for those who wanted to spearhead the opening up of a market economy. So whether the political elites were encouraged or oppressed by Gorbachev's reforms, the overall effect was that the elites became differentiated.

The big question, of course, is whether Gorbachev realized the potential impact of his policies for communism in Eastern Europe.[25]

Clearly, the genesis of the collapse of communism goes beyond the Gorbachev era and the immediate events that precipitated the collapse. In fact, to understand the genesis of the collapse in each case in Eastern Europe, one should look at the manner in which communism arrived and survived in each case. We should not only look at factors such as the impact of Gorbachev's reforms and Western demands for liberalization as a prerequisite for financial aid and development as mentioned already, but we must also focus on the social, economic, political and ethnic make-up of each of the countries of this so-called bloc. Communism collapsed in Eastern Europe and later in the Soviet Union, but it collapsed in different ways and to different degrees in each of these countries.

When academics and journalists talk of the domino effect, that is, the ripple effect of the collapse of communism in Poland and Hungary being repeated across Eastern Europe, it is important to remember that this was not just a case of some inevitable and deterministic dynamic. Much deeper and state-specific processes underpinned each episode of change. In order to understand these specific circumstances, we must look into the history and experiences of each of these countries, both before and after the establishment of the People's Democracies after the Second World War. We must understand the specific experience of communism in each state if we are to understand how structural and external factors, including the Gorbachev phenomenon, combined to precipitate regime change across Eastern Europe in 1989.

This volume sets out to establish how communism collapsed in Poland. The Polish case is crucial because of its demonstration effect across Eastern Europe in 1989.[26] It is also crucial because of the speed and timing of regime change. Understanding the sequence of events and the dynamics of the process that led to the PZPR's loss of power facilitates explication of the mindset, motivation and calculus of communist elites in the region more generally. In tracking the sequence of events both before and during the Polish Round Table, this volume offers detailed insight into the decision and calculus of PZPR negotiators. The approach applied here and insights gained from this exercise would surely prove a useful heuristic in the context of the analysis of the collapse of party power in other Eastern European regimes in 1989.

As was argued earlier, conflicting theoretical, case study and methodological literature underpin the central question that this volume will address. In Chapter 2, we will examine these explanatory approaches in order to assess their relevance to the explanation of political change and democratic transition. In particular, we will assess whether or not these various approaches provide the explanatory leverage required to offer an account of why communism collapsed in Poland when it did. In the first place, we will differentiate between structural and actor-based explanations and address the question of the classification of the events of 1989. The problem here is the issue of whether it is appropriate to classify the regime changes experienced in various countries across Eastern Europe as an evolutionary or revolutionary phenomenon or indeed whether either category provides a useful heuristic device.

This discussion is followed by an evaluation of previous explanations, which leads on to an account of why the analysis of regime change in Poland in 1989 is more usefully characterized as a collective-action problem. In this context, it is posited that reform-oriented members of the PZPR including the first secretary, General W. Jaruzelski, recognizing that the regime was facing economic collapse, responded as political entrepreneurs to bring about a resolution of the collective-action problem or regime crisis in the hope of securing the nation's economic fate and, thus, ensuring their own power in the new order.

At this point, however, it is important to reiterate that, while exclusively top-down or bottom-up explanations alone have not provided a plausible account of why communism collapsed in Poland in the summer of 1989, this volume will start from the premise that structural conditions provided the necessary but not the sufficient conditions for change at the end of the 1980s. In the context of classifying regime change as a collective-action problem and in pursuing an actor-based explanatory framework, this volume responds to the work of Adam Przeworski[27] and Josep Colomer[28] who have offered conflicting accounts of the genesis, nature and path of the fourth wave of change and transition in Eastern Europe since 1989. Przeworski has concluded that rational, well-informed actors could only work to maintain the authoritarian status quo or a 'broadened dictatorship',[29] and that an agreed transition to democracy could be the outcome only of misinformed or miscalculating actors' strategies. However, Colomer takes the view that 'Self-interested, rational actors can play the main part in the transition from authoritarianism to a democratic regime.'[30]

In his analysis of transition interactions, Colomer assumes that actors are playing non-cooperative and non-repeated games. Relying on the conceptual framework proposed in Brams's 'theory of moves',[31] Colomer posits that actors can react and counter-react to their choices before the game ends and that they do not make simultaneous or blind choices of strategies but make choices in the expectation of other actors' reaction. It is worth quoting from Colomer at some length in order to clarify the parameters of the debate between these two scholars and to indicate the broad outlines of the hypotheses that will be examined in the course of this volume:

> It is also assumed that actors do not merely look at their immediate interests but can make future-oriented calculations anticipating other actors' reactions and counterreactions [*sic*]. Instead of future repetitions of the game (which in our case are highly unlikely to exist), some foresight of the actors is assumed.[32]

In essence, then, Przeworski regards democratic transition as the result of a misperceived strategy on the part of regime actors who sought a broadened dictatorship, while Colomer posits that actors' foresight, or long-time horizons, facilitates the emergence of what he calls 'intermediate regimes'.[33] According to Colomer, 'intermediate regimes' provide a safety net for incumbents and a 'way to create a relatively stable situation away from the dictatorship but short of democracy'.[34]

In the course of his discussion, Przeworski exhorts scholars to empirically test his analytical framework and hypotheses.[35] This volume responds to this challenge and sets out to apply the underlying assumptions underpinning both Przeworski's and Colomer's analysis in order to assess which approach comes closest to providing an explanation of the collapse of communism in Poland. It is most important to note that Colomer specifically points out that the Polish case tends to support Przeworski's 'pessimistic interpretation of human rational choices'[36] in that the incumbents there 'were badly defeated in their self-confident expectations to retain power by electoral means'.[37] Colomer attributes this self-confidence to the fact that the Polish process of change was temporarily ahead of the other processes of change in Eastern Europe. However, he also points out that, in the midterm, the unanticipated democratic outcome proved relatively favourable for Polish communists who transformed themselves into Social Democrats and became the leading party in a coalition government formed in 1993.

It is important to note that Colomer makes a distinction between the rulers' decision to negotiate or not to negotiate a political compromise with the opposition and decisions made during the process of the subsequent negotiations.[38] According to Colomer, the key question is whether the behaviour of regime leaders can be characterized as far-sighted at the point when the decision to negotiate or not to negotiate is made. It is this pre-negotiation stage that Colomer regards as the focus of both his and Przeworski's analysis. In attempting to assess whether or not regime actors conform to the hypothesis posited by Colomer, he argues that it is essential to distinguish between rational behaviour, which is based on actors' available information, and perfect information, which is not a necessary condition for a rational decision. In this context, it is argued that unintended outcomes can be produced even by the most rational and best-informed decisions.

A number of points follow from the foregoing analysis. First, any attempt at estimating the rationality of PZPR actors prior to their decision to negotiate with the Solidarność-led opposition must be explicit about the available information upon which the decision was made. It follows that a crucial goal here is to discover whether or not the PZPR's decision-making was premised on the evaluation of all of the information it had at its disposal or whether information that may have had the potential to influence decision-making was ignored or not sought out. Second, if it can be shown that regime actors made the decision to negotiate without fully assessing the available information, then this would tend to cast doubt on Colomer's hypothesis. Third, while Colomer's analysis concentrates on the initial decision to negotiate or not to negotiate, it is plausible to argue that if actors are far-sighted and rational in their hopes and goals at the point when the decision to negotiate has been made, this behaviour will continue throughout the subsequent negotiation process.

With this in mind, we will explore a range of bargaining and decision-making scenarios, prior to, during and in the immediate aftermath of the Round Table negotiations, in order to assess whether the evidence tends to support the idea that PZPR actors operated on the basis of a far-sighted time horizon or whether they made a series of strategic mistakes that led to the unanticipated collapse of their power. In order to track the gap between actors' strategic expectations and actual outcomes, we will set out an informal set of observable implications for each of the hypotheses in each scenario evaluated. Put simply, the PZPR's Round Table bargaining will be analysed to assess whether party actors were well informed and far-sighted in their behaviour or whether their bargaining and decision-making reflects Przeworski's contention that democratic transition only results from the misperceived strategies or simple errors of authoritarian incumbents.

While Przeworski and Colomer employ the formal tools of game theory to construct and illustrate their analysis of political change, this study will follow the form of an analytic narrative. Following Bates *et al.*, the methodological approach employed here seeks to 'trace the sequences of actions, decisions and responses that generate events and outcomes'.[39] By analysing contemporary documents, secondary sources and new interview material gathered by the present author over time with a number of key Round Table players, this volume seeks to understand PZPR negotiators' preferences, their perceptions, their evaluation of alternatives, the information they possessed, the expectations they formed, the strategies they adopted and the constraints that limited their actions. In doing so, it is hoped to construct the story that accounts for the particular outcome. Put simply, this is a process-driven account which seeks to expose the underlying mechanisms, interactions, motivations and strategies that led to the collapse of communism in Poland in the summer of 1989.

The analytic narrative form employs 'thin' reasoning and is theoretically driven. Rather than simply telling the story of what happened in relation to each of the bargaining scenarios examined, each event will be analysed in order to track the extent to which the empirical data supports the strategic, hypothesis of far-sightedness posited by Colomer or supports Przeworski's mistakes hypothesis. The observable implications of both hypotheses will be informally stated at the outset of each narrative. In other words, a simple statement of what might be expected, given either the assumptions of Colomer or Przeworski, will be set out prior to the analysis of each bargaining scenario. The advantage of this method is that because it is 'based on rigorous deductive reasoning as well as close attention to empirical detail, analytic narratives are tightly constrained'.[40] As Bates *et al.* point out, both logic and the empirical record discipline analytic narratives.[41] Later on, in Chapter 3, it will be argued that process-driven accounts that set out to compare data with hypotheses and their observable implications provide a transparent, replicable and deeper explanation of how and why change occurred in the way it did.

Apart from a discussion of the methodology employed here, Chapter 3 provides biographical information concerning the Round Table actors and players with whom interviews were conducted. While the present analysis is based on an extensive series of interviews conducted between the summer of 1989 and spring 2000, this analysis is underpinned by interviews and research carried out in Poland since July 1980 when the Gdańsk shipyard strike spawned Solidarność. Given the focus, the bulk of the interviews quoted are with PZPR leaders and negotiators. Many of these interviews, including those with PZPR's first secretary, General W. Jaruzelski, Poland's last communist prime minister, Mieczysław Rakowski and party ideologue and negotiator, Professor Jerzy Wiatr, were conducted over time. The fact that many of the interviews were not once off but conducted at different time points enhances the reliability of the information and interpretation offered by these interviewees. In many cases, the interviewees were asked the same or similar questions about personal motivation and role in the Round Table process in the course of a number of interviews conducted several years apart and, as a result, it has been possible to cross-reference these answers and compare them with contemporary documents. This undoubtedly obviates any questions that might be raised concerning the reliability of the accounts of interested actors.

It has already been made clear that this analysis is informed by actor-based explanatory approaches and assumes that the structural preconditions necessary for change created political disequilibrium in Poland and the rest of the Soviet-dominated bloc during the late 1980s. Chapter 4 will examine the context, structural preconditions and historical background to the PZPR's decision to initiate talks with the Solidarność-led opposition. Having provided a biographical account of the backgrounds and motivations of the PZPR interviewees in Chapter 3, Chapter 4 gives an account of the game these actors thought they were playing when they initiated the Round Table process and sought direct talks with the Solidarność-led opposition in the autumn of 1988. The analysis of these interviews as well as contemporaneous documents is informed by the conflicting assumptions of the Przeworski and Colomer hypotheses. At the end of this chapter, an appraisal is offered of the relative merits of these two hypotheses in light of the empirical data. This chapter assesses a range of evidence in order to confirm or negate the hypothesis that in deciding to initiate talks with Solidarność; PZPR actors thought they were engaging in a process of incremental and controlled political change. It will be argued that these actors did not expect that the initiation of talks with the opposition would lead to immediate democratization or the collapse of communist hegemony.

Chapter 5 evaluates PZPR negotiators' motivations and strategies in relation to three bargaining scenarios. First, the issue of the relegalization of Solidarność is analysed. The fundamental question here is how PZPR players evaluated the impact of relegalization. Was relegalization part of a far-sighted plan or did party actors fail to assess the potential impact of this decision? Again, the discussion is underpinned by the assumptions of the Przeworski and Colomer hypotheses. It has been argued that the PZPR's desire to get Solidarność's agreement to a strong presidency was part of its plan to retain political control and power.[42] However, in order to get Solidarność's agreement to the new presidential office, PZPR negotiators agreed to the establishment of a freely elected Senate. It is arguable that the consequences of the party's failure to win any of the 100 freely elected Senate seats was an even greater psychological blow than the collapse of its vote in the election to the *Sejm* (Lower House) where only two of its candidates were elected from its 35-member national list.[43] In this context, this chapter will provide an evaluation of the motivation of PZPR negotiators in pursuing these three institutional bargains and assess whether the evidence tends to support the far-sighted and strategic or mistakes hypothesis.

It has been argued that the biggest mistake made by the PZPR at the Round Table was its negotiators' bargaining over the electoral law. With his counterfactual analysis of the election result, Marek Kamiński has shown that almost any other voting system would have produced a more favourable result than the electoral collapse produced under the majoritarian rule adopted by the party for the contractual election on 4 June.[44] Chapter 6 offers an analysis of the process that led to the choice of the electoral system and voting formula in order to assess whether or not PZPR negotiators were far-sighted and strategic office-seekers. In this context, the analysis will focus on three separate questions: first, whether or not errors were made in relation to the choice of electoral system and voting formula; second, whether or not PZPR negotiators made choices on the basis of reliable information concerning their true support levels and third, whether PZPR actors behaved judiciously in the conduct of their overall electoral strategy.

In his analysis of the PZPR's election campaign, written just a few months after the election, Paul Lewis notes that many commentators said that the party had given up the ghost before the election campaign had even started.[45] Chapter 7 analyses the key features of the PZPR's election campaign in order to assess what PZPR strategists thought they would achieve from a range of campaign decisions. The fundamental question is what this campaign can tell us about the motivation and conduct of the PZPR's electoral strategy. Was the party behaving tactically in allowing Solidarność leader Lech Wałęsa to engage in a television debate with the party's trade union boss Alfred Miodowicz? What was the motivation behind the decision to run a 'personality first'[46] campaign blurring the distinction between PZPR and Solidarność candidates? These and other issues will be addressed in order to assess whether we can deduce far-sighted or erroneous strategies at the heart of the party's campaign plan.

Przeworski notes that one PZPR Round Table participant, Professor Jerzy Wiatr, has somewhat provocatively described the Round Table agreement as having been the outcome of a pact between the Catholic Church and the army.[47] Given the importance of the role played by General W. Jaruzelski and General C. Kiszczak in gaining communist party support for the initiation of the Round Table process and the fact that both of these men developed extremely positive relationships with senior members of the hierarchy,[48] there is clearly more than a hint of truth in Wiatr's claim. Wiatr's remarks highlight this most fascinating aspect of the behind-the-scenes play that facilitated the Round Table accord, that is, the warm relationship between senior members of the Catholic Church hierarchy and the PZPR. Chapter 7 offers an evaluation of the impact of this relationship on the strategic choices made by the PZPR in order to assess what this relationship has to tell us about the Przeworski and Colomer hypotheses.

The final chapter offers a review of the extent to which the new interview material, documentary evidence and the historical data tend to support the proposition that the collapse of communism in Poland was the unintended consequence of the strategic misperception of PZPR Round Table negotiators who had sought controlled and incremental political change when they initiated the process. The evidence in relation to each bargaining scenario is evaluated and explicit conclusions are drawn about the impact on the Przeworski and Colomer hypotheses. The central issue addressed in this volume is why the communist party collapsed in Poland in the summer of 1989. It will be shown that this particular *ancien régime* did not intentionally give up. Through a blow-by-blow analysis of each of the party's Round Table bargaining scenarios, it will be shown that in some cases, most particularly the initial decision to enter into talks with Solidarność, PZPR actors were far-sighted and strategic in intention but that a series of subsequent mistaken strategies produced the unexpected collapse of the party's hegemony long before it planned to share power self-interestedly with the opposition.

2 Explaining change

The paucity of the agency–structure debate

Two basic approaches can be distinguished in the literature on regime change and transitions to democracy. One approach emphasizes the structural prerequisites of democratization while the other treats political regimes as the outcome of strategic processes of change. As Colomer has noted, the structural approach was dominant in the 1950s and 1960s when comparisons focused on the stable democracies of Anglo-American countries and the failure of democratic experiments in continental Europe between the two world wars.[1] In this explanatory approach, the emergence and survival of democracy was associated with socio-economic development and political culture:

> As a logical reaction to the deficient performance of the structural approach, the role of political incentives and leadership decisions has been remarked in order to explain the attainment of elites' compromises leading to the establishment of democratic regimes.[2]

Responding to this 'deficient performance',[3] Adam Przeworski described 1989, the 'Autumn of the People',[4] as a dismal failure for political science. He argues that 'any retrospective explanation of the fall of communism must not only account for the historical developments but also identify the theoretical assumptions that prevented us from anticipating these developments'.[5] In this context, therefore, it is important to distinguish between analytical frameworks and categories that help us to understand and explain the process of change that occurred in Eastern Europe in the late 1980s and those conceptual tools that have been found wanting. Leaving aside for a moment the fact that 'not one of the structural preconditions for democracy postulated in the sociological approach existed in Communist Europe',[6] the events of 1989 posed other categorization problems for scholars used to defining change as either revolutionary or evolutionary.

As has been argued, much of the literature that seeks to explain regime change is underpinned by both the structure–agency debate and the problem of the applicability of the revolutionary–evolutionary framework. It is, therefore, important to examine the specific problem of regime change in 1989 and assess whether it is possible to define the phenomenon as either revolutionary, evolutionary or perhaps neither.[7] We do this in order to be clear about the nature of the phenomenon we seek to analyse. We will then move on to an analysis of previous approaches and review the extent to which the tools supplied in a purely structural or actor-based account help us to explain the case at hand. In this context, it will be argued that structural accounts alone provide little or no leverage in the explanation of the fall of communism in Eastern Europe, and while some early actor-based accounts focused on the interaction of regime players, the analysis was still embedded in structuralist discourse.

Actors' preferences were often assumed and were not specifically set out in advance of the empirical analysis. Przeworski noted that the 'result was an intuitive micro approach often couched in macro language'.[8] Having determined the elements of the individualist or actor-based literature, which have been more successful in explaining regime change, we will move on to argue that the problem of regime change is best understood as a collective-action problem:

> The collective action problem defines a central paradox generated by our individualistic motivational assumptions. If a group of rational people behave so as to maximize their individual welfare, then they produce a state of affairs that is worse for each of them, individually, than if they had adopted more co-operative behaviour.[9]

In the specific case of Poland at the end of the 1980s, the collective-action problem can be understood in the context of the catastrophic deterioration of the economy and the collapse of the PZPR's confidence that it could resolve this problem alone without Western support. It became apparent to a number of the PZPR's most senior players[10] that regime reform of some type was the answer but the problem was in whose interest was it to carry the cost of attempting to bring about the changes that would allow for the gradual marketization of the economy and the attraction of Western capital? Laver points out that a 'solution to certain collective problems may be provided by a political entrepreneur, who organizes various forms of collective endeavour on behalf of the group'.[11] In the case of Poland, it will be argued that elements of the reformist wing of the PZPR, including General W. Jaruzelski, should be understood as political entrepreneurs who, recognizing the decreasing cost of initiating political change in the Gorbachev era, acted in the hope of maintaining incumbency and power in the new order.

Before moving on to an overview of academic approaches to the explanation of revolution, democratic transition and regime change, it is evident that, following Dankwart A. Rustow, a distinction must be made between the causes and conditions that maintain democracy and the conditions that initiate the democratization process itself: 'Explanations of democracy must distinguish between function and genesis.'[12] Rustow's approach underscored the importance of choices made by identifiable political actors in crafting democratic institutions. In describing Rustow's analysis, Lisa Anderson has written that he

> never denied the significance of structural and cultural conditions to the maintenance and stability of existing democratic regimes. However, he was more interested in identifying the factors that brought such regimes into

existence in the first place. These factors he found to be a more varied mix of economic and cultural pre-dispositions with contingent developments and individual choices.[13]

Defining regime change in 1989

It goes without saying that for a democratic transition to take place some form of political and social change or revolution must occur in the first place. It, therefore, follows that research aimed at explaining the nature of transition must a priori deal with the causes of change itself. In her book *States and Revolutions*, Theda Skocpol offers research students three basic analytical strategies.[14] She argues that the state and organizations are at the centre of explanations of social revolutions because revolutions do not happen without the breakdown of the administration and coercive power of the *ancien régime*. Her second point is that a focus on international and world historical contexts is crucial to an explanation of the outbreak, conflicts and outcomes of social revolution. Her fundamental argument is for a structural and non-voluntarist or purposive approach to revolutions. She criticized theorists for imposing what she calls a reified collective will on revolutionary origins and outcomes:

> Wilful individuals and acting groups may well abound in revolutions, I maintained, but no single group, or organization, or individual creates a revolutionary crisis, or shapes revolutionary outcomes, through purposive action. It will not do, I asserted, to explain revolutions simply by propositions referring to mass social psychologies, or by propositions referring to class interests or actions, or by propositions referring to the ideological outlooks and derivative actions of vanguard revolutionary leaderships.[15]

Skocpol champions a social–structural approach to the explanation of revolution. She argues that most 'recent attempts to explain either revolutions per se, or some broader class of phenomena explicitly conceived as subsuming revolutions'[16] can be identified primarily with one or another of three major approaches. First, she identifies aggregate-psychological theories, which attempt to explain revolutions in terms of people's motivations for engaging in political violence or joining oppositional movements. The second group she describes is 'system/value-consensus theories',[17] which attempt to explain revolutions as violent responses of ideological movements to severe disequilibrium in social systems. Her third category is political conflict theories, which argue that conflict between governments and organized groups contending for political power should be the focus of attention:

> Thus I will be arguing that a major theoretical reorientation – away from social psychological and universalist-deductive modes of explanation, and toward a structural and comparative-historical approach – is required if progress toward the adequate explanation of revolutions is to be made in the social sciences.[18]

Przeworski takes a different view. He highlights the fact that top-down and bottom-up models often compete to explain liberalization but they are too crude. He makes the case that 'short of real revolution'[19] decisions to liberalize combine elements of top-down and bottom-up forces. Perhaps the key phrase here is 'short of real revolution': it brings into focus the fact that even the simple characterization of 1989 for research purposes is problematic:

> For even in those cases where divisions in the authoritarian regime became visible well before any popular mobilization, the question is why the regime cracked at a particular moment. And part of the answer is always that Liberalizers in the regime saw the possibility of an alliance with some forces that up to then had remained unorganized, which implies that there was some force in the civil society with which to ally. Conversely, in the cases in which mass mobilization antedated visible splits in the regime, the question remains why the regime decided not to repress it by force. Again, part of the answer is that the regime was divided between Liberalizers and Hardliners. Liberalization is a result of an interaction between splits in the authoritarian regime and autonomous organization of the civil society. Popular mobilization signals to the potential Liberalizers the possibility of an alliance that could change the relations of forces within the power bloc to their advantage; visible splits in the power bloc indicate to the civil society that political space may have been opened for autonomous organization. Hence, popular mobilization and splits in the regime feed on each other.[20]

Przeworski is not alone in arguing for a more holistic research agenda. J. A. Goldstone argues that there is no conflict between micro and macro approaches to the causes of revolution:

> [P]rocess models of group recruitment, solidarity, and rational action suggest that a wide range of collective action phenomena – including rebellions and revolutions in traditional societies, social protest movements, and revolutions in modern neo-patrimonial and communist states – are capable of being brought together in a common framework involving group identity, popular mobilization, elite divisions and disaffection, and changes in state strength and effectiveness.[21]

Piotr Sztompka makes the point most effectively when he charges Skocpol with forgetting that human beings 'thinking and acting (however haphazardly) are the mediating link between structural conditions and social outcomes'.[22] He argues that structural conditions do not dictate absolutely what humans do; they merely place certain limits on human action or define a certain range of possibilities. Sztompka says that what is needed is a synthetic, multidimensional approach. He criticizes Skocpol for treating structural analysis and voluntarist analysis as mutually exclusive opposites rather than as two necessary elements of a complete sociological explanation.

It has been argued that one of the fundamental questions raised by the collapse of communism is whether it took the form of a revolution or whether it was an evolutionary phenomenon. The answer is important from a number of perspectives. One obvious question is whether the term 'revolution' is an appropriate analytical concept in the case in point. Kazimierz Poznański is an evolutionist.[23] He argues that 'the decay process of communism could be seen as a slow but systematic rejection of an artificial implant or foreign body, where a successful defence mechanism prevents an unhealthy "population" from intruding and overtaking an existing system.'[24] Using a metaphor from natural science, Poznański sees communism as an implant that was initially stabilized within the Eastern European system. Such implanted bodies are then isolated and, finally, neutralized by the 'healthy, normal part of a given self-contained organism'.[25] Essentially, Poznański rejects the 'revolutionary' tag and argues that 1989 was the product of an evolutionary process.

In the context of whether the collapse was initiated by economic failure or ideological breakdown, Poznański argues that the evolutionary weakening of the official doctrine was not necessarily synchronized with economic misfortunes. He points out that critical revisions of ideology often took place despite a relatively good economic performance, though he concedes that the worsening of the economy was 'most likely stimulating the critical search for an adequate ideological guidebook'.[26]

In the context of arguments about agency and structure, Poznański, perhaps somewhat simplistically, argues that if it can be shown that particular social groups were central to the process of change, then a 'revolutionary' approach is justifiable. However, if no single identifiable group can be found to have played a vital role, then the 'evolutionary' theory receives support. But here, again, we find that the arguments stack up on both sides because of categorization problems. Focusing on the Polish case, Poznański asks whether it was the workers or the intellectuals who led the 'revolution'. Poznański quotes from M. Burawoy who argues that the industrial workers were responsible for putting an end to communist rule. He calls the struggle, launched in 1980 by the independent unions under Wałęsa, the first – in the Marxian sense – true revolution. Burawoy supports his claim by arguing that Solidarność involved the massive participation of factory workers who were self-led rather than directed by dissident, 'vanguard'[27] intellectuals.

V. Tismaneanu also talks about the revolutionary dismantling of the party by society in Eastern Europe but sees the decisive force behind it as not the workers but rather the opposition intellectuals.[28] To him, what happened in Eastern Europe (less so in Poland and more so in Czechoslovakia and Hungary) was the first revolution in modern history by intellectuals, resulting in their capturing power from the communist apparatchiks. On the other side of the coin, S. Meuschel argues that East Germany was an example of society-centred collapse in that revolution occurred without truly identifiable revolutionaries.[29] 'This was a most strange example of a revolution executed by nobody or everybody, though, similar to the French Revolution, ignited in the name of "liberty" '.[30]

Poznański argues that to understand the forces that brought the system down, one has to look to the communist party itself.[31] In many cases, the apparatus self-destructed. But what would have been the communist elite's motives for such a move? One answer is that it was unintended self-destruction by incompetent, sterile cadres. Another answer might be that they gave way through the collapse of their belief in the party and the system. There was, in other words, a collapse of their ideological belief system. Poznański posits an alternative view of why party elites may have collaborated in the self-destruction of the party:

> A more accurate picture is that by and large, and not only at the end of communism, the members of the 'nomenklatura' were destroying the political system as peculiar counter-revolutionaries, though not always damaging themselves as discrete actors. This was not only rational behaviour but, importantly, was driven largely by concern for various types of personal gain.[32]

Poznański provides further support for the hypothesis that it was in the interest of party elites to cause the system to self-destruct because they were already involved in 'nomenklatura' capitalism. He cites both Hungary and Poland as examples:

> The escalation of so-called nomenklatura capitalism during the last years of communism – as in Hungary and Poland where the party passed the most favourable regulations in 1987 – represented another step in the effort by the party to expand its wealth. Large portions of public capital were handed over during that period to the power elite at extremely discounted prices. By mid-1989 in Poland, there were about 1800 so-acquired nomenklatura enterprises, mostly small scale, but some rather large entities as well.[33]

Poznański argues that party or state actors did not act as an organized group but rather as individuals sharing more or less similar concerns. Individual members of the elite tried to maximize their personal gains at the expense of society but they were competing among themselves as well:

> In this game, the fittest were not only gaining the most by securing the most valuable economic assets, they were also assuming the least vulnerable political positions and thus were better prepared for growing anti-communist attacks.[34]

Erzsebet Szalai's analysis of the impact of Janos Kadar's New Economic Mechanism in Hungary supports Poznański's argument.[35] Szalai has shown that communist party elites were the direct beneficiaries of economic liberalization in Hungary and argues that what effectively appears to have happened in Hungary was an unspoken deal between the large enterprise managers and the communist party giving them ownership rights on the condition that they kept the economy afloat.

Poznański's account of communist decay in Eastern Europe and the Soviet Union is convincing. It offers the thesis that communism did not collapse through a revolutionary act but rather through evolutionary forces. He argues that the questioning of ideological principles undermined the regime more decisively than its economic failures and that the party–state apparatus, together with society, 'brought the institutions of communism down, as neither could live with the constraints imposed on individual preferences and actions'.[36]

Poznański leaves us with an account that highlights the motivations of both elite and societal actors who respond to systemic problems, conscious of the constraints imposed on their individual preferences. These groups of individuals, bound by their separate but coinciding needs, acted to abolish the constraints imposed on their preferences and in so doing brought about the end of communism. While Poznański's justification of the evolutionary hypothesis is supported by the historical evidence of the gradual disintegration of state socialism in Eastern Europe, it does not help us with an explanation of why the communist party collapsed in Poland in 1989. Jerzy Wiatr argues:

> Revolution involves the rapid, mostly forceful, overthrow of the existing power system. What happened in Poland was not a revolution in this sense. Evolution involves a long process of gradual transformation. That also was not what took place in Poland. There is a third category – political reform. Such reform sometimes takes place in a short time (like a revolution) but is done without the use of force and within the framework of the existing institutions (through their transformation). There are two pure types of reform: negotiated reform and reform from above (Spanish v. Brazilian model). Poland was the case of a negotiated reform.[37]

Wiesław Władyka has commented that the

> attempt of the Communist Party and the opposition to create the common Round Table was a means of looking for a synthesis between revolution and evolution, and what is the most important – they succeeded.[38]

Solidarność leader, Lech Wałęsa, later Poland's first non-communist president, had this to say when Władyka asked him if the Round Table should be regarded as a success or failure:

> It depends on the conception. In the evolutionary understanding, in seizing the opportunities the Round Table was a momentous event. However, in the revolutionary understanding it was a poor affair. In fact, there is no straightforward answer to this question.[39]

It, thus, appears that regime change in Poland in 1989 was a case of neither revolution nor evolution, but a hybrid case where changes in the structural conditions played their part in the evolution of disequilibrium. This political disequilibrium prompted dissatisfied regime actors to seek self-interested political change or negotiated reform, as Wiatr describes it.

If categorizing the events of 1989 as a case of revolution or evolution has proven problematical, other conceptual problems arise when explanatory frameworks, formerly applied to authoritarian regimes, are used unquestioningly to explain the collapse of communism. There is an assumption implicit in using such models that the end result of transition from authoritarian and communist rule should or will be the same. A second problematic assumption is that 'democracy' and the desire for it was the motivating factor for those who facilitated the process. C. G. A. Bryant and Edmund Mokrzycki are particularly critical of the idea of mixing the two areas of research.[40] They argue that the collapse of communism is different from the defeat or the collapse of fascism and authoritarianism in so far as it involves not just political transition but also fundamental economic change. In short, it is argued that there is neither a model nor a precedent for the transition from 'real socialism' to democracy and capitalism. They make the point that the very language of transition assumes an outcome that in reality is far from guaranteed. Bryant and Mokrzycki quote from Stark who says that seemingly descriptive notions like 'transition to capitalism' and 'transition to a market economy' hide 'teleological constructs in which concepts are driven by hypothesized end-states. Presentist history finds its counterpart here in futurist transitology.'[41]

Explanations of regime change and democratic transition

As was noted earlier in this chapter, academic explanations of democratic transition have moved from structural to agent models. For Seymour Martin Lipset, the engine of change was modernization.[42] He identified certain social conditions for the emergence and survival of democracy. It followed that the breakdown of democracies was associated with undeveloped socio-economic environments. Samuel Huntington, working in a similar vein, also associated democratization processes with industrialization and economic development.[43] Colomer has pointed out that Gabriel Almond and Sidney Verba 'added a cultural mediator between basic social processes and the political level'.[44] Almond and Verba emphasized political culture as the driving force behind the stabilization of democracy.[45] However, in his analysis of the relevance of these approaches, Adam Przeworski has characterized the macro-historical comparative sociological approach of Barrington Moore, Seymour Martin Lipset and their academic descendants in the following terms:

> The method characteristic of this approach is to associate inductively outcomes, such as democracy or fascism, with initial conditions, such as agrarian class structure. In this formulation the outcome is uniquely determined by conditions, and history goes on without anyone ever doing anything.[46]

Przeworski has also noted that 'the macro-historical approach was unappealing, even to those scholar-activists who resisted the intellectual assumptions of the micro perspective, because it condemned them to political impotence'.[47] More recently, Colomer has pointed out that the structural approach has come under attack both theoretically and empirically.[48] It has been argued that the notion of identifying conditions with causes for the emergence of democracy was antiquated while the correlation of socio-economic and political culture variables with processes of democratization underestimated the possibility that the relationship could also work the other way round. The changes in Eastern Europe proved particularly problematic for the structural framework, given the fact that in very few cases were there necessary or sufficient structural conditions to facilitate democratic transition. However, despite the structuralists, regime change did occur in Eastern Europe in 1989.

In more recent times, analytical frameworks have moved towards theories promoting actor models and 'modes' of transition, as is evidenced in the work of Juan Linz and Alfred Stepan,[49] Guillermo O'Donnell and Phillippe C. Schmitter.[50] In his analysis of the failure of democracy in Spain and Germany in the 1930s, Linz highlighted the importance of leadership, institutions and belief systems for a stable democracy. Structural conditions were deemed necessary but not sufficient for democracy to survive. As this vein of analysis developed, the impetus was moving away from deterministic approaches and towards analysis that focused on the role of politics. It is fair to say that a striking feature of the literature on this 'third wave' of democratization has been the prominence of theories that mirror Rustow's emphasis on strategic interaction and negotiation.

Terry Lynn Karl and Phillippe C. Schmitter identify four ideal types of regime transition: pact, imposition, revolution and reform.[51] They conclude that pacted transition, the mode with the greatest odds of success, or transition through imposition produce restricted democracy because the old elites retain power in some shape or form. O'Donnell and Schmitter's essay, 'Tentative Conclusions about Uncertain Democracies' in *Transitions from Authoritarian Rule*, is another important contribution in the same vein. In the same tradition as Rustow, Linz and Stepan, they highlighted contingent choice:

> the high degree of indeterminacy embedded in situations where unexpected events (fortuna), insufficient information, hurried and audacious choices, confusion about motives and interests, plasticity and even indefinition of political identities, as well as the talents of specific individuals (virtu) are frequently decisive in determining outcomes.[52]

As Colomer has argued, uncertainty was regarded as an essential feature of political change in the context of the work of O'Donnell, Schmitter and Whitehead. This new approach emphasized subjective factors 'while structural conditions were now considered to be not only insufficient but even unnecessary for attaining political aims'.[53]

Przeworski was one of the first to point out the problems associated with the early versions of the strategic approach. Essentially, he noted that, while the language was that of strategic interaction, the analysis was embedded in structural assumptions. Adopting arguments from public choice, Przeworski has used the distinction between hardliners and softliners to develop a game-theoretic model of authoritarian withdrawal. Staying in the realm of bargain making, Donald Share and Scott Mainwaring have developed a 'transactional approach' to the process of transitions,[54] while Samuel Huntington has examined transition in the context of the relative power of government and opposition.[55] Not only bringing people back in, but also putting them centre stage, Giuseppe DiPalma characterized democratization as the 'crafting' of alliances in the transition process.[56] In their analysis, John Higley and Richard Gunther attributed democratic consolidation to 'elite settlements' and 'elite convergence'.[57] While offering a critique of what she claimed was the excessive voluntarism of such approaches, Terry Lynn Karl built her scheme around a typology of transition paths that rested ultimately on the possibilities of elite pact making.[58] In 'The Political Economy of Democratic Transitions', Stephen Haggard and Robert Kaufman argue that

> the specifics of these approaches differ in important respects, yet they converge on a number of points that can be traced directly to Rustow. First, the key actors in the transition process are political elites, whether in the government or opposition, not interest groups, mass organizations, social movements, or classes. Second, actors are typically defined in terms of their orientation toward regime change (hard-liners–soft-liners, moderates–extremists) rather than by interests rooted in economic structures and conditions or institutional roles. Third, actors behave strategically; their actions are influenced by expectations concerning the behaviour of allies and rivals. Finally, democratization is the outcome of explicit or implicit negotiation; new institutions are 'bargains among self-interested politicians'.[59]

It is, therefore, clear that current academic orthodoxy lies firmly within the agency or elite model of transition. However, the usefulness of some streams of this analysis remains problematic. In a 172-nation comparative study of the preconditions of democratization, Tatu Vanhanen points out that the problem with O'Donnell, Schmitter and Whitehead's study in *Transitions from Authoritarian Rule* is that it does not test any clearly stated hypothesis nor produce such hypotheses.[60] Oddly, O'Donnell and Schmitter seem quite proud of this:

> We did not have at the beginning, nor do we have at the end of this lengthy collective endeavour, a 'theory' to test or to apply to the case studies and thematic essays in these volumes.[61]

As Vanhanen has observed, their study clarifies the final stages of the process of democratization, but it does not provide any theoretical explanation for democratization. As Przeworski points out, much of this exhaustive literature bore no fruit. Although O'Donnell and Schmitter focused on strategic analysis and looked at the problem from the perspective of actors, their work shied away from

> adopting a formalistic, ahistorical approach inherent in the abstract theory of games. Given that the macro-language of classes, their alliances, and 'pacts of domination' was the dominant vocabulary of the time, the result was an intuitive micro approach often couched in macro language.[62]

Empirically, it seems that there is strong evidence supporting actor-based and elite settlement theories of the initial phase of democratization. In the context of the most recent wave of transitions the cases of Poland and Hungary provide the most obvious examples. The problem is that, unlike earlier theories, including Lipset's modernization approach, these new approaches lack predictive power and do not sufficiently allow for hypothesis testing. Unni Edvardsen agrees with this view.[63] He argues that the actors-and-process paradigm has failed to account for political actors' choice of strategy. He makes the point that Karl and Schmitter's four 'modes' of transition are assumed to be the prime determinants of whether democracy emerges.

Yet their model is not based on a decision rule. Being purely descriptive the model lacks predictive value and fails to explain two issues. The first problem is why an actor prefers one strategy to another in any context. Second, the model does not explain why one mode is more likely to bring about democracy than another. In particular, Edvardsen argues that there is no basis for Karl and Schmitter's conclusion that the pact mode has the greatest likelihood of success in a democratic transition. In short, assumptions are made about the motivations and goals of actors and elites, but if such approaches are to offer any leverage in the explanation of change such models must be underpinned by theoretical assumptions and testable hypotheses.

As has already been noted, Przeworski has exhorted scholars to test the hypotheses he has generated. In 1991, he pointed out that as the events in Eastern Europe unfolded scholars were on the verge of having enough cases to test these hypotheses systematically.[64] By adopting individualistic or rational-choice assumptions, Przeworski has moved the strategic approach forward from a point where the preferences of actors were simply assumed to an analytical framework that is underpinned by explicit a priori statements about the expected behaviour of strategic players. The scholarship of Colomer and Geddes,[65] amongst others, follows in this vein. Because these authors have conducted their analysis of the process of transition within the context of an explicitly laid-out set of theoretical assumptions, and because they have used the tools and formal models of game theory, it is possible to both replicate and build upon their scholarship.

We have so far concluded that it is not appropriate to examine the case of regime change in Poland as either an evolutionary or a revolutionary phenomenon; we have also found that structural scholarship failed to predict the possibility of change in Eastern Europe more generally and that, while actor-based strategic approaches provide a more accurate account of what occurred in this last wave of democratization and regime change, this approach has generally not been underpinned by explicit theoretical assumptions. The work of Przeworski and Colomer is a response to this lacuna. Unlike much of the previous strategic analysis, their work is underpinned by the formal individualistic assumptions of rational choice and game theory.

At this point, we move on to a discussion of the analytical framework upon which this study of regime change in Poland will be based. The starting point for this discussion is the characterization of regime change as a collective-action problem.

Regime change: collective action as a framework of analysis

Michael Laver has defined the 'collective-action problem' in the following terms:

> It arises when rational people desire collective consumption of goods from which they cannot economically be excluded, and when each individual's contribution to the production of these yields a directly consequential benefit

that is less than the cost involved. Rational individuals will then have strong incentives to enjoy the benefits of the good without paying for it, and in this sense to take 'free rides' on it.[66]

The ultimate collective-action problem is the abolition of the existing order or regime and the supply of a new order and a new set of rules supplying more beneficial outcomes. This was precisely the scenario that regime reformers and opposition activists faced in Poland throughout the 1980s. Elinor Ostrom and James Walker have used the public choice paradigm to analyse recent transitions[67] and they have defined the problem in the following terms:

> The problem of collective action is finding a way to avoid deficient outcomes and to move closer to optimal outcomes. Those who find a way to co-ordinate strategies receive a 'co-operation dividend' equal to the difference between the payoffs at a deficient outcome and the more efficient outcome.[68]

Ostrom and Walker argue that, in the context of Russia and Eastern and Central Europe, it is important to explore how a wide diversity of institutions 'that are neither markets nor states'[69] operate to enhance the joint benefits that individuals achieve in collective-action situations. Ostrom and Walker point out that participants in a self-governing or anarchic process constitute many of these institutions. They have not been imposed by external authorities and are obviously not statist solutions. Ostrom and Walker further argue that the very creation of these institutions is itself a collective-action problem and that understanding how individuals solve different types of collective-action problems is of substantial analytical and normative importance:

> To understand how institutions that are neither markets nor states evolve and cope with collective action problems, we need to unpack larger and more complex problems into a series of transformations that occur between the provision of any good and its consumption. For each transformation process we need to understand the kind of behaviour that individuals adopt.[70]

In Poland, as in other parts of Eastern Europe at the end of the 1980s, the collapse of the command economy as well as the collapse of the socialist project more generally created a collective-action problem. As Oberschall points out, communist discourse had become empty rhetoric and the erosion of regime legitimacy had been facilitated by the private acceptance by regime elites that the system had failed.[71] The problem was how to extricate both state and society from the game being played under the clearly suboptimal rules of the command system. When we look at how individuals and groups come together to achieve a goal, in this case, a change in the rules of the game, we are in fact analysing the art of crafting institutions. Ostrom and Walker argue that crafting such institutions can be viewed as one of creating co-ordinated strategies for players in multilevel games:

> Two types of co-ordinated strategies enable participants to extricate themselves from collective action dilemmas: one exists when individuals

agree upon a joint strategy within a set of pre-existing rules; another when an effort is made to change the rules themselves by moving to a collective choice or constitutional choice arena. The possibility of switching arenas is frequently ignored in current analyses of collective action problems.[72]

Ostrom and Walker work on the assumption that rules are a public good and that agreement on better rules 'affects all individuals in the group whether they participate in the reform effort or not'.[73] Anticipating the 'free rider' problem, they point out that the temptation to free ride in an effort to craft new rules may be offset by the strong interest that most individuals have in ensuring that their own interests are taken into account in any set of new rules:

> Further, the group might be 'privileged' in the sense that one or a very small group of individuals might expect such a high return from provision that they pay the full cost themselves.[74]

This is the context, I argue, in which party reformers or softliners took on the role of political entrepreneurs:

> The entrepreneur supplies 'political services' for a fee. These services may include enforcing agreements made by group members, imposing sanctions on free riders, or getting more deeply involved in the co-ordination and generation of collective action – for example by identifying strategies that allow group members to generate collective action, or even producing goods and services directly and using limited powers of coercion to 'tax' the group with enforced payments for these. To save ink, let's call the 'political entrepreneur' a *politician* and the 'group to which political services are supplied' the *public*. The portfolio of political services that are provided might be thought of as a *regime*.[75] (emphasis added)

It is being argued that General W. Jaruzelski and the communist party reformers who initiated the Round Table process were political entrepreneurs. As political entrepreneurs, they were the agents of regime change. This group was prepared to absorb the costs of creating the new rules of the game in anticipation of the rewards they would accrue in the new game. In an article entitled 'Economic Theories of the State', Russell Hardin observes that it may be in each individual's interest to support an extant order that is generally defective.[76] Hence, it may be that, although citizens would benefit from a change in regime, no individual would benefit enough to take the costly action necessary to change it. He makes the point that in general the logic of collective action can be devastating for any hope that we can collectively provide ourselves with collective benefits:

> An odd analogue of that logic applies just as forcefully to the burden of switching from a defective to a more beneficial co-ordination. But if a Gorbachev comes along to take the lead in moving us from a defective to an alternative co-ordination, we may find it remarkably easy to switch.[77]

The role of political entrepreneurs and their clients

Frederik Barth has written one of the earliest treatments of the role of the entrepreneur in social change.[78] He argues that there are several reasons why anthropologists should investigate the entrepreneurial activity in the societies they study. Barth points out that entrepreneurship is closely associated with general leadership and the social structure of communities. Also, it very frequently involves the relationship of persons and institutions in one society with those of another economically more advanced one, and the entrepreneur becomes an essential 'broker' in this situation of culture contact:

> But in the most general sense, one might argue that in the activities of the entrepreneur we may recognize processes which are fundamental to questions of social stability and change, and that their analysis is therefore crucial to anyone who wishes to pursue a dynamic study of society.[79]

Barth *et al.* set out to look at the entrepreneurial career as a process or as a chain of transactions between the entrepreneur and his environment. In setting out to describe the social aspects of that environment, Barth *et al.* argue that such descriptions should emphasize the reciprocity of the transactions between the entrepreneur and those around him:

> In other words, we need to see the rest of the community as composed of actors who also make choices and pursue strategies, and we must analyze routinized, institutionalized community life in terms of the choices that are available and the values that are ascribed – factors to which the entrepreneur, through his relations with other people, is subject, but which he also by his very activity may modify and change.[80]

From this perspective, all social activity may be analysed as the result of constrained choices and, thereby, connected with the variables of 'value' and 'purpose'. It hardly needs to be said that the goods that are obtained through entrepreneurial activity are clearly not restricted to purely monetary, or even material, forms but may take the form of power, rank or experience and skills. If politics is viewed as an enterprise, the problem the political entrepreneur faces is how to locate clients. He does this by at first locating unsatisfied needs or by nurturing such needs in a population:

> A political entrepreneur is a person who works to attain desirable power positions. He can only achieve these, within this political structure, by obtaining the stewardship of votes from clients; and clients render him votes on the understanding that he acquires for them – by means of his expertise – specific, culturally defined goods.[81]

Political entrepreneurs in Eastern Europe

The two most obvious groups of individuals that may be described as political entrepreneurs come from the reform wings of the various Eastern and Central

European communist parties and from the moderate ends of the opposition elite or counter-elite. In the Polish case, Catholic Church activists are also strong candidates for the role of political entrepreneurs. Another obvious group is enterprise managers, as are individuals who were active in Kadar's second economy in Hungary. This coincides with the views of regional specialists such as Elemer Hankiss who have argued for a Grand Coalition theory of regime change in Hungary.[82] In 1990, he argued that a new ruling class, a grand bourgeoisie, had entered the political arena. He saw the emergence of an alliance of four social groups:

> the most dynamic members of the younger generations of the Kadarist oligarchy; second, the same type of people coming from the upper and upper-middle layers of state bureaucracy; third, from the managerial class, i.e. the managers of great state companies and agricultural co-operatives (called the 'red' and the 'green barons'); fourth, the most successful members and families of the emerging entrepreneurial class.[83]

Hankiss was not alone amongst area specialists in predicting such a coalition of interests. Another Hungarian writer, Szelenyi, detected a coalition of the 'reform-minded cadre elite, the technocracy, and the new petty bourgeoisie'.[84] Hankiss argues that the ruling elite gave up its coercive and bureaucratic power without too much resistance and took the risk of a radical transformation of the political system because it realized that it had a good chance of converting the power it had possessed in the old system into a new kind of power which would be relevant and workable in the new system.[85]

Defining payoff and utility

So what is the payoff or the utility for the political entrepreneur? Specifically, what did the reformist group around General Jaruzelski hope to achieve with its attempt to change the rules of the game? Clearly, the hope of future incumbency under new rules is one form of payoff. However, in the case of many 'party reformers' there were two kinds of potential payoff. Arguably, particularly in the Hungarian case, some hoped to be able to exchange political power for economic power after the communist parties lost exclusive power. Second, many reformers recognized the inevitability of change and sought to exert as much influence as they could on the transformation process and thus secure a stake in the new order.[86]

In the *fin de siècle* situation of Eastern Europe, the actors involved did not have perfect information; all kinds of mistakes were made and actors did not always know the moves that others were making. However, given that the game was about shaping or indeed controlling the future, it follows that an actor's utility could only be realized in the future. Following Michael Laver, I assume that

> the less an individual discounts future utility, the more likely that he or she is to find it rational to stick to a conditionally co-operative strategy, and the greater the consequent prospect of resolving the collective action problem concerned.[87]

Political entrepreneurs expect potential rewards and, thus, are prepared to underwrite the costs of overthrowing the *ancien régime*. For the opposition activist, the rewards include becoming part of the new ruling elite, shaping the rules of the new game to suit individual interest, approval and reputation benefits. For the party reformer, enterprise manager, technocrat or financial entrepreneur, there is the twin chance of economic power through privatization as well as the hope of retaining political influence.

Defining costs and benefits

In analysing stability and institutional change, Douglass C. North has described the agent of change as the 'individual entrepreneur responding to the incentives embodied in the institutional framework. The sources of change are the changing relative prices or preferences'.[88] North allows for the grey, fuzzy bits where people's preferences and perceptions come in:

> we are at something of a loss to define, in very precise terms, the interplay between changes in relative prices, the ideas and ideologies that form people's perceptions, and the roles that the two play in inducing changes in institutions.[89]

From the perspective of regime change, the big question is when do relative price changes lead to institutional change and when are they simply a source of recontracting within the framework of the existing rules? North argues that the easiest way to think of these issues is in an equilibrium context:

> Institutional equilibrium would be a situation where given the bargaining strength of the players and the set of contractual bargains that made up total economic exchange, none of the players would find it advantageous to devote resources into restructuring the agreements. Note that such a situation does not imply that everyone is happy with the existing rules and contracts, but only that the relative costs and benefits of altering the game among the contracting parties does not make it worthwhile to do so. The existing institutional constraints defined and created the equilibrium.[90]

Clearly, the relative costs of opposition and bargain seeking changed because of internal and external political developments in Eastern and Central Europe and the Soviet Union. In the context of the collective-action problem, that is, the overthrow of the communist regime, the international political environment in which Eastern Europeans existed was provided with an external political opportunity in the form of Mikhail Gorbachev. In the domestic context, a political opportunity was created by the gradual delegitimizing of communist power. There are two key factors here. First, there is the gradual collapse of the command economy and the private acceptance by regime elites that the system had failed. Regime opponents were also provided with political opportunity by the failure of attempted reforms and by the subsequent division within the regime elites occasioned by the economic failure and the erosion of legitimacy.

As we noted earlier, Anthony Oberschall has remarked, in the context of the collapse of communist party legitimacy in Eastern Europe, that communist discourse and frame had become empty rhetoric: 'When a regime lacks or loses legitimacy, the challenger's discourse and frame prevail.'[91] Przeworski has identified two factors that led to the destabilization of the communist monolith and the destruction of the party's legitimacy. The first was the embourgeoizement of the party elite, which diminished the elite's ability to crush dissent. His second point is that implicit in the concept of 'goulash communism' was the admission that the model was flawed. Once Khrushchev and later party chiefs publicly identified Western living standards as something to be aimed at, the cat was out of the bag. In the context of the relative costs of opposition, the balance sheet was steadily slipping in favour of those capable of arbitrating change. As Przeworski has argued:

> By 1989, party bureaucrats did not believe in their speech. And to shoot, one must believe in something. When those who hold the trigger have absolutely nothing to say, they have no force to pull it.[92]

Following Olson, Gordon Tullock has offered his by-product theory of revolution.[93] Essentially, a critique of the public goods approach, Tullock argues that revolutions should be analysed in the context of the private rewards for those who participate in them:

> The largest profits from revolution are apt to come to those people who are (a) most likely to end up at the head of the government, and (b) most likely to be successful in overthrow of the existing government. They have the highest present discounted gain from the revolution and lowest present discounted cost. Thus from the private goods theory of revolution, we would anticipate senior officials who have a particularly good chance of success in overthrowing the government and a fair certainty of being at high rank in the new government, if they are successful, to be the most common type of revolutionaries.[94]

Tullock points out that superficial examination of history would seem to indicate that the private goods theory is upheld by the empirical data. Another obvious area for empirical investigation concerns the expectations of revolutionaries. Bearing in mind the problem of categorizing 1989 as a 'revolution', it is worth noting Tullock's point that research is required to establish whether his impression that revolutionaries generally expect to have a good position in the new state is correct:

> Further, my impression is that the leaders of revolutions continuously encourage their followers in such views. In other words, they hold out private gains to them.[95]

Morris Silver's argument provides support for those who might want to test the hypothesis that revolutionaries have made a calculated choice.[96] He argues that in the private interest framework, the revolutionary is viewed as having made an occupational choice to become a 'ruler' and to this end devotes a portion of his time to politics of a certain type:

> Revolutionary activity itself is a form of 'investment' in human resources:
>
> (1) it creates a position or, one might say, an annuity for the revolutionary;
> (2) it provides the revolutionary with some of the organizational, communications, and military skills needed to earn the 'wage' paid by society to its rulers for producing 'order'.[97]

Hankiss provides convincing support for those who would argue for a private reward theory of revolution or regime change in the context of Eastern Europe in 1989. He makes the point (in relation to Hungary) that it was not only the threat of economic collapse and loss of power that prompted the members of the ruling elite to implement radical reforms. An important factor, according to Hankiss, was the knowledge that they had a fairly good chance of transferring their power into a new and more efficient socio-economic system:

> This would be the consummation of a historical process: the new ruling elite of 1948, which began to rule in the 1950s as a small, despotic vanguard and became a parasitic oligarchy in the 1960s and 1970s, has found in the late 1980s the ways and means to establish itself, for the first time since it came to power, as part of a strong and legitimate ruling elite or ruling class, forming a 'grand coalition' with the managerial and the emerging entrepreneurial class. I have warned that – depending on how far the country will be able to develop the institutions of a constitutional democracy and those of welfare state – their rise to power may limit as well as increase the freedom of society.[98]

Rational choice, game theory and 1989

It is an implicit assumption in many of the explanatory approaches reviewed above that 1989 can be categorized as a revolution. While this notion is highly contested,[99] the idea of regime or rule change as a collective-action problem is a useful heuristic device in the conduct of academic analysis of the phenomenon. Furthermore, approaches such as Tullock's by-product theory of revolution and North's cost–benefit analysis of institutional equilibrium and change open up the possibility of researchers tracking the relationship between the initiation of political or regime change and alterations in the cost–benefit structure of actors' preferences.

Many scholars question the application of game theory to non-institutionalized settings or indeed moments of crisis.[100] It is argued that periods of regime change are implicitly inappropriate canvasses for the application of game-theoretic models where it is presumed that actors are rational and in possession of perfect information. Given the nature of the complex range of external, internal and economic factors that affected the choices made by political actors in Eastern and Central Europe following the initiation of Gorbachev's reforms, it can be taken for granted that national regime leaders made such choices without perfect information. G. Tsebelis argues that

> As the actor's goals become fuzzy, or as the rules of the interaction become more fluid and imprecise, rational choice explanations will become less applicable.[101]

However, Tsebelis concedes that the validity of the rational-choice approach increases where elites are involved, and in addition he argues that the results (of applying rational-choice models) are more likely to be fruitful in iterated situations in which people learn or are naturally selected than in non-iterated games. Tsebelis continues that behaviour will more closely mirror rational-choice prescriptions when the issues are important and that the degree of approximation will vary with the level of information. With these provisos in mind, it seems clear that the repeated elite interaction between communist regime actors and the Solidarity opposition in Poland throughout the 1980s satisfies Tsebelis's conditions; the game was iterated and the issues were unquestionably important. That said, the problem of the lack of perfect information remains.

More recently, Josep Colomer has argued that both rational choice and game theory are appropriate analytical platforms for the study of processes of political change:

> Transition from a nondemocratic regime by agreement between different political actors is a rational game. If rulers are unable to maintain their unchallenged domination and the opposition is not powerful enough to impose its preferred regime alternative, two possible outcomes can result. The first is a civil war...the second possible outcome is a compromise of rational actors with different preferences on an intermediate formula between dictatorship and democracy.[102]

Colomer specifically posits that his reasoning differs from other analyses in holding that an agreed transition to democracy could be the outcome only of misinformed or miscalculating actors' strategies. He disputes Przeworski's analysis that rational well-informed actors could not promote a process leading to democracy but could only work to maintain the authoritarian status quo or a 'broadened dictatorship'.[103]

The central issue that arises in the context of the Colomer and Przeworski debate is the question of whether actors will operate on the basis of a 'farsighted criterion of choice'[104] during periods of regime crisis given the long-term consequences for the rules of the game:

> The assumption that rational actors can have some degree of foresight is postulated for situations of regime crisis which involve decisions with long-term consequences – the choice of the rules of the game – and do not usually

appear very often in individuals' lives (perhaps once in a generation). Actors participating in a transition process can have strong incentives to make calculations anticipating the foreseeable consequences of their choices if they believe that they are not likely to have the opportunity to repeat the game soon thereafter.[105]

Colomer's argument in relation to far-sighted time horizons is a central plank of his analysis of the process of democratic transition in Poland and is also central to his refutation of the Przeworski hypothesis that Eastern and Central European regime actors sought only 'broadened dictatorship' and not full democratization.[106] Colomer also rejects the view that political equilibrium and perfect information are necessary conditions for the appropriate application of game theory models:

> Usually, transition actors have noncoincident expectations regarding their relative strength in the future... These different expectations are compatible because the transition process is characterized by a relatively high degree of uncertainty in comparison with more stable political regimes... The uncertainty of such an open situation induces actors to make some concessions in pre-electoral bargains.[107]

While it is hard not to agree wholeheartedly with Colomer's attack on structuralist scholarship which failed to predict the collapse of communism and the transition process in Eastern Europe, his rejection of Przeworski's contention that democratic transition only results from the miscalculated strategies of party elites is more problematic. Colomer posits that in certain situations actors operate on the basis of a 'farsighted criterion of choice', which, he says, induces non-myopic equilibrium instead of short-term-looking myopic equilibrium. Colomer further argues that rational actors can anticipate other actors' reactions and counter-reactions to their decisions in order to avoid undesirable and inefficient results and that this condition 'can be associated with a process of regime change in which actors can remember a previous failed experience of civil conflict or believe (themselves) to be playing a game that is very unlikely to be repeated soon'.[108]

While it is plausible to argue, as Colomer does, that past memories of failed bargaining induce non-myopic strategic behaviour, it is arguable that his view that actors will perfectly anticipate each others' moves and, thus, avoid inefficient outcomes is more problematic. First, there is the issue of actors' access to information and, second, there is the matter of disequilibrium and uncertainty at times of regime crisis. Third, Colomer's contention that this non-myopic behaviour only applies to the decision to negotiate or not to negotiate and not to any subsequent round of bargaining leaves us with only a partial explanation of actual outcomes. If it is deemed that regime actors may be far-sighted at the outset, how do we characterize their behaviour during subsequent rounds of the game? In the specific context of the Polish Round Table, Colomer argues that the agreement was 'viable because it gave the actors reasonable expectations of satisfying their priority interests: freedom of association for Solidarność and maintenance of the

Communist's dominant role, respectively'.[109] However, because the Polish reformers were ahead of the rest of the Eastern European transitions, 'mistaken expectations'[110] about the party's prospects in competitive elections led to unexpected defeat. Colomer concludes that because of a 'stroke of bad luck'[111] the results of the June election produced a 'political upheaval'.[112]

But contrary to Colomer's analysis, it will be shown here that the outcome had nothing to do with bad luck, but a lot more to do with the fact that PZPR strategists did not make informed evaluations in relation to a range of Round Table institutional bargains and, in particular, the party's expected performance in the election. It will be shown that party actors did not behave rationally in that they did not assess the available information at their disposal. The question that arises is a simple one: what would have been the effect of perfect information on the PZPR's decision to enter into talks with Solidarność or, indeed, on the institutional bargains negotiated by the party at the Round Table; consequently, what are the implications of the answer to this question for Colomer's theory of strategic transition and Przeworski's contention that democratic transition only results from the miscalculated strategies of party elites?

This volume will provide a process-driven analysis of a range of institutional bargains negotiated at the Round Table in order to assess whether the strategic misperception of PZPR negotiators produced the almost immediate collapse of communist power and not the broadened dictatorship that had been expected. With this aim in mind, it is argued that regime change in Poland in the late 1980s is best understood as a collective-action problem and that political entrepreneurs such as General W. Jaruzelski and the reform wing of the PZPR initiated the Round Table process as a way of resolving that problem with the provision of new rules of the game. It is argued that these reform-oriented entrepreneurs, or apparatchiks, initiated this process in the hope of securing future incumbency and political gains in the new order.

In subsequent chapters, we will examine each of the key Round Table bargaining scenarios in order to assess whether PZPR negotiators were strategically far-sighted, as Colomer posits, or merely seeking the broadened dictatorship posited by Przeworski. While Colomer's expectation of non-myopic behaviour applies only to the initial decision of regime actors to negotiate, it is hoped that by applying these two hypotheses to the various Round Table bargaining scenarios, it will be possible to demonstrate the gap between actors' strategic expectations and actual outcomes. Examining subsequent rounds of bargaining in the light of these two hypotheses provides a heuristic with which to gauge the empirical record and, thus, explore in a systematic fashion the behaviour of PZPR negotiators.

3   Explaining the collapse of communism in Poland

There is an implicit assumption in much of the case study analysis of the collapse of communism in Poland that the PZPR made a number of strategic mistakes that precipitated the party's demise. Such accounts have given the notion that PZPR participants blundered in their negotiations at the Round Table. Osiatyński quotes President Aleksander Kwaśniewski who told him that the PZPR had mistakenly believed it was strong enough to retain power and to enforce any compromise that might be reached at the Round Table:

> This illusion saved us from the Romanian experience. If the Party leadership realized how weak it was, there would never have been the roundtable talks and peaceful change.[1]

Kamiński has shown that the communists made two critical mistakes at the Round Table talks by agreeing to certain details of the future electoral law. The first one was the error of estimation. The communists estimated their level of political support from non-adjusted polls. 'Such polls were doomed to paint an overly optimistic picture'[2] of the likely electoral outcome. As Kamiński argues, the second mistake was an error of omission. The PZPR proposed single-member district majority run-off (in short, MR) as the electoral law. This gave them worse outcomes than Single Transferable Vote (STV) or Proportional Representation (PR) Party List systems would have produced.

The results of the June 1989 election unleashed political chaos.[3] Solidarność negotiators had agreed to a 65:35 division of seats for the 'contractual' *Sejm* at the Round Table. This arrangement, amongst other institutional agreements reached during the talks was designed to ensure the party's control of the legislative process. This division reserved 65 per cent of *Sejm* seats for the communist party and its allies while Solidarność and opposition candidates could contest the remaining 35 per cent. Only 2 of the 35 communist party candidates on the national list election to the contractual *Sejm* reached the 50 per cent requirement and were elected on the first round.

While the PZPR's allies, the Peasant Party, managed to get three candidates elected to the *Sejm* on the first round, the result was that only 5 of the 299 seats reserved for the ruling coalition were secured on 4 June. This performance contrasts with that of Solidarność whose candidates secured 160 of the 161 seats reserved for the opposition in the first round. In the election to the Senate, which was fully contested, Solidarność took 99 of the 100 seats, with the communist party failing to secure a single seat (the other seat was won by an independent millionaire). The party's electoral collapse precipitated a crisis and made the implementation of the Round Table accord problematic. Although both Solidarność and PZPR negotiators moved quickly to patch up the crumbling agreement, 'the planned chronology was rapidly overtaken by the new pace of events'.[4]

Much of the analysis of the PZPR's collapse has concentrated on the PZPR's fatal choice of a majoritarian electoral system. So, while these contributions explain how the outcome might have been different had alternative choices been made, they do not explain why or how these choices came to be made. This analysis will show that this error over the choice of electoral system was part of a bigger pattern of PZPR strategic errors in their negotiations over a range of institutions during the Round Table process. Tracing the genesis of the Round Table process and examining a whole range of PZPR strategic choices will expose the matrix of decisions and institutional outcomes that led to the party's collapse. Previous accounts have assumed that the PZPR contained softliners and hardliners and that these internal divisions played a major role in the party's lack of a coherent game plan or strategy.[5] However, it will be shown here that a very small group within the party elite propelled the Round Table process and that younger party players were able to hijack the negotiations when this elite lost control of the bargaining process in the context of the dynamic of change they had initiated.[6]

This analysis is premised on the assumption that while structural and external factors created the necessary conditions for regime change in 1989, there were not sufficient conditions to precipitate the collapse of communism in Poland. However, external factors, including Gorbachev's reforms and his abandonment of the Brezhnev Doctrine, created institutional disequilibrium within Poland and elsewhere in Eastern Europe towards the end of the 1980s. The most significant impact of this disequilibrium was a change in the relative costs and benefits of the preferences and available political alternatives of communist regime players. A number of additional theoretical assumptions underpin this framework of analysis. First, it is assumed that PZPR Round Table negotiators were rational, goal seeking and utility maximizing. The validity of the rational choice assumption is increased given the tight nature of the elite group that negotiated on behalf of the communist party. Second, it follows that rational behaviour can be modelled and that rational PZPR actors would not have knowingly made suboptimal choices that would lead to the collapse of communist power. In the context of the theory of games, it is, therefore, argued that false expectations and miscalculation on the part of PZPR negotiators precipitated the fall of communism.

In their seminal work on the Polish transition, Josep Colomer and Margot Pascual argued that the misinformation of actors made the Round Table pact possible and that this put Poland ahead on the path towards change.[7] Colomer and Pascual take the view that had the players had true information about the Polish voters' preferences and had Solidarność understood its own strength, then neither side would have agreed to the Round Table compromise. The more likely scenario would have been sharp conflict followed by repression.

Marek Kamiński's counter-factual analysis of the outcome of the June 1989 contractual election also assumes that PZPR players made ill-informed strategic choices at the Round Table.[8] As we have already remarked, Kamiński has shown that the PZPR's consent to the elections was founded on an overly optimistic estimate of its popular support. An alternative electoral law, the STV, would have been mutually acceptable to Solidarność and the coalition government and would have been critically better for the communists. Kamiński's argues that

> the configuration of social, economic, and geo-political factors in Poland in 1989 were not sufficient for the fall of communism. I argue that the collapse of the communist regime in Poland could quite likely have been prevented if the communist rulers hadn't committed a series of mistakes.[9]

Kamiński argues that both STV and PR would have been acceptable to Solidarność:

> This mistake, the choice of a weakly dominated proposal, was probably due to the complexity of the decision-making environment, the lack of technical knowledge about electoral rules and their properties, and finally, the fact that under communist estimates about the distribution of voter preferences, alternative laws produced similar outcomes.[10]

While Kamiński's seminal work is, perhaps, the most important explanation to date of why the Polish communist party lost power when it did, it is, nonetheless, limited to the analysis of the PZPR's bargaining over the electoral rules. Kamiński has stated that his goal was not to reconstruct the political history of the fall of communism. His interest lies in the Round Table bargaining process that produced the voting procedures and the subsequent political games. However, given the relevance of Kamiński's analysis and conclusions to the debate between those who argue the case that democratic transition may be the strategic, far-sighted goal of regime actors and those who take the view that such transitions are the outcome of the strategic mistakes of regime liberalizes, it seems more than worthwhile to expand upon Kamiński's framework of analysis and examine a range of Round Table bargaining scenarios to see what they can tell us about these two conflicting perspectives.

This volume builds on the works of Przeworski,[11] Colomer and Pascual,[12] Kamiński[13] and Colomer[14] and posits that dynamic change was precipitated in Poland in 1989 because both the PZPR and Solidarność opposition actors were playing the political game in conditions of uncertainty without full informational resources. Przeworski and Colomer propose two conflicting individualist explanations of the collapse of communism and subsequent transition in Poland. Our main task here is to assess which of these explanations provides the most explanatory leverage. Following King, Keohane and Verba, a desirable property of any theory is that it should generate as many observable implications as possible.[15] In other words, readers should be told in advance what behaviour or consequences they should expect to see given theory A or theory B.

It also follows that in order to track the extent to which a hypothesis stands up, it is necessary to outline the observable implications prior to the actual analysis. In each case of institutional choice discussed in the course of this volume, the observable implications will be informally stated at the outset so that an assessment can be made of how the facts of what happened conform to either the predictions of Przeworski or Colomer. With these two conflicting explanations in mind, we will first examine the PZPR's decision to initiate talks with Solidarność in order to assess whether the party was far-sighted and strategic or not. This will be followed by an analysis of the party's expectations in relation to the relegalization of Solidarność. Did PZPR negotiators methodically evaluate the consequences of relegalizing the union?

We then move on to investigate the PZPR's expectations from the establishment of a strong presidency followed by an analysis of the party's agreement to the introduction of a freely elected Senate. It has been argued earlier that the choice of a majoritarian electoral system proved fatal to the PZPR's electoral prospects: we will now elaborate on Kamiński's analysis of the bargaining over this institution in order to assess what it tells us about the party's motivation and behaviour. We also look at the PZPR's conduct of the electoral campaign and its expectations in relation to the role of the Catholic Church in that campaign.

Colomer argues that the Round Table should be understood in the context of an 'agreed project [that] was a redefinition of the rules of the political game according to the estimated bargaining power of the players'.[16] If this was the case and both Solidarność and the PZPR coincided in their strategies and sought an 'intermediate formula',[17] then it follows that a number of observable implications can be elaborated. First, we would expect that each institutional bargain should reflect the relative strengths of the regime and opposition, as perceived by PZPR and Solidarność negotiators at the time. We would also expect that party negotiators would plot each move or strategic choice on the basis of the most up-to-date information at their disposal. We also expect, as Colomer posits, that the PZPR would 'react and counter-react to their choices before the game ends'.[18] In other words, if PZPR negotiators make mistakes in a bargaining arena then we expect them to try and rectify that error or mistake. We also expect to see PZPR actors making future-oriented calculations when making strategic choices or agreeing bargains. In simple terms, we do not expect to see PZPR negotiators make calculations on the basis of immediate short-term interest alone.

Przeworski posits that 'misperceptions lead liberalization to transition'[19] and that regime liberalizers want 'democracy that will keep them in power'.[20] A number of observable implications flow from Przeworski's hypothesis. First, we would expect to see PZPR actors evaluating each strategic move on the basis of its capacity to preserve incumbency. If, as Przeworski posits, liberalizers only seek 'broadened dictatorship',[21] then the PZPR should only agree to the creation of institutions that it can realistically hope to do well from. Unlike Colomer, he does not expect actors to be far-sighted in their calculus. If as Przeworski posits, misperception leads to liberalization, then we expect to see the PZPR making flawed evaluations and strategic errors arising out of a failure to update information in the bargaining arena.

Having outlined the observable implications and expected behaviour that flow from the hypotheses of both Przeworski and Colomer, we now move on to a description of how we will go about evaluating these conflicting explanations. It has been argued earlier that game-theoretic forms of rational choice have been most effective in the study of highly institutionalized settings in the developed world.[22] Moments of transition are, by their very nature, unstable because the institutional settings are also unstable and the rules are undefined. Such situations are, as Przeworski has argued, moments of maximal uncertainty.[23] In moments of transition, people may not know where their interests lie and so it is arguable that political transition seems to defy rational forms of analysis. In their analysis of the cases of Zambia and Yugoslavia, Bates *et al.* argue that spatial models proved too limited and sought to use 'games of incomplete information'[24] where the limitations of rational choice became evident.

Bates *et al.* argue that the 'cultural' knowledge required to complete a rational choice explanation reveals the complementarity of interpretivist and rational choice approaches. In criticizing the game-theory method, they argued that game theorists often fail to acknowledge that the approach requires a complete political anthropology. They argued that if game theory is to provide explanatory leverage, a detailed knowledge of the values of individuals and of the expectations that individuals have of each other's actions and reactions is required. Furthermore, they argued for a detailed and fine-grained knowledge of the precise features of the political and social environment within which individuals make choices and devise political strategies:

> To construct a coherent and valid rational choice account, then, one must 'soak and poke' and acquire much the same depth of understanding as that achieved by those who offer 'thick' descriptions.[25]

According to Bates *et al.*, the phrase 'analytic narrative' captures their conviction that theory linked to data is more powerful than either data or theory alone.[26] While the narrative form has been the dominant form for explaining human behaviour, it is recognized that they often mobilize the mythology and hagiography of their times. This led many social scientists to reject the method and instead adopt quantitative methodologies. Bates *et al.* argue that in seeking a logically rigorous approach they have returned to the rich, qualitative and descriptive materials that narratives offer. In exploring a concrete historical case, such as the Round Table process and the collapse of communism in Poland, we are examining the choices of individuals embedded in specific settings. In examining such choices, we need to unpack and trace the sequence of actions, decisions and responses that generate events and outcomes. Following Bates *et al.*, the analytic narrative approach seeks to account for outcomes by identifying the mechanisms that generate them. However, rather than representing a return to 'thick' description, the analytic narrative method employs rational choice theory and, thus, 'thin' reasoning to produce tightly constrained accounts based on rigorous deductive reasoning grounded on close attention to empirical detail. As we noted earlier, both logic and the empirical record thus discipline analytic narratives.

In the particular case we examine here, we will explore a range of the Round Table bargaining scenarios in the context of the specific observable implications of the conflicting Przeworski and Colomer hypotheses. In explicitly laying out the expected behaviour, given each hypothesis in each bargaining scenario, it will be possible to evaluate each explanation in order to see if the interview data, historical records and other sources support the logic and implications of either account. Following Bates *et al.*, this analysis will locate and explore the particular mechanisms that have shaped the interplay between strategic actors involved in the Round Table. In so doing, it will be possible to model the process that generated the collapse of communism in Poland and will capture the essence of the story of that collapse.

The present analysis and conclusions are based on an extensive series of interviews conducted with key party players, opposition negotiators and observers carried out between 1989 and 2000. However, this analysis builds on research conducted in Poland prior to, during and in the year after the Gdańsk shipyard strikes in August 1980. During 1980 and 1981, interviews were conducted with Solidarność leader, Lech Wałęsa, the founding members of the Free Trades Union of the Coast, the Solidarność presidium, Catholic Church hierarchy, priests and activists as well as a wide range of dissidents.[27] The conclusions have also been drawn from a close examination of Politburo records, Round Table documents and the work of other academics. Previous accounts have not highlighted the fact that PZPR negotiators were warned of the dangers of choosing a majoritarian electoral system for the election to the Senate. It will be shown that two electoral experts[28] advised the party, in writing, against opting for a majoritarian electoral system but that this advice was ignored. By tracking the series of events and decisions and showing that this electoral error was part of a wider pattern of strategic misperception which produced the institutional arrangements agreed at the Round Table, it will be possible to offer a more comprehensive explanation of the collapse of communism in Poland.

Given the emphasis on actors and actor-based explanation, it is important to establish the credentials and credibility of the interview data gathered for this analysis. Many scholars eschew interviews with actor stakeholders on the basis that such persons will seek to tell the story that serves their best interests or fits the legacy they wish to leave. Several factors obviate that perception in this case. First, many of the key PZPR players were interviewed over time. For example, the PZPR first secretary, General W. Jaruzelski and the last communist prime minister, Mieczysław Rakowski, were interviewed by the author on two separate occasions,[29] while Professor Jerzy Wiatr was interviewed on five occasions during the 1990s.[30] Lengthy and detailed interviews (not all quoted from in this volume) were conducted with PZPR spokesman, Jan Bisztyga, immediately after the election in June 1989 and on two subsequent occasions in 1990 and 1992.[31]

Interviews with less well-known players have also been conducted over time. In the case of opposition dissidents and Solidarność activists (subsequently post-Solidarność elected representatives), including Lech Wałęsa, interviews have been conducted on several occasions between 1980 and 2000.[32] The fact that the interviews have been conducted over time has allowed the author to check the consistency of actors' stories. It has been possible to compare the analysis and information of PZPR interviewees to ascertain whether their stories conflict with each other. Conducting the interviews over several time periods has also made it possible to ask interviewees to respond to the accounts of other actors where differences have occurred.

As Bates *et al.* point out, a narrative 'possesses a background or setting, a beginning, a sequence of scenes and an ending'.[33] For the purposes of this analytic narrative, we, therefore, need to know the background and setting of the actors or interviewees from whom we have sought information so that we can evaluate their motivations in the context of the version of events they relate. In order to help the reader to follow those motivations, we now move on to provide brief biographical details of the actors interviewed in the course of the research for this book. Before doing so, it is important to note that the prime source of information for this analysis is a series of interviews conducted in May 1999. At that time, a range of PZPR and ex-Solidarność actors were asked the same set of questions concerning the Round Table process. These questions are related to the conditions that facilitated the initiation of the contacts between Solidarność and the PZPR; what the PZPR expected to achieve from the initiation of talks with the opposition; what the PZPR expected to achieve with the relegalization of the union; what party actors expected from the institutional agreements they reached with Solidarność as well as a range of questions that sought information on the PZPR's disastrous choice of electoral rules. Questions were also posed concerning the PZPR's relationship with the Catholic Church and the conduct of the election campaign.

Interviewees: biographical information[34]

Stanisław Ciosek

Born in 1939, Stanisław Ciosek was a member of the Polish United Workers' Party (PZPR) from 1959 to 1990. He held a variety of administrative posts within the party. He was awarded a degree in oceanic studies from the College of Economics in Sopot in 1961 and served for the next 14 years in the administration of the Union of Polish Students. Ciosek was a deputy to the *Sejm* from 1972 until 1985, and from 1975 to 1980, he was a regional first secretary in the PZPR. He served on the Central Committee (Komitet Centralny, KC) from 1980 to 1981 and from 1986 to 1990. He was also a member of the Council of Ministers between 1980 and 1985. In the years leading up to the Round Table negotiations

(1986–8), he was the general secretary of the KC PZPR and general secretary of the National Council of the Patriotic Movement for National Rebirth (PRON). Ciosek served as Poland's ambassador to Moscow between 1990 and 1996. In 1996, Ciosek became President Kwaśniewski's adviser on international affairs. Ciosek was centrally involved in the ongoing talks between the Catholic hierarchy and the PZPR during the 1980s. He was one of a small group of key party figures who drove the process that led to the Round Table.

Professor Stanisław Gebethner

Stanisław Gebethner is a professor of Political Science at the University of Warsaw. He represented the government coalition at the subtable on Political Reform at the Round Table. Regarded as a non-party intellectual who was close to but not a member of the PZPR, Professor Gebethner also had links with the PZPR's coalition partner, the Democratic Party. Professor Gebethner is a consti-tutional and electoral expert. Subsequent to his role at the Round Table, Professor Gebethner has advised various parliamentary committees on the relative merits of various electoral formulae and constitutional issues. Apart from his teaching and advisory work, Professor Gebethner writes extensively on Polish politics, in particular on constitutional and electoral matters.

General Wojciech Jaruzelski, first secretary of the PZPR

> Mr Jaruzelski is a dramatic person in Polish history. In his personal biography one can see the dramatic destiny of many Polish people and elites. Jaruzelski, a representative of the gentry and intelligentsia, becomes a communist because he thinks that it was the great hope for the world. Having served the interests of communism and the Soviet Union, he then sees it collapse in the eighties. And what is left? His national feelings and patriotic sentiments! Now I believe that Mr Jaruzelski is a different person – and this different person I have learned to respect.[35]

Bronisław Geremek's assessment of Jaruzelski encapsulates the key points in his biography. Jaruzelski's father was a volunteer in the war against the Bolsheviks in 1920. Later, he was deported to Siberia along with his father who died there. As a young man, he attended a training school for Soviet officers and joined the Soviet-inspired Polish First Army and took part in the liberation of Poland as well as the suppression of anti-communist resistance. He joined the Polish Workers' Party in 1947. General Wojciech Jaruzelski, first secretary of the KC PZPR, chairperson of the Council of State of the PRL, was appointed prime minister in February 1981. One of the central issues surrounding Jaruzelski is whether he should be regarded as a Polish patriot or traitor arising out of his role in the introduction of martial law in December 1981.[36] Jaruzelski was the key figure behind the PZPR's decision to enter into talks with Solidarność in the late 1980s.

Jaruzelski claims that it was the realization that it was impossible to reform the economy without social support that precipitated the initiation of the Round Table process.[37] Jaruzelski was elected as the first president of post-communist Poland in August 1989 but retired from public life after his presidency came to an end in December 1990. In 1992, he published his book *Stan wojenny dlaczego...* (Martial law why). Jaruzelski has been a prolific defender of his role in both martial law and the Round Table process. His most recent work is *To Differ Wisely. How Did Marshal Law Come About?*[38] On 16 October 2001, General Jaruzelski went before Warsaw district court, accused of being the chief perpetrator behind the bloody suppression of demonstrations in Gdańsk and Szczecin in December 1970.

Lech Kaczyński

Lech Kaczyński was a Round Table participant on behalf of Solidarność. He was born in 1949 (one of identical twin brothers) and graduated from the University of Warsaw's Faculty of Law in 1971. He was later awarded a doctorate from the University of Gdańsk. During the 1980s, Kaczyński was the director of the dissident-led Bureau for Intervention of the Workers' Defence Committee (KOR) and advised striking workers in the Lenin shipyards in Gdańsk in 1980. He was a member of the Helsinki Committee in Poland between 1982 and 1989 and played a prominent role in the opposition throughout the 1980s. He was an adviser to Lech Wałęsa both before and after the collapse of communism and was a member of the Citizen's Committee between 1988 and 1991. He became a Senator representing the post-Solidarność Civic Parliamentary Club in 1989. He was later elected to the *Sejm* for the Centre Alliance and served as a presidential adviser on issues of national security. He was the Minister of Justice from June 2000 until July 2001. He has held prominent positions in Prawo i Sprawiedliwość (PiS) and is currently the mayor of Warsaw. He is also professor of Law at the Catholic Theological Academy in Warsaw.

General Czesław Kiszczak

General Kiszczak likes to style himself as the 'Father of the Round Table'. While Mieczysław Rakowski was the last communist prime minister of Poland to actually head a government, General Kiszczak was the last PZPR prime minister of the People's Republic of Poland. He was in office from 2 to 15 August 1989 but was unable to form a government. In the first non-communist government of Tadeusz Mazowiecki, Kiszczak served as vice-prime minister until July1990. Kiszczak is best remembered for his role as Minister of the Interior, a position he held for most of the 1980s. He was extremely loyal to General Jaruzelski and, in January 1989, threatened to resign with his first secretary when the Tenth Plenum of the KC PZPR resisted their Round Table initiative. Kiszczak is bitter about the outcome of the Round Table and feels that the Solidarność opposition hijacked the project. He maintains that his role in the Round Table is not fully appreciated.

Since 1993, General Kiszczak has been facing a series of charges in relation to the killing of miners at the Wujek mine in Katowice. In 1994, Kiszczak's trial began in Warsaw's Provincial Court. He was accused of breaking the constitution of the Polish People's Republic. In 1996, he was acquitted. In 1997, the Court of Appeals rejected General Kiszczak's acquittal and the court case started in the court of first instance. The trial started again in May 2001. In March 2004, Kiszczak was given a two-year suspended sentence.

Aleksander Kwaśniewski

President of Poland (serving two terms – 1995–2000 and 2000–2005), Aleksander Kwaśniewski was born in 1954 and helped to initiate the Round Table negotiations. He was co-chair of the subtable on Union Pluralism at the Round Table. Kwaśniewski studied international business at the University of Gdańsk and was a member of the PZPR from 1977 until 1990. He was active in the youth wing of the party and was leader of the Union of Polish Students and editor of the student weekly *Itd*. He was the Minister for Youth Affairs between 1985 and 1987 and chair of the Committee for Youth and Physical Fitness from 1987 to 1990. Kwaśniewski played a significant role at the Round Table and was responsible for proposing that the election for the Senate would be competitive. He played a central role in the creation of the post-communist SdRP and was leader of the SLD (Democratic Left Alliance) until he became president in 1995.

Adam Michnik

Adam Michnik has been a lifelong human rights activist and Polish dissident. He was adviser to the Solidarność movement and negotiator for the opposition at the Round Table. He is a renowned intellectual, historian, author and is editor-in-chief of *Gazeta Wyborcza* since it was launched in the spring of 1989 (then a pro-Solidarność election gazette). Michnik was imprisoned between 1968 and 1969 following his expulsion from the University of Warsaw after the protest marches in March 1968. He was a founding member of the KOR in 1977 and a lecturer in the 'Flying University' which brought workers and intellectuals together in unofficial seminars. Michnik was imprisoned again between 1981 and 1984 and from 1985 to 1986. After the Round Table, he served as a *Sejm* deputy for the post-Solidarność Civic Parliamentary Club until 1991.

Bishop Alojzy Orszulik

Father Alojzy Orszulik was made bishop of Łowicz in 1982 and played a key role in the process that led to the Round Table. Bishop Orszulik lectured in canon law until 1989 and held several positions in the Polish Episcopate including director of the Press Department between 1963 and 1993. In 1980, he began serving as a member and secretary of the Joint Commission of the Government and Episcopate of Poland. Bishop Orszulik's Round Table memoir is an important source of information concerning the relationship between the PZPR and the Catholic Church in Poland.

Mieczysław Rakowski

Mieczysław Rakowski was prime minister in the months leading up to the Round Table. Born in 1926, he was an officer of the Polish People's Army from 1945 until 1949. Rakowski received a doctorate in history from Warsaw's Institute for Social Sciences in 1956. He became a member of the Polish Workers' Party in 1946 and, from 1948 until its dissolution, was a member of the PZPR. He served on the KC from 1975 to 1990.

Rakowski was editor-in-chief of the weekly magazine *Polityka* from 1958 until 1982. In 1990, Rakowski became editor-in-chief of *Dziś*, a political magazine. He was a member of the PZPR's Politburo from 1987 to 1990 and the last first secretary of the party. Rakowski has always insisted that he was on the reformist wing of the party although this opinion was not universally accepted. He was not a central figure in the contacts between the party and the opposition in the run-up to the Round Table as he was prime minister during the period. However, he argues that he was the first to invite the opposition to join the coalition government in the autumn of 1988 in the hope that the move might help to resolve Poland's economic crisis. Rakowski is the author of numerous publications on Polish politics.

Professor Janusz Reykowski

Janusz Reykowski was born in 1929 and is a professor of psychology at the University of Warsaw since 1972. Since 1980, he has directed various psychological institutions including the Institute of Psychology at the Polish Academy of Sciences. He also founded the private Higher School of Social Psychology in Warsaw in 1996. He was one of the two co-chairs of the subtable on Political Reform at the Round Table and negotiated on behalf of the government. He was a member of the PZPR from 1949 until 1990 and served on its KC and Politburo between 1988 and 1990. Reykowski became editor-in-chief of the journal *Studia Psychologiczne* in 1972 and is a member of several international psychological associations. Reykowski describes himself as being surprised by the PZPR's request that he negotiate on the party's behalf at the Round Table[39] as he does not regard himself as having been a party insider. The timing of Reykowski's appointment to the KC and Politburo is worth noting.

Professor Andrzej Werblan

Born in 1924, Andrzej Werblan was professor of Political Science at the Silesian University in Katowice. He was a member of the Polish Socialist Party and joined the PZPR at its foundation in 1948. He became a member of the PZPR KC in the 1950s and served as head of the Science and Education Department of the KC. In the 1970s, he became one of the secretaries of the KC as well as deputy speaker of the *Sejm* in 1971. He was a member of the Politburo for a few months in 1980, but resigned in December. He lost his *Sejm* seat in 1985 and was no longer involved in leadership positions from that time. During his active role in the party, he was on the reformist side in 1956, then drifted to the mainstream but was later identified as a reformist leader in 1980–1. In 1968, he became associated with the nationalistic faction of General Moczar, for which he was often criticized in liberal circles. He was not active in the PZPR at the time of the Round Table negotiations but was in regular contact with party activists. In particular, he was in contact with Professor Reykowski and telephoned him in relation to the proposed electoral rules. He also contacted Prime Minister Rakowski who notes, in a published collection of his letters, that Werblan's advice against the use of the majoritarian system for the June 1989 election was ignored because he had not actively participated in the creation of the government or the PZPR's policy-making in the late 1980s.

Professor Jerzy Wiatr

Born in 1931, Jerzy Wiatr is professor of Sociology at the University of Warsaw. He has held various academic positions in Poland and abroad, including the presidency of the Polish Political Science Association and vice-presidency of the International Political Science Association. From 1981 to 1984, Wiatr was director of the Institute of Marxism–Leninism of the PZPR KC. He was a deputy to the *Sejm* and a negotiator for the party at the subtable on Political Reforms at the Round Table. He was a founding member of the Social democracy of the Republic of Poland following the dissolution of the PZPR in 1990 and a member of the SdRP's National Council between 1991 and 2000. He was chairman of the party's Warsaw Council between 1991 and 1996. Wiatr was an MP from 1991 until 2001 and Minister for Education between 1996 and 1997 in the government of Włodzimierz Cimoszewicz.

Sławomir Wiatr

Sławomir Wiatr has played a prominent role in post-communist government in Poland including a position as campaign chief in the country's negotiations with the European Union prior to membership. He was awarded a PhD degree in Journalism and Political Science at the University of Warsaw in 1980. From 1979 until 1983, Wiatr worked at the Warsaw University Methodology Centre for Political Sciences, followed by a job at the Polish Academy of Science (PAN) Centre of Management Sciences (1983–9). In the academic years 1981–2 and 1986–7, he lectured at the Institute of Political Science of Vienna University. In 1984, he completed an internship at the Institute of Political Science of the University of Heidelberg. In 1989, Wiatr was appointed as the head of the youth department of the PZPR KC and from July 1989 he was appointed as a secretary of KC.

Sławomir Wiatr was head of the PZPR KC on youth in 1989 and founder member of the post-communist SdRP along with his friend, Aleksander Kwaśniewski.

He participated in the Round Table talks and was a deputy in the tenth *Sejm* – the last before the fall of communism. In 1991, he became involved in business, introducing the Austrian Billa supermarket chain to Poland. Other companies with which he was linked were active in social research, marketing, promotion and construction. From 1980 to 1989, he was an activist of the Polish Society of Political Science, acting as chairman of its Warsaw branch and a member of the Central Board. From 1990, he chaired the Kazimierz Kelles–Krauz Foundation. Sławomir Wiatr is the son of former Education Minister Jerzy Wiatr.[40] He is a friend of his contemporary, former President Aleksander Kwaśniewski.

In this chapter, it has been argued that the analytic narrative 'offers a method for moving from the context rich world of events and cases to explanations that are logically rigorous, illuminating and insightful'.[41] It has also been shown that by explicitly laying out the observable implications of hypotheses, in this case of conflicting theories of Adam Przeworski and Josep Colomer, it is possible to empirically assess which of these theories provide the most explanatory leverage. It has also been argued that the interview material gathered for this volume is unlikely to yield false information given the fact that many key actors were interviewed over time and because it has been possible to check the veracity of stated positions with other contemporary documents. Finally, in providing a brief biographical note, it is hoped that readers will be able to follow the motivation and logic behind interviewees' statements more easily.

We now move on to the analytical narratives themselves. In Chapter 4, we examine the context of the initiation of the Round Table process and try to determine the strategic goals and expectations of PZPR negotiators at the start of the process.

4 PZPR strategic goals

Expectation and outcome

> The compromise was built on the weakness of Solidarność and the party. The party was too weak to liquidate us and we were too weak to gain power.[1]

The structural context

Any credible analysis of the context of the collapse of communism in Poland must take into account the overall structural background conditions in Eastern and Central Europe in the 1980s. Zbigniew Brzeziński's argument that communism entered into a general crisis in the late 1980s was noted in the introductory chapter.[2] Other authors have referred to systemic exhaustion.[3] In simple terms, the command economy system was no longer capable of being reformed by *ad hoc* interventions. In retrospect, it can be seen that several factors, including economic decline and the destabilizing impact of cyclical attempts at economic reform and partial marketization contributed to this systemic exhaustion. Virtually all of the Polish communist party leaders spoken to in the course of this research have confirmed that the main motivation behind the initiation of talks with Solidarność and the opposition in 1988 was the realization that the PZPR's economic reform effort had failed.[4]

Another important contextual factor was modernization. Although spotty in the Soviet bloc, modernization created demands that could not be dealt with in the context of monocentric politics. In Poland, Hungary and Yugoslavia, various attempts and varieties of party reform ended in different degrees of failure. But perhaps the key factor which created the mindset for change in Poland and the rest of the Soviet bloc was the collapse of the ideological belief and commitment to communism. Adam Przeworski has observed that, by 1989, party bureaucrats did not believe in their own propaganda. And not believing in their own speech, lessened their authority as well as their ability to enforce that authority.[5] The decomposition of communist elites was another factor of varying importance in the destabilization of communism across the Soviet bloc. This was a particular problem in Poland where factionalism had always been rife. However, after 1980 when General Jaruzelski suppressed Solidarność with the introduction of martial law, the differences between the hardliners and party reformers became more acute.

The fatal blow, as has been noted earlier, was, of course, Gorbachev's abandonment of the Brezhnev Doctrine. It is arguable that the communist system of governance in Eastern Europe would have struggled on had party reformers not been given the green light to initiate economic and social change. The removal of the threat of Warsaw Pact intervention cannot be overestimated as a factor in the collapse of communism in 1989.

In the Polish case destabilization was not confined to the party–state arena alone. A separate but equally important change in the balance of power was occurring within NSZZ Solidarność, in the late 1980s. Voytek Zubek has shown that, by 1988, the Solidarność leadership under Lech Wałęsa was on the run from the younger and more militant elements with its ranks.[6] Initially, some PZPR-oriented commentators and party leaders took pleasure in the Wałęsa leadership's discomfiture. Soon, however, most of the PZPR's leaders began to realize that the dangers stemming from the inception of the new, more radical, movement within Solidarność were incomparably greater than the possible benefits that the party could gain from a weakening of the 'old' Solidarność leadership. There was a growing fear that if left unchecked, the new movement would inevitably continue to develop its new leadership and would find followers among radical intellectuals.

The effect of this realization combined with the impact of Gorbachev's reforms 'even further isolated Poland's besieged communist elite'[7] and encouraged the internal reform of both Solidarność and the PZPR. The overall impact of the radicalization of younger Solidarność members and the various pressures being experienced by the PZPR led both the party and Solidarność to engage in exercises designed to rid themselves of their more radical elements. As the Solidarność theorist Adam Michnik notes earlier, the perceived mutual weakness of both the government and opposition created a context where compromise was the rational and self-interested strategy for both players.[8] It is this context that underpins our analysis of the expectations of PZPR actors responsible for the initiation of the talks process with Solidarność.

Wiktor Osiatyński has argued that the PZPR's main purpose in opening up negotiations was to seek a compromise that, while giving the opposition some say, would secure for the party overall control over developments in Poland.[9] In this scenario, the ideal situation was a distinction between economic and political reforms:

> The Party elite would have preferred to solve economic problems first, and only then move on to political reforms, having thus secured a better starting position for such negotiations. According to Aleksander Kwaśniewski,[10] this turned out to be impossible, 'for economic change requires many years, while political reforms are faster and easier to implement'.[11]

As Osiatyński remarks, the party's bottom line was that it had to retain control of the reforms and negotiations. Even for the party reformers, the idea of democracy was limited to democracy in which the PZPR could not lose.

The initiation of the Round Table process

Was this a far-sighted strategic move aimed at preserving the long-term interests of PZPR actors or a short-sighted strategy designed to retain incumbency?

In order to evaluate the relative merits of the respective hypotheses of Przeworski and Colomer, we must return to the observable implications or expected behaviour and strategies that flow from these conflicting theories. It follows that, in the light of Colomer's strategic transition theory, we would expect to see PZPR actors evaluate their strategic options in the context of their assessment of the relative strengths of the party and the opposition. We would also expect to see PZPR negotiators attempting to perfect and update the information at their disposal as they plot each strategic move. Furthermore, we would expect regime players to react and counter-react to the moves of opposition negotiators. In general terms, we would expect to see actors focusing on long-term interests. In the light of Przeworski's hypothesis, we expect that the preservation of short-term incumbency will be the focal point of PZPR strategies. If broadened dictatorship was the goal of these actors, then we would also expect to see them only agreeing to the creation of new institutions they can hope to dominate and do well from. If, as Przeworski posits, transition results from the misperceived strategies of regime liberalizers, then we expect to see actors making flawed evaluations that are not in the PZPR's best interests as a result of a failure to update and improve the information at their disposal.

Author interviews with PZPR Round Table negotiators

Professor Janusz Reykowski

The psychologist, Professor Reykowski, argues that there was a growing awareness of the ineffectiveness of the command economy among the political elite towards the end of the 1980s and that this was a prime factor in the move to initiate talks with the opposition:

> In my conversations with people in the leadership at the time I learned that they thought there would either be fundamental economic reform or the economic system was likely to collapse or at least not be able to meet the basic needs of society. So the problem was how to reform the system and there was some plans and programmes. And towards the end of the eighties the authorities learned that they themselves do not have the social approval for deep reform. So there was an intensive search to get this approval. One attempt was a kind of referendum in 1987.[12] It failed and there was no clear idea as to what to do next. The problem was how to get the public's approval. So during the eighties there was a crossroads. Either the system is going to be more and more repressive and sooner or later face a major confrontation with part of society or some completely new solution would have to be attained. And this new solution was an attempt at reaching an agreement with the opposition. The idea was that if the opposition became part of the political system then it would give an opportunity to make reform because the attitude of society in general would be different.[13]

Professor Reykowski provides an interesting insight into the private motivation of the elite to which he belonged. He points out that the situation of the nomenklatura played a part in the elite's decision to seek an accommodation with the opposition:

> The living conditions of the nomenklatura, the people at the highest level here, was approximately that of a lower middle class person in the west. Of course there were many privileges in comparison with ordinary people. But this privilege from today's perspective was a joke. For example as a Politburo member, as I was in 1989, I had no problem buying shoes. I had two or three pairs of shoes to choose from and the ordinary person had no choice – only one pair. Ordinary people had to stay in line to buy a TV, but I could buy one in one week. So there was a privilege – there were stores behind the yellow curtains for the governmental elite. But these stores were very low quality in comparison with an ordinary provincial store in Poland at present. What I am saying first is that this ruling class was very economically frustrated – especially those people who had contact with the west. They knew that people in a similar position in politics in the west lived completely differently.[14]

Apart from the personal economic frustration of the elite, Professor Reykowski remembers a pervasive feeling of the ineffectiveness of the system of governance in Poland:

> They [members of the elite] were not able to pursue any rational plan. Even people at the top level felt helpless. They perceived the system as irrational. Both these aspects – the economic situation and the inability of self-realization in professional life meant that people were ready to search for deep change. There was of course a large group of party activists – the party leadership in the large factories and the large voivodships [districts] who were trying to protect the status quo. They didn't want to have any radical change except the change of leadership.... In the second part of the seventies – the elite was transformed. New people had joined the party. Most of them were university educated – most of them in the best Polish universities. A high proportion had contact with the west. So what I am saying is that there were social processes within the system that made the system more inclined to change. At the same time there were also highly conservative factions who would interfere with any change. An important factor was that after martial law, in the second half of the eighties, Jaruzelski eliminated the more conservative elements from the leadership.[15]

Professor Reykowski points out that the goal of those seeking talks with Solidarność at the end of 1988 was not very clear or defined:

> The idea was that the opposition should become part of the political system. But what does it mean to become part of the political system? It means, at least, to be in the parliament. The idea to recruit the opposition had come

earlier. Prime Minister Rakowski wanted to have ministers from the opposition in his government. But the opposition argued that if they were recruited into government they would be of no value because their supporters would perceive them as traitors and not as independent political actors. They would be seen as part of the system. I think that for quite a long time in the Polish leadership there was not a clear awareness of this situation. But in early '89 it was possible to agree that Solidarność was [of] no use if it was perceived as being in the same position as PSL [Peasant Party] or other so-called satellite parties. It was then understood that the opposition must be independent and be an independent political agent. And for that to be the case, it cannot be a part of centralized and a mono-party system.... There must be a new form of political game. It was hoped that parliament would be a new area – a new institution where this new political game can be played. But nobody was very clear how this new game could be played. There was a vague premonition that the next step would be more fundamental change in the political system. Nobody was thinking very far ahead.... But the main idea... was to transform political conflict from the streets into the parliament and into the political arena.... It was hoped that if Solidarność was in parliament that the conflict will be rationalized in this form and not by demonstration. Of course the aim was not clear or highly articulated![16]

MP Professor Jerzy Wiatr

MP Professor Jerzy Wiatr identifies three conditions that facilitated the convening of the Round Table:

First Gorbachev and the new Soviet policy! Second the elimination of the hardliners from the PZPR, which took place gradually and was completed at the tenth Party Congress. And then, the third factor was Solidarność. Two things happened within Solidarność in 1988 that were important for future compromise. One was that the leaders of Solidarność – the people around Wałęsa realized that they were strong enough to negotiate from the position of strength but not strong enough to win if they rejected negotiation. This kind of feeling was probably consolidated by the strikes in the summer of 1988. And then the second thing was that for the first time, the Solidarność leadership realized that they had been challenged by a younger and more radical generation. So for them it was now or never! By the way, it explains to some extent why among the radical and younger militants of Solidarność there is now so much criticism of the Round Table. In a sense the Round Table was stealing the chance from these younger more radical people. It was probably the last moment for the old leadership. Had Wałęsa and the people around him made a mistake and rejected the offer of compromise then probably they would have been replaced by the younger, more radical generation of Solidarność. The results would probably have been worse for the party but also worse for the then leadership of Solidarność.[17]

So, what were the PZPR's perceived alternatives to opening negotiations with the opposition? Wiatr argues that other alternatives were being considered:

> I would call it the Brazilian alternative rather than the Spanish model. Amongst those of us who were in power in the late eighties on the national level, nobody could be described as conservative anti-reform. But there were distinctively different approaches. Everybody knows what is meant by the Spanish way. So what is Brazilian – it is reform from above without consultation about changing the system. Change is imposed, but the essence of what *abertura* meant in Brazil was keeping power. It meant marginalizing the opposition but at the same time democratizing the system to the point where Brazil became a democracy. So it was a different channel. I think that Rakowski[18] was actually the strongest and most serious exponent of the Brazilian strategy even if he would not have called it by that name. You cannot describe Rakowski as a conservative anti-reformer. He was for democratic change long before many people were in favour of this option! But at the same time he was very emotionally anti-Solidarność and rather sceptical about the prospects of negotiation and hoping that he would be able to reform the system from above. He could not achieve this aim for many reasons; one of them being that he was given the chance too late. But there are also other factors in the Brazilian case – the fact that the opposition was destroyed much more radically in the coup of 1964 than was the case in Poland after martial law. Also the Brazilian economy was doing very well as compared to the dismal state of the Polish economy. I think it explains why the Brazilian road was closed for Poland. That's my view. The only road that was open if Poland was to avoid a confrontation was a negotiated transition and that was what Jaruzelski opted for. I think that at a certain point Rakowski joined the team, but that was a different story.[19]

Wiatr argues that there was a sense of there being no turning back from the process of change among the reform-oriented elite who played the central role in initiating the Round Table:

> At the time, the aim as I saw it was a form of contractual democracy, which was another way of saying negotiated power sharing with the objective of democratizing the system later on. When we discussed this question of what would come later I remember asking [Professor Janusz] Reykowski and [Mieczysław] Rakowski whether the PZPR would be in power or opposition when the system becomes fully democratized? In fact history has shown that we would be both in opposition and in power. So both sides were proved to be right. But one thing was obvious that the power sharing was not an arrangement for another half-century. Sharing power would allow Poland to transit through the very difficult period of reforms. The idea was, and we were probably over optimistic, to try and reach a socially acceptable situation in a few years and then compete in a fully democratic election – not from the position of extreme political weakness but from a position of sharing the credit with Solidarność for the improvement in society. We didn't want a situation where

one side was only to be blamed for the failures and the other side could be seen as the only hope. That was certainly my view. People had various expectations but the realization that there was no return was fairly common.[20]

General Wojciech Jaruzelski

General Wojciech Jaruzelski argues that a turning point in his analysis of the options open to the PZPR was the government's failure to win the 1987 referendum on the party's economic reform package:

> It was the best example of how the rulers of Poland were so naïve. It was decided to count the votes on the basis of the people eligible to vote rather than on the basis of the actual turnout or vote. In any country there is no such formula – it was more than democracy. It was stupid. If you count the votes of those who came – then over 70 per cent voted. Looked at this way the referendum was won by the government – but if you calculate on the basis of 100 per cent total electorate then we lost with just over 40 per cent supporting the reforms. This state considered to be totalitarian in 1987 honoured the result. But it was a signal that the necessary reforms would be painful and that we needed to enlarge the basis of social support. We were looking to widen the base of support and we were using the church. Publications were emerging, a pro-reform coalition was being suggested and anti-crisis pacts were being mooted in the press. The whole conception, before the strikes.[21] was to introduce the opposition to the system of power, but doing it smartly on a restricted basis...we did not want to formalize the opposition as Solidarność. But we were looking for ways to exploit, to invite the opposition to help us reform the economy.... It is worth noting that some important steps were made under Rakowski[22] and they were very close to those continued by Mr Mazowiecki[23] ...but Mr Mazowiecki was enjoying a state of national euphoria and so people were ready to take risks. But we did not have that luxury – even our own trade unions[24] started to strike. But the big change came both from the political and psychological point of view.[25]

General Jaruzelski took the view that he was under no immediate pressure to initiate talks with the opposition groups. However, he did feel that the moment was optimal from a strategic point of view. The Solidarność-led strikes in the spring and late summer of 1988 had not been universally supported across the country and there were elements within Solidarność who were questioning the capabilities of Lech Wałęsa and the group around him:

> The strikes were finished very quickly. And there was a lot of opposition from within the party and reservations about me personally and about the fact that I was starting talks with the opposition. The situation was not pressing...but I believed it was an optimal moment to make the move. Because when there is a winner and loser it is hard to say that negotiation or a compromise is going on – because there is someone who lost and someone who won. But in 1988

during and after the strikes one cannot say there were winners and losers. Solidarność was weak and the strikes were waning. Even the first move toward the government was from Solidarność. Professor Andrzej Stelmachowski, who had the blessing of the church, approached the government about the possibility of talks. But it is true to say that the government was weak. We knew the result of the referendum (1987) and we were unable to carry out the reforms without broad support. So it was a very good moment to start talking about negotiations. It took more than half a year to set it up and the church played a major role. But the main barrier was the question of Solidarność's legalization. The party members were thinking about giving the opposition part of the power, some part of the *Sejm*. Rakowski was offering to share ministries with Solidarność – but the party was afraid. There were bad memories of 1981 and fears that we would have strong trade unions making demands. We were afraid of aggression that would hurt the economy.[26]

General Jaruzelski makes the point that he was not afraid of Solidarność as a political force, but he was afraid that the union would create chaos if it was relegalized and allowed to organize in the factories. Jaruzelski's notion of the political role Solidarność would play was coloured by the PZPR's perception of the strength of its own organization:

I was more thinking of [Solidarność as] an additional party – like a Christian Democratic party. We were not afraid of political competition. We had strong political structures of our own. We had our own knowledge that the support for Solidarność was not so strong. But we were afraid that if we relegalized Solidarność, they would create chaos when they entered the factories. It is hard to imagine Solidarność re-entering the factories and saying 'work harder and eat less'.... The state-controlled unions were afraid of the competition from Solidarność, and so before relegalization, they had started being more aggressive. They were going to make demands because they were afraid that Solidarność would snatch away their members. So we were expecting a wave of demands after relegalizing.[27]

General Czesław Kiszczak

Interior Minister General Czesław Kiszczak likes to be described as the 'father of the Round Table'. Almost fanatically loyal to General Jaruzelski, on 11 September 1986 Kiszczak announced an amnesty for political prisoners. He regards this as the masterstroke and first move in the effort to initiate talks with the opposition: 'The basis of the communist system was terror... so our move had great significance and much influence.'[28] Kiszczak says that he wanted to create

the environment for political talks with the opposition so that we could discuss the possibility of improvement of the country. It is important to remember that no serious member of Solidarność would talk to the party while his friends were in prison.[29]

As with all interviews with political actors, it is necessary to exercise great caution in the assessment of General Kiszczak's testimony given his desire to be remembered as having played a key role in the Round Table process:

> The party was very weak. There was a pretence that the party exists – as in the rules and the constitution. But three people ruled Poland – Jaruzelski, Siwicki[30] and Kiszczak. We wanted to legalize Solidarność at the tenth Plenum (of the Central Committee of the Party) on 17 January 1989. We wanted agreement from the party. We wanted to spread the responsibility for legalizing the union. A paper was presented and there was a great debate – but we anticipated the problem. We three – Jaruzelski, Siwicki and myself – arranged a trick. Jaruzelski threatened to resign. Rakowski got to hear of it and he joined in. We all [the three] withdrew in a dramatic fashion. There was a discussion. Henryk Jabłoński led the discussion – the party was afraid of discussion.[31]

Having secured the approval of the Tenth Plenum to enter into talks with the opposition, a meeting was arranged between Solidarność leader Lech Wałęsa and General Kiszczak for 25 January. Kiszczak argues that the timing was right for the opening of talks because both sides were weak:

> It was a chess game. Nobody could make a move to win. Solidarność tried their 1980 strategy – they tried strikes to demonstrate their power one more time. The April–May [1988] strikes failed for Solidarność. They only got the partial support of the workers. In August – they tried again in Gdańsk. Geremek[32] and Wałęsa went up to try and get support. Only 300[33] workers out of thousands joined the strike. The same in Kraków – Nowa Huta! There only 300 or so joined in. Overall only a thousand or so went on strike in the whole country. The people were tired – they'd had enough. Solidarność was weak. They were having an internal crisis. But in the party, people were not happy either. We couldn't manage the economy. People's expectations were not satisfied. The socialist system, the economic model was not reformable. The military men had thought that the army way, discipline, would reform the economy but we didn't succeed. The country needed systemic change. No government with communists and the peasants could introduce reforms. The changes needed required belt-tightening, and for that, public support was required. We were not going to get that. We needed the support of society. But we would not get co-responsibility for the economy and the changes without co-opting the opposition.[34]

Kiszczak argues that the PZPR could have adopted other strategies:

> We could have started the talks differently. We could have made problems for the opposition. We could have talked to the non-Solidarność opposition or with certain wings of Solidarność, for instance the 'August 80'[35] opposition. Also we could have talked to the AK[36] army people. But all of that had the potential to create chaos within the opposition. But we didn't want to do this.

The public had greater respect for Wałęsa than the rest of the opposition. That's why I chose Wałęsa. We didn't mean to harm the opposition.[37]

Kiszczak emphasizes that the goal, the reason for initiating the Round Table talks process was to generate the social support necessary to reform the economy. Limited political change was the means to an end – not an end in itself: 'We thought about reform, market economy *à la* Balcerowicz – we wanted to loosen the straightjacket. We thought about press freedom. But we didn't aim to give power to the opposition.'[38]

Stanisław Ciosek

The political scene in 1988 was the following: Solidarność was weakening – they'd moved from 10 millions down to 2 millions. It was not possible to count exactly but it was weaker and the spirit of Solidarność was getting weaker. That can be checked. One of the mysteries is why the party was going to agree for a free election! And the answer – maybe because Solidarność was getting weaker – so we hoped for a better result. The idea of competition for political elections in 1980 would have been to give up – political suicide. But the party felt in 1988–9 the chances were more or less equal – that is the party against Solidarność. The economy was down the drain despite the attempts at reform with no significant results. Brezhnev was gone... so the climate was different.[39]

Ciosek rejects the notion that the PZPR had no alternative but to negotiate with Solidarność:

Of course there was an alternative. Keep the old way. It would have been stagnation – helpless. We would keep our posts. We could rule for a number of years with the old ways. It was not a tactical move to allow the free election – this whole Round Table compromise. It was not a tactical move – it was a strategic move and change. It was a clear and conscious drive to change the whole situation and system in Poland. It was a deliberate attempt to change the system. It was not to give power to Solidarność – but it was a power-sharing idea. The idea was to try and rule together. But the situation changed.[40]

Ciosek is emphatic that the initiation of the Round Table talks process did not result from some immediate sense of pressure:

The direct goal – the basic goal – the reason was intellectual. There was no physical pressure. The strikes were weak. It was a deliberate intellectual decision! It was not a result of pressure. We were seeking the solution to the current situation and problems. The other countries around Poland were growing at a greater rate. So we could rule in stagnation as it was in 1988. Most probably if we had started to change the face of socialism but leaving the leading role of the party, there would be other solutions. But we decided to allow the opposition to share power. Maybe it was a naïve approach to invite the opposition to power share.... Of course, my instincts were telling me that it was the end of an era – the end of absolute rule! In my opinion everyone was realizing that the relegalizing of Solidarność is the effective end of the leading role and sole ruling of the party.[41]

Unlike Kiszczak who, as we saw, argued that the main aim of the Round Table was to initiate a process of economic reform, Ciosek claims that the aim was to start the process of democratization in Poland. He does not accept that the PZPR made any strategic mistakes at the Round Table:

> It was clear gamble! We were devising the change of a system – so it was a conscious gamble concerning this. The real aim of the changes was not about the economy or socialism to capitalism. It was about a democratization process – a fuzzy democracy.... In the Round Table there is no sign of a free market concerning the economy. The Mazowiecki government made the true choices relating to the political and economic system in Poland.[42]

Mieczysław Rakowski

Mieczysław Rakowski supports the idea that the Round Table process arose not just out of systemic exhaustion but also from the personal exhaustion of the elite players:

> We realized in the second half of the 1980s that the economic crisis [and] the political crisis had not been resolved. We used preventive measures against underground Solidarność and especially in the second half of the 1980s – the underground was still very active. They were publishing a lot of papers, etc. We could see that the system was tired but the main reason and the most important was that since September 1986 there were no political prisoners. All prisoners were released on the 11 September. This meant that the activists were operating in public. Solidarność was openly organizing in many facto-ries. There were two trade unions, the old one, the OPZZ[43] and Solidarność. In 1988 there were strikes in Kraków. The August strikes showed that Solidarność was also weak. Solidarność knew it. Bugaj[44] said that they were like officers without an army. Both sides were tired. Each side was looking for something new and so – the Round Table.[45]

Rakowski says that there was no alternative to negotiation, but he did not expect that the opening up of the Round Table talks process would result in the PZPR losing power:

> We aimed to include the opposition into the existing system of power in the country. I suggested when I was forming my last government that we offer four ministries to Solidarność but they rejected the idea. That was September 1988! To repeat – the general idea was to include the opposition into the system of ruling![46]

Sławomir Wiatr

In 1989, Sławomir Wiatr was an active member of the PZPR. He completely rejects the idea that the collapse of communist power resulted from a mistaken strategy at the Round Table. He admits that many people in the PZPR had a different attitude to the prospect of political change than the generation he represents. He argues that young party reformers like himself and Aleksander Kwaśniewski actively sought deep change in order to position themselves for the creation of a new post-communist social democratic party:

> We were in a sort of situation where we looked at this process, maybe not without emotion, but with an awareness that we had to change our PZPR suit. People with the experience of Rakowski saw it as the end of the world. It was difficult for them to imagine what would happen the day after. That's why the younger generation took an active role in 1989. That's not to decrease the role of Jaruzelski and the group around him because without him nothing would have happened. I have read Rakowski's notes from this period and it displays that he was sceptical about the idea of the creation of a new system in Poland. We were in a totally different condition, intellectually and politically because we believed that we would be weak for a while, but we were also sure that we would achieve important positions in the new system for many reasons. Some reasons were internal. We thought we were more politically talented and that we understood the country and the mechanisms better.[47]

Sławomir Wiatr concedes that the potential outcome was far from clear at the beginning of 1989:

> We wanted the best results. Some people even thought it was possible that we could win the elections.... It was clear that after the elections that there would be a change in the system of power and it was also clear that Solidarność would join this system.... We thought and the Solidarność people thought that the structures from the old system would exist in the new system for some time. Even after the election and the agreement between Wałęsa and the ZSL and SD[48] which gave Solidarność a majority, it was still clear that some posts in the ministries would go to people from the PZPR. The idea of that was more to do with geo-politics than with internal affairs. When you look at it now – and there were a lot of emotions at the time of the 4 June elections – for the more aware and astute end of the PZPR, it was clear that it was the end of the system and the end of the party. From the beginning of 1989, we were intellectually prepared for the organization of a new left-wing party. It was to be a party that would meet the standards of European social democracy. It was also clear that it would be a revolution of the generations. It was clear that this party would be created by the 35-year-old generation. There were two kinds of thinking. One way was from people in the parliamentary structures or people with party roles. So these people were inside this new system created by the Round Table. And

the other approach was that we were preparing for the creation of the SdRP, which happened in January 1990.... At the beginning of 1989 – it wasn't like today – there were going to be great changes between 1989 and whatever happened next. People would have different skins. We knew we would be in a new formation. We didn't know how many left wing parties there would be or how many Solidarność parties there would be, but we knew it would be different.[49]

Wiatr points out that this desire for less radical change was not just a preference of the older generation of the PZPR:

I remember unofficial talks, which were important for the consensus about the election. Bronisław Geremek and Adam Michnik[50] argued that in the future the political scene would not be conducted through parties, but through social movements. They hoped for something that we knew could not happen except in a quasi-totalitarian system. They wanted to keep the organizational integrity of Solidarność. And we knew that the sooner we finished the PZPR, the sooner the decomposition would occur on the other side.[51]

Adam Michnik

Adam Michnik played a central role in the contacts and later on in the negotiations between the union and the government:

HAYDEN: To what extent do you agree that the party negotiated itself out of power politically in order to reinvent itself in the new order?

ADAM MICHNIK: Fairytales! You should read the documents. Till the end, they did not believe that they would lose power and have to give power to Solidarność. They were totally astonished – surprised.[52]

The conditions of change

The evidence from PZPR documents, memoranda, pre-Round Table exchanges and the contemporaneous notes of Catholic Church negotiator, Bishop Alojzy Orszulik.

General W. Jaruzelski has consistently argued that the economic imperative played a major role in the decision to make contact with the 'constructive opposition' in the late 1980s. One of the key aims of the initiation of contacts with Solidarność was the desire to create an environment where Western governments would end the economic sanctions imposed on Poland after the introduction of martial law in 1981. Given the fact that economic aid from within the Soviet bloc did not compensate for the loss of Western aid and capital, the need to appease Western demands for the inclusion of the Polish opposition became more acute as economic conditions deteriorated in the Soviet Union. General Jaruzelski visited Prague in February 1989 for a meeting with the general secretary of the Czechoslovak communist party, Milosz Jakesz, and President Gustav Husak. He used the opportunity of the visit to explain the *raison d'être* behind the PZPR decision to enter into a talks process with Solidarność. The memorandum provided to the Polish Politburo following the trip is the equivalent of a cost–benefit analysis of the determinants of PZPR strategy in the late 1980s.[53] Jaruzelski began his meeting with Jakesz by justifying the introduction of martial law in December 1981:

> The introduction of martial law was a necessity (there was a threat of a catastrophe), in military terms it was a victory but politically it was a defeat. Conclusions had to be drawn from that, the position of socialism had to be rebuilt in people's heads and hearts – something that was not fully successful.[54]

Jaruzelski then explained the reasoning behind the 'round table' and the opening of discussions on political and union pluralism in Poland:

> It is necessary to take such steps as a result of a difficult economic situation that requires unconventional methods and difficult decisions aimed at overcoming inflation and improving the market. This, in turn, would not be possible without the understanding and backing (or at least neutrality) of all significant social forces. The objective, therefore, is to neutralize 'Solidarność' in order to pass successfully through a difficult period of 1–2 years when all these problems will become particularly striking.[55]

Jaruzelski told Jakesz that the PZPR needed

> to create a reality that would allow breaking of the West's economic discrimination. Out of this necessity came the idea of seeking solutions that would lead to the weakening of the opposition's hostility. It is a lesser evil than eventual confrontational solutions and at the same time provides a chance of creating a wide front of national agreement and holding parliamentary elections on a joint platform and with a high attendance of electorate. The accepted course of action therefore provides a chance of reaching a situation that would be safe for socialism and would include the opposition in joint responsibility. Also important in this matter is the position of the Church: currently that means objective support for our efforts.[56]

Jaruzelski said that he was aware that the opposition had its long-term objectives. He said that the aim was to keep the process under the party's control and force the opposition not to incite strikes but to counteract them. Jaruzelski spoke of the conditional opportunity to initiate change:

> It is assumed that insofar as the anticipated process will develop successfully and 'Solidarność' will be able to operate legally, it will be a different 'Solidarność' than the one in 1981. Then it was an anti-Soviet movement, today it declares itself in favour of *perestroika*; then its extremist wing could not be isolated, today there is a very apparent split within it, something that gives us an additional chance.[57]

Jaruzelski also described changes in the attitude of the Catholic Church which created opportunities for the PZPR:

> The relationship between the Catholic Church and the USSR has changed. The Church, to large extent, as a result of the Vatican's eastern policies, is interested in peace in Poland and does not want the emergence of anti-Soviet feelings. It has a moderating impact on the stance of the opposition.[58]

In weighing up the cost and benefits of the PZPR's new strategy, Jaruzelski also provided Jakesz with an assessment of the international situation:

> The other significant element is the international situation. The non-confrontational tendencies weaken the US and Western pressure for destructive actions in Poland. Whereas in 1981 the West was attempting to cause a break out of conflict, now it has adopted a longer term policy of gradually winning different social forces for strengthening pro-western tendencies. This is however a process that can be appropriately won over.
>
> Poland's foreign debt is a serious problem since it impedes the acceleration of the economic development. We are aware that without changes in our domestic policies there is no chance of the West changing its attitude towards our country. Introduced changes create an opportunity to improve our economic relations with the West and also give us a chance to improve economic situation of our country which would, in turn, strengthen the party's position and provide wider opportunities for its policies.
>
> It is possible to adopt such a direction in our solutions because: in the current situation we don't do it under pressure but on our own initiative; there appears to be a positive opinion of the government's work; part of the opposition (Wałęsa, etc.) changes its rhetoric and working methods (from aggression to agreements, strike prevention, compromise). Being fully aware of the dangers, we believe that the above circumstances allow us to take a step that, with due caution, should be, on balance, beneficial to us.[59]

Jaruzelski warned that the success of the 'round table' 'is not a foregone conclusion. The responsibility for its failure should not fall on us'.[60] He told Jakesz that a central part of the deal would be Solidarność's agreement to abstain from strikes for two years:

> This year is an important one. Being fully aware of dangers and differences in political make-up of the opposition the issue at stake for our system is to try to absorb the opposition and to make it participate in shaping of the system. It is a great historical experiment, which, if successful, may have implications reaching beyond Polish borders.[61]

General Jaruzelski's exposition of the reasoning behind the decision to initiate the talks was clearly intended to highlight the fact that the PZPR was starting a process it intended to control. While the Prague memorandum deals with the generalities of the aims of the talks process, other PZPR documents provide more detailed accounts of the specific institutional changes envisaged. A confidential report prepared by a PZPR 'Interdepartmental Team' in September 1988 following the Eighth Plenum of the KC PZPR clearly shows that the party intended to design institutions it expected to dominate.[62] According to this document, the establishment of an upper chamber and the office of the president could be introduced through amendments to the existing Constitution. Acknowledging the fact that a 'deep process of social and political changes'[63] was taking place, the interdepartmental team explained that a new constitution should be the end, rather than the beginning of the process.

In a later chapter, I will provide a detailed analysis of the PZPR's bargaining over institutions, including the presidency and Senate at the Round Table. At this juncture, however, a number of points should be made. First, the characterization of the functioning of the new Senate, as outlined in the departmental team report, clearly shows that the PZPR envisaged it as a vehicle for incorporating the opposition onto a body that would ultimately be controlled by the PZPR itself. The selection mechanism for the Senate would give the president control over one-third of the seats while nominally independent organizations would nominate the other two-thirds. However, given the fact that these organizations would be nominated by the PZPR-controlled *Sejm*, and the fact that the president would always come from within the ranks of the party, it is clear that the party elite saw its future being secured in the context of the creation of a strong presidential system of government.

The fact that a number of members of the PZPR's senior elite were actively thinking about ways of including the opposition in the state's institutions towards the end of the 1980s is not contested. However, as late as June 1988, two years after Kiszczak's amnesty for political prisoners and a mere year before the con-tractual election of June 1989, Polish Catholic Church authorities were surprised to hear that the PZPR was considering the possibility of including the opposition in the formation of a coalition government. Bishop (then Father) Alojzy Orszulik played a key role as a go-between for the PZPR and the opposition during the 1980s. He kept a contemporaneous account of his meetings with both government and opposition representatives.[64] Father Orszulik met with Stanisław Ciosek on a regular basis during the course of 1988 and early 1989:

> Ciosek said that a proposal of creating the Senate or an upper house of the Parliament is being considered. In the *Sejm*, the governing coalition would secure 60–65 per cent of seats. But, in the Senate, it would be the other way round. The Senate would have the right to put forward a motion ordering controversial decisions of the *Sejm* to be voted again, but they should then be supported by two-thirds of votes. Ciosek stated that political pluralism was needed in Poland adding, however, that he did not support trade union pluralism. He returned to the concept of merging Solidarność with existing trade unions, but, according to him, they would not have to be of a party

type. Ciosek added that neither the Americans nor Germans had trade-union pluralism.[65]

The limits of the PZPR's ideas of political pluralism are clear in a note from Father Orszulik's talks with Stanisław Ciosek in November 1988.[66] Father Orszulik reports Ciosek's annoyance at remarks made by Solidarność spokesman, Janusz Onyszkiewicz, concerning free elections:

Ciosek complained about Onyszkiewicz who had demanded free elections in the interview for 'Confrontations'. The party is not prepared for that. For the present, it is being proposed that the party would keep 60 per cent of seats in the Parliament. Ciosek said that their intention was to change the state's structures significantly in the future: We should move gradually towards free elections.[67]

On 4 January 1989, Father Orszulik asked Prime Minister Rakowski if he could envisage free elections in four years' time and whether it was possible for the PZPR to be in opposition.[68] Prime Minister Rakowski acknowledged that free elections might be possible in 4–8 years. He commented that the PZPR was weak and cautioned that the notion of elections in April (1989) was an idea 'discussed in a small circle, not a proposal':[69]

Personally, I am not afraid of confrontational elections. We have at our disposal Security Forces, the party machine and the mass media, but it will be another split which will solve nothing. External conditions make it possible that the conflict in Poland can be resolved. This will lead to social and political order at the end of this millennium.[70]

This chapter begins with a quote from historian and dissident Adam Michnik who played a central role in the Round Table process. As a historian, Michnik has been particularly concerned by the tendency to alter the historical record so as to fit today's political needs. At a conference in Michigan to mark the tenth anniversary of the Round Table, he vehemently rejected the claim that the PZPR had voluntarily handed power to the opposition:

There are two myths that accompany the debate about the Round Table. The first myth, popularized by politicians and columnists associated with the former communist party, talks about the benevolence of the party leaders, who simply turned the power over to the opposition as soon as it became possible. The second stereotype talks about the conspiracy of 'the reds with the pinks.' However, there was neither benevolence nor conspiracy. The strategic goal of the communist party was to gain a new legitimacy for the communist rule in Poland and abroad, and allowing some form of legalized opposition was to be the price for that. The strategic goal of the Solidarność opposition, on the other hand, was legalization of Solidarność and launching the process of democratic transformation.[71]

Conclusion: a 'fuzzy democracy'

This chapter set out to discover whether PZPR actors were far-sighted, as posited by Colomer, or motivated by more short-term interests, as posited by Przeworski, when they initiated the process of contacts with Solidarność. In general, we were seeking to assess whether PZPR actors sought incremental and controlled political change that would facilitate a broadened dictatorship in the short term or whether they looked to their strategic long-term interest and a process of deeper change. We now return to the observable implications or expected behaviour that flows from the hypotheses of Przeworski and Colomer to evaluate what the material, discussed in preceding pages, tells us about these conflicting propositions.

It is clear from the preceding analysis of both interviews with party actors and PZPR documents that the initiation of the Round Table process was enabled by political disequilibrium in the Soviet bloc at the end of the 1980s. Senior PZPR actors, led by General Jaruzelski, understood that the cost–benefit calculus of initiating systemic reform had changed as a result of the abandonment of the Brezhnev Doctrine. Interviews with General Jaruzelski, General Kiszczak, Mieczysław Rakowski, Stanisław Ciosek, Janusz Reykowski and Jerzy Wiatr have clearly identified that the key motivating factor in the decision to initiate talks with the opposition was a fear of economic collapse.

In the context of the Przeworski hypothesis, PZPR actors were motivated by short-term interest and retaining power and so we expect them to try and dominate any institutions agreed in the opening round of contact with the opposition. We also expect to see mistakes arising out of flawed strategic evaluation and incomplete information. We have found evidence to support Przeworski's hypothesis in the contribution of Professor Janusz Reykowski who points out that the goal at the outset of the talks 'was that the opposition should become part of the political system'.[72] Reykowski also states that 'nobody was very clear how this new game could be played'[73] and 'nobody was thinking very far ahead'.[74] General Jaruzelski also supports this perspective. He noted that

> the whole conception, before the strikes, was to introduce the opposition to the system of power, but doing it smartly on a restricted basis.... We were looking for ways to exploit, to invite the opposition to help us reform the economy.[75]

It is clear that General Kiszczak thought of the project in limited terms: 'We didn't aim to give power to the opposition.'[76] Prime Minister Rakowski echoes this view: 'we aimed to include the opposition into the existing system of power in the country'.[77] The Prague document could not be more explicit on the short-term interest that was to be served by the initiation of talks between the PZPR and Solidarność.[78]

Jaruzelski told his Czechoslovak colleagues that the 'objective is to neutralize Solidarność...the accepted course of action therefore provides a chance of reaching a situation that would be safe for socialism and would include the opposition in joint responsibility'. The PZPR's Interdepartmental Team report clearly shows that, in September 1988, party strategists only envisaged the creation of institutions it could expect to control.[79] The Presidential office was to act as the party's guarantee of continued power. Finally, Bishop Orszulik's memoirs confirm the fact that as late as November 1988, Stanisław Ciosek was angered by and rejected Solidarność spokesman Janusz Onyszkiewicz's demand for free elections.[80]

In the context of the Colomer hypothesis, PZPR actors should be strategic and far-sighted; they would be expected to carefully evaluate their options in relation to the relative strengths of the party and Solidarność. We would also expect PZPR actors to react and counter-react to the moves of other players and to have sought to update their contextual knowledge before making choices. A number of statements support Colomer's analysis. First, Jerzy Wiatr argues that the aim was 'a form of contractual democracy, which was another way of saying a negotiated power sharing with the objective of democratizing the system later on'.[81] This conception supports Colomer's contention that liberalizers will seek to create an 'intermediate regime' as they extricate themselves from authoritarianism. Wiatr's son, Sławomir, who would later play a leading role in the formation of the post-communist SdRP, is clearly far-sighted when he talks about the group around him believing that they would 'achieve important positions in the new system'.[82] This group looked to the future and the creation of a new 'left-wing party'.

Stanisław Ciosek, who emphasized that the PZPR perceived Solidarność to be weakening in the latter part of 1988, provides clear support for the expectation that actors will evaluate their options in relation to the relative strength of the opposition.[83] Ciosek says that, in the context of an election, it was thought that the chances of the PZPR and Solidarność 'were more or less equal'.[84] Ciosek confirms the fact that Solidarność's weakened position was seen as the PZPR's opportunity to drive a hard bargain for the union's support for the government's economic reform package. Ciosek, who as we shall see in later chapters, has always claimed that he was involved in a 'deliberate attempt to change the system',[85] describes the initiative as a 'clear...conscious gamble'.[86] However, Ciosek's remarks highlight the limits of the PZPR's plans at the start of the Round Table: 'It was a democratization process – a fuzzy democracy'[87] or perhaps an 'intermediate regime' as Colomer posits.

In the light of the mixed evidence, it is difficult to conclude that PZPR actors were exclusively far-sighted or short-sighted when they initiated the talks process with Solidarność in late 1988. Actors had differing conceptions of the end goal and often displayed elements of both short- and far-sighted behaviour during the period. However, it does seem fair to conclude that PZPR negotiators, albeit gambling negotiators, expected to be able to control the process they had unleashed and engage in incremental and controllable change. They were to learn very quickly that this was a flawed evaluation of their prospects.

5 Strategies and outcomes

Part 1 – institutional choices of the PZPR

The relegalization of the union was Solidarność's main goal at the start of the Round Table. Olson argues that this objective was easily and quickly met.[1] However, he points out that the political conditions surrounding that main goal were much more difficult to define and took much more time to resolve. Ultimately, the PZPR was prepared to relegalize the union in order to achieve its main goal, that is, Solidarność's agreement to participate in contractual elections so as to legitimize the party's economic reform effort. However, the institutional bargaining between the two sides created a dynamic in which new institutions emerged as a result of offer, counter-offer and compromise. So, while it can be seen that both sides had clearly defined objectives at the start of the Round Table, the potential impact of many of the institutional bargains, which emerged out of the dynamic process, had not been comprehensively evaluated. As Olson has argued, the creation of the new Senate was not only haphazard but was also one of the most fateful decisions made at the Round Table. Solidarność wanted free elections as the price it would pay for conceding the strong presidency and, while the PZPR was not prepared to abandon its reserved seats in the *Sejm*, its negotiators, much to the surprise of many involved, offered the opposition a freely elected Senate: 'A government negotiator, apparently without advance consultation on his side, offered the Senate with elections.'[2]

Once the negotiations began, both sides were drawn into a contingent and evolving dynamic. Round Table co-chairman Bronisław Geremek has said that the opposition's acceptance of the principle of non-confrontational parliamentary elections was linked to three bargaining scenarios.[3] The first of the scenarios was the negotiations over the restricted *Sejm* elections, the second was the free elections to the Senate and the third was the creation of the office of president.

This chapter will focus on three Round Table bargaining scenarios: the relegalization of Solidarność; the PZPR's preference for the introduction of a strong president and its bargaining over the introduction of the Senate. The bargaining over the electoral system and voting formula for both the *Sejm* and the Senate will be discussed in Chapter 6.

While the PZPR's negotiators were drawn from the reform-oriented wing of the party, it would be incorrect to regard them as behaving as a single actor at all times. As we have seen, many scholars talk about the PZPR's goals and objectives at the start of the Round Table. While acknowledging the splits between hawks and doves, many of these scholars fail to register the range of opinions that permeated the small clique who conducted the negotiations. So, while there is wide knowledge of the hurdles that Jaruzelski *et al.* had to cross on occasions, such as the Tenth Plenum, when only the threat of resignation forced the party to back his decision to open talks with the opposition, there is less analysis of the differing expectations of the PZPR elite who negotiated on the party's behalf. As a consequence, there is even lesser analysis of how these differing conceptions of the outcome of the talks affected individual bargaining scenarios. It is being argued here that differing conceptions of the purpose and expected outcome of the talks had a major impact on institutional bargaining and outcomes at the Round Table.

We now move on to an evaluation of the hypotheses of Przeworski and Colomer in the context of the relegalization of Solidarność, the PZPR's preference for a strong presidency and the concession of a new and freely elected Senate. In the context of the Przeworski hypothesis, we expect that the PZPR's decision to relegalize Solidarność will be part of a short-sighted strategy to co-opt the opposition and create a 'broadened dictatorship'. We also expect that they will only agree to the creation of new institutions that they can realistically hope to do well from. Finally, we also expect PZPR negotiators to make flawed evaluations in relation to institutional choice due to a lack of contextual information. However, in the context of Colomer's analysis, we would expect that the PZPR's decision to relegalize Solidarność was part of a far-sighted plan aimed at opening up the political space to opposition actors. We would expect to find that, having evaluated the relative strengths of the party and the union, the PZPR sought the creation of institutions that reflected that strength. We also expect that, in the course of the negotiations over new institutions, PZPR negotiators would react and counter-react to moves and offers on the basis of updated information.

The relegalization of Solidarność

Professor Janusz Reykowski emphasizes the fluidity and strategic incoherence that was prevalent in the PZPR at the end of 1988 and the beginning of 1989.[4] He points out that there were different ideas within the party about the purpose and significance of the offer to relegalize Solidarność:

> At the initial stage of the negotiation – it was a trade-off. Solidarność agrees to participate in a not fully democratic parliament and for that get legalization. I am not sure to what extent this idea was accepted in the party leadership at the end of '88 or the beginning of 1989. What I remember is that part of us opposed this kind of approach. I think Ciosek, Kwaśniewski[5] and others were thinking that legalization of Solidarność was part of a broader process of the change of the political system and not the price paid for Solidarność's participation in the system of government. In this concept, legalization was a necessary step towards the transformation of the system. But I cannot say when awareness of this point of view became common enough to become part of the policy![6]

An examination of internal party documents indicates that, as late as September 1988, within days of the first historic meeting between Lech Wałęsa and General Kiszczak, senior PZPR members were still being reassured as to the impossibility of any restoration of Solidarność. In a document entitled 'Solidarność – Why Not' distributed on the instructions of General Jaruzelski to members of the Politburo and party deputy secretaries, the writer engages in a Jesuitical distinction between the evil inclination of Solidarność as an organization, an acknowledgement of the 'just protest'[7] of 1980 that led Poles to support the union, and the acceptance that 'many leading (Solidarność) activists... have changed over the years'[8] and have now developed into 'realists':[9]

> Poland is open today to far-reaching changes of relations and structures, development of liberties, democracy and diversity. However, there are limits to the changes and they are unsurpassable at the present stage in history. In the interests of Poland's existence a line must be drawn that cannot be crossed. This, among other things, is the reason why the restoration of 'Solidarność' is not possible.[10]

In the course of the rest of this document, Solidarność is accused of extremism, of breaking agreements, of making 'immoderate... pay claims',[11] of jeopardizing Polish statehood by engaging in anti-Soviet actions, as well as a range of other crimes, including being paid indirectly or directly out of the American state budget:

> The name 'Solidarność' was intrinsically associated with actions that cannot be reconciled with the aspirations to strengthen, purge, and transform socialism that dominate today in the USSR, Poland and some other countries in our camp and that are historical process of reforms called the second revolution.
>
> So, even if we assumed today theoretically that a new, hypothetical 'Solidarność' becomes a real trade union organization for working people. cut off from its roots and traditions, taking the platform of revival, reconciliation and reform, severing links with Western centres of control and dollar payments – even then the name itself would be a burden for all those positive aspirations and would undermine their credibility.
>
> Besides, at present, the introduction into a workplace of two or more competing trade unions would encourage competitive bidding in social and pay demands making rational management of the economy difficult and overturning reforms.
>
> The 'Solidarność' chapter must be, therefore, finally closed since the current activities of illegal structures of the organization show that they continue all harmful tendencies from the period of legal activities and from the times of full conspiracy.[12]

The same document later goes on to talk of the 'positive achievements of Solidarność, its constructive ideas and human potential hav[ing] their lasting place in the life of Poland'.[13] While the message is clearly designed to reassure the more hardline elements within the PZPR, it also highlights the fluid nature of the political scene towards the end of 1988:

> Nobody wants people from 'Solidarność' to feel defeated or rejected. Simply we must look into the future and not into the past, we must put common good above old and present antagonisms. The situation is changing, people are changing, socialism is changing and new relations require new structural forms. And this also applies to former 'Solidarność.'[14]

Two things appear clear from an analysis of this document: first, General Jaruzelski was preparing the way for a broadening of the dialogue between the government and the public approved at the Eighth Plenum of the PZPR KC on 27–28 August, and second, it was not envisaged that Solidarność would reemerge in its old form as a result of these contacts.

As mentioned earlier, the 'Solidarność – Why Not' document was distributed three weeks after the historic first meeting between Lech Wałęsa and Interior Minister, General Kiszczak. In a *Radio Free Europe* situation report, J. B. de Weydenthal noted that while the meeting was a 'political milestone', the 'uncertainties surrounding the meeting are not surprising'.[15] De Weydenthal points out that the recent plenum of the party's Central Committee reiterated its long-standing opposition to the reinstatement of Solidarność and there were no grounds for assuming that this policy will be quickly reversed. He further notes that Solidarność has repeatedly said that any talks between the union and the party would have to deal with the issues of pluralism and the relegalization of Solidarność and that it was unlikely that the union would abandon its position in the near future.[16]

Radio Free Europe's situation report also notes remarks made by Politburo member, Władysław Baka on 31 August, the same day as the Wałęsa–Kiszczak meeting. In an informal meeting with Western journalists, Baka is reported to have said that Solidarność activists 'might be allowed' to take over certain chapters of official unions in particular factories but that the 'restoration of the Solidarność organization seems unlikely'.[17]

Solidarność's insistence on the primacy of the relegalization issue was one of the factors that delayed the opening of the Round Table talks which had initially been envisaged for the autumn. Millard notes that, following the first meeting between Kiszczak and Wałęsa, both sides came under considerable pressure from within their own ranks.[18] Wałęsa was criticized by elements within Solidarność who perceived any negotiation with the government as a sell-out[19] and by radical groups such as 'Fighting Solidarność' and 'Solidarność 80'. Meanwhile, Jaruzelski and other reformers faced the continuing opposition of the party's hardliners as well as the strident antagonism of the PZPR's trade union ally, the OPZZ, who rejected the idea of trade union pluralism outright. A sense of confusion and conflicting signals was the key feature of the end of 1988 and the beginning of 1989. Millard notes that when the two sides met for the preparatory meetings on 15–16 September in Warsaw, both Jaruzelski and Kiszczak were 'clearly prepared not only to talk to Solidarność but to concede its legalization'.[20] The problem was that at this stage of the game neither the party as a whole nor a majority of the Politburo were prepared to go as far as the reformers were to appease Solidarność in order to get the union to share responsibility for the much-needed economic reform.

The period between September and the end of January was both intense and divisive for the PZPR. On 19 September, the Messner government resigned after a televised parliamentary debate which was highly critical of its performance. Mieczysław Rakowski became prime minister and immediately offered the opposition a number of places in his cabinet. Solidarność rejected his offer not least because the union did not want to be co-opted in the way other segments of the opposition in Poland had been, but because Solidarność did not wish to be in any way encumbered in its negotiations at the Round Table. Meanwhile, Jaruzelski and the close circle around him pursued their Round Table strategy by making key changes to the Politburo so as to rid themselves of the hardline elements opposed to the talks. As was noted in the 'Solidarność – Why Not' memorandum quoted earlier, the 'situation is changing, people are changing, socialism is changing and new relations require new structural forms'.[21] However, despite Jaruzelski's manoeuvres, there was still opposition to the idea of the Round Table at the start of the second leg of the Tenth Plenum of the PZPR KC in January 1989. General Kiszczak explained how they finally got the Central Committee's approval for the leadership's position on the question of political and trade union pluralism:

> At the Tenth Plenum on 17 January 1989 we wanted to legalize Solidarność. We wanted agreement from the party. We wanted to spread the responsibility for legalizing the union. A paper was presented – there was a great debate – but we anticipated the problem. We three – Jaruzelski, Siwicki[22] and myself – arranged a trick. Jaruzelski threatened to resign. Rakowski got to hear of it and he joined in. We all withdrew in a dramatic fashion. There was a discussion. Henryk Jabłoński led the discussion – the party was afraid of discussion.[23]

Colomer and Pascual argue that Jaruzelski and Kiszczak's tactics at the Tenth Plenum 'implied new priorities on the part of the communist leaders which can be precisely defined as new preference orders'.[24] While this new preference order underpins the tactics and strategy of Jaruzelski's immediate entourage, and possibly most of the small group entrusted with the task of negotiating with the opposition, the vote did not change the fact that a large segment of the party was opposed to the very idea of the Round Table and had only voted under threat of the leadership's resignation. The daily, *Trybuna Ludu*, noted after the plenum that

> statements by KC members provided the party leadership with a clear signal that the course of action it had proposed raised numerous doubts, questions, and serious fears.... There were also accusations that party policy was incomprehensible, flawed, and at times contradictory to the expectations and views of party members.[25]

Perhaps a more important qualification is the fact that even those party actors committed to the idea of the Round Table were not *ad idem* on the concessions they were prepared to make once the negotiations began. Jaruzelski *et al.* wanted the opposition to share responsibility for the economic reforms and for this they were prepared to relegalize Solidarność. However, the precise consequences of this concession and subsequent concessions had not been fully formulated. In the week before the Round Table was due to commence its first formal session, both sides were still at loggerheads over the relegalization issue.

On 27 January 1989, a team of opposition representatives, including Solidarność leader Lech Wałęsa, met a PZPR team led by General Czesław Kiszczak at Magdalenka near Warsaw. The meeting, which took place from 11.30 a.m. to 10.15 p.m., was highly charged and centred on the relegalization issue. General Kiszczak opened the meeting by telling those assembled that the PZPR regarded the meeting as the final one before the first plenary session of the Round Table. He set out his side's preference that the question of elections to the *Sejm*, changes in the political system and the possibility of the creation of trade union pluralism 'including Solidarność'[26] should be discussed. Senior Solidarność negotiator, Tadeusz Mazowiecki, intervened immediately to say that the relegalization issue should be dealt with first. While Kiszczak agreed that the relegalization issue should top the agenda, a row immediately ensued about the question of how the union would be relegalized. Solidarność wanted one single reregistration and not a branch-by-branch registration so as to avoid the chaos that surrounded Solidarność's registration in 1980. Stanisław Ciosek got to the heart of the problem straight away when he told the Solidarność side that the OPZZ objected to the top-down relegalization process. The OPZZ wanted Solidarność to 'follow the same route as the OPZZ, to rebuild its structures from the bottom up'.[27] The exchanges that followed provide a fascinating insight into the hardball being played on both sides of the table:

L. KACZYŃSKI (SOLIDARNOŚĆ): If the version of legalizing 'Solidarność' in one single step cannot be implemented, then the government is not going to have a partner for a very long time ...

A. GDULA (PZPR): There are many things, which tie our hands. There is a split reaction amongst our grass roots, which blames us for selling out the interests of socialism. We have great problems with OPZZ. Their position yesterday and the absence today of their representatives at this table is not a game of pretence. This is political fact that we have to take into consideration. Also, the existing legal arrangements cannot be disregarded.

   In my opinion, we must show wide-ranging moderation. The objective of our discussion is consensus on non-confrontational elections, which shall be followed by the process of the legalization of 'Solidarność'.

L. WAŁĘSA (SOLIDARNOŚĆ): We must see and understand the barriers, but we must not erect or build new ones.

T. MAZOWIECKI (SOLIDARNOŚĆ): We understand fully iunctim between the legalization of 'Solidarność' and the elections. However, we cannot enter into agreement earlier, before we obtain guarantees of 'Solidarność's' right to exist. We are discussing the framework and how to 'tie-up' the 'round table'. Its results will ensure the implementation of changes in the Cabinet's resolution and the legalization of 'Solidarność'. We decisively want this to happen on the basis of one legal act. As to the OPZZ's argumentation, it is historically outdated. If we are to build a new chapter, then let us put the past aside, and not give ourselves a conflict card. You've got problems with the OPZZ, but this is your worry. The party was backing OPZZ cells then the party should convince them about the concept of a dialogue. We want a single-step act also in your interests. If this is going to be a 'bottom-up' and slow process, then at the bottom we have to take into account the resistance of the party apparatus. This is an exceptionally conflict generating situation.

B. GEREMEK (SOLIDARNOŚĆ): I wish to say it openly: 'Solidarność' is interested in dragging the issue. For us, the slow pace of the process is not dangerous, does not create conflicts at the grass roots, as it gives the new trade union personnel time to develop and to mature. However, let us not think separately about the interests of each side. Let us find ways to reconcile those interests. I assure you, that the creation of trade union structures from 'bottom-up' does not lie in the interests of our country.

S. CIOSEK (PZPR): Thank you for your sincerity. We see the global interest of our country differently. The process of the creation of 'Solidarność' should be something that would finalize the social conflict, and not open it into a new phase. The bases for everything, which we are discussing here, are material issues and the possibility of an economy-based conflict; one must enter into a social agreement, in which we [ought to] determine intentions as to the economic reforms and the position of the trade union movement. As a 'finale' of the 'round table', we see the arrangement being achieved on the social compromise, the renunciation of strikes and the commencement of the process of creating 'Solidarność'.

If we were to manage stopping the vindication strikes, then we would have a card to tackle trade union-related matters. But we see the order [of these matters] as follows: a formal act to rebuild 'Solidarność' that follows the arrangements on the issue of social order. You must understand us; we have already crossed the Rubicon. We do not intend to go back, but the rebuilding of the legislation on trade unions requires a longer period of time.

L. WAŁĘSA (SOLIDARNOŚĆ): We cannot provide declarations of strike guarantees, if we don't have an organization that would be able to hold back the vindication. We don't want to blackmail with strikes, but we are more responsible than our colleagues from the OPZZ and cannot provide such guarantees.

J. REYKOWSKI (PZPR): How one should move forward from the declaration that 'Solidarność' will ensure the stabilization of the atmosphere in factories to its implementation? What mechanism would guarantee the safety of the partners?

L. WAŁĘSA (SOLIDARNOŚĆ): We can work and reason towards that but we cannot give you any guarantees. We could write [something to that effect], but that would achieve nothing. Such guarantees might be given by various institutional bodies, but also not in 100 per cent.

B. GEREMEK (SOLIDARNOŚĆ): I propose that the social order declaration be treated as an undertaking to renounce actions that disrupt order.

W. FRASYNIUK (SOLIDARNOŚĆ): Prompt creation of 'Solidarność' is a guarantee of ensuring peace and order. The lack of any movement in this matter increases the tension and fuels speculations. We want a 'top-down', single-step registration, and temporary regulations should be created that would make it possible. You, Gentlemen, are afraid of your grass roots. We also are afraid of grass roots, especially the inexperienced activists; those, who became activists at five past twelve. They don't know anything about martial law; they did not stick their necks out, but now proclaim radicalism...

T. MAZOWIECKI (SOLIDARNOŚĆ): Let's find common ground on the issues of social safety. We don't want to run away from it today, but we see this as a very difficult problem. Maybe it should be worked out at a 'small' table? Only the programme for social order that is based on concrete solutions could bring us closer to [our] objective. Today we won't be able to resolve it, we can only make a declaration.

CZ. KISZCZAK (PZPR): I propose to close the discussion on this subject as follows: 'Having agreed a formula for the social agreement, we shall submit to the Cabinet a request to change the Trade Unions legislation and we shall determine at the 'round table' the date for the commencement of the creation of 'Solidarność'.

T. MAZOWIECKI (SOLIDARNOŚĆ): Who is going to be party to the social agreement?

CZ. KISZCZAK (PZPR): The signatories of the 'round table'![28]

It is abundantly clear from the exchanges quoted earlier that it was not only the PZPR side that had to deal with its hardline faction. Lech Kaczyński bluntly told his interlocutors that the failure to concede a single-step registration process would lead Solidarność to withdraw from the negotiations, while Bronisław Geremek was effectively saying that time was on the union's side and that they were prepared to sit the economic crisis out. Gdula's plea that the party's hands were tied and that the OPZZ posed many problems for the PZPR is met with the blunt riposte from Mazowiecki that the OPZZ is the party's worry. Ciosek's argument that 'the commencement of the process of creating Solidarność'[29] should follow an agreement on social compromise and the renunciation of strikes clearly indicates that, for him at least, the idea was that Solidarność would be rewarded after it delivered the conditions in which the party would be able to introduce economic reform. Perhaps one of the most revealing of all of the contributions is from Władysław Frasyniuk who points out that the manoeuvrability of the PZPR and Solidarność is constrained by threats from the grass roots in both organizations. Frasyniuk was effectively saying that if the party did not concede single-step and top-down registration it might well find itself left to negotiate with inexperienced union radicals whose demands would not be constrained by the memory of martial law.

An internal party memorandum entitled 'Information Concerning the Magdalenka Talks on 27 January 1989' notes that

> [T]he most difficult negotiations were concerned with the issue of the timetable for the legalization of 'Solidarność'. The 'Solidarność' side remained categorically on the position that the commencement of the process of creating 'Solidarność' must precede their agreement for the conclusion of an election pact. In a very difficult and heated discussion we finally worked out a conditional formula for the setting up of 'Solidarność'...[and by] March we shall request the Cabinet to change the resolution, which is blocking trade union pluralism. At the same time we shall put forward a legislative initiative to amend the Trade Union legislation in a way that would enable the creation of a professional union from the top, enabling also joint trade union representation in the work place. This formula has a condition that it will be valid only when we obtain necessary authorization in this matter. Otherwise, we can withdraw from it. The 'Solidarność' side made the reservation that it would like to hear this declaration in the opening speech of the 'round table' negotiations. If this does not happen, then they shall consider the idea of the 'round table' invalid.[30]

In another PZPR memorandum dated 30 January, it is noted that in accordance with arrangements made during the preparatory meeting on 27 January that the work of the Round Table will be divided into three working groups: a group on the economy and social policy, a group on political reforms and a group on union pluralism. A team under the leadership of comrade W. Baka will lead the PZPR side of the negotiations as the table on union pluralism. It is further noted that

> [I]t is proposed to hold this week the meetings between the proposed comrades and the persons responsible for each particular group. The aim of these meetings should be to agree the tactic and the preparation of working material necessary for the future work of groups.[31]

The question arises, given the short amount of time between the party's agreement to open the negotiations on trade union pluralism and the commencement of the first plenary session of the Round Table on 6 February, as to the quality and thoroughness of the negotiating tactics and strategies of Comrade Baka's team.

A key question in the evaluation of PZPR strategy at the Round Table is whether the party anticipated the impact on the institution of one-party rule of legalizing Solidarność. Janusz Reykowski's account of the PZPR's reaction to the first meeting of the Political Table at the Round Table provides an interesting insight into the mixed and confused feelings of participants:

> People don't think clearly! At the one side – it is true what you have said that nobody anticipated [the impact of relegalizing Solidarność], but on the other

hand there were many situations where people considered the possibility that the whole system would collapse and Solidarność would get power. I repeat often a story from the first meeting of the political table – at the beginning of February – when one member of the table (PZPR) wrote to me saying that this was not a real negotiation about the sharing of power but about giving up the power to Solidarność. So I gave the letter to Ciosek, and he gave it to Jaruzelski, and he sent me a message saying that our side should discuss what our view of this was. So I organized a meeting and I invited, besides the members of the negotiation group, also people from the top leadership. The discussion was hot and the general agreement was that the author of the letter was likely to be right and that we should seriously consider that it is an outcome. But in order to understand our position we have to consider what are the alternatives. What – if not negotiation? And there was quite a common agreement that if we did not negotiate that after the next few years – two [or] three years – there would be a physical confrontation in Poland with the younger generation, the post-martial law generation – who were not demoralized and who were quite radical. So we either seek a negotiated solution or we accept the possibility that there will be a sharp confrontation in the near future. I remember one speech – where he ended by saying – 'after all they [Solidarność] are Poles.' It wasn't giving away the basic values of the nation to some foreign power, but to other Poles. In other words, in some part of the minds of those involved in decision making there was consideration that things may go in this direction [Solidarność would eventually take power]. But the dominant thinking was not like that. Of course there will be four years of cohabitation and during this time the party would become much more effective. This bureaucratic organization [the PZPR] would become more able to act politically. In fact it did happen – after four years – between 1989–93, it [the party] became able for the political game in the democratic system. It was not expected that in the meantime our power would be taken away by Solidarność.... Expectations were vague – there were some dominant trends in thinking but the same people could think conflicting things at the same time.[32]

Professor Jerzy Wiatr thought that the party's purpose in offering relegalization was very clear:

The aim was to give it [Solidarność] a share of power. Not just legal existence of the union, but a share of power! On that I have no doubt.[33]

While Wiatr maintains that the party's goal was clear, he argues that the PZPR had not worked out the potential consequences of relegalizing Solidarność:

That was probably the weakest elaborated part of the strategy. Obviously the party had to change but most of us did not realize before the election how fundamentally the party was unprepared for the new situation. I can speak of myself. I was astonished by the degree to which the party was unable to operate in the relatively open political context of the election of 1989. It was totally unprepared. It had unrealistic image of the situation.[34]

Wiatr goes further and claims that the PZPR negotiators had 'no plan and no strategy'[35] going into the Round Table process:

On our side it was one big improvisation. Reykowski was often alarmed by the degree to which our side was unprepared. Many things were just impro- visations. Elements of the new proposals had been elaborated in a small team that we had formed half a year before the Round Table. We – meaning Janusz Reykowski, Mikołaj Kozakiewicz, myself and Stanisław Gebethner – we weren't all in the party. Kozakiewicz was in the Peasant Party and Gebethner was a non-party academic. We did it under the umbrella of PRON.[36] It was a kind of convenient way to do it. There were some ideas elaborated. I was the author of the proposal to have a presidential system, a strong president – as a way to stabilize and democratize the system. Not through strengthening the party – it was beyond repair. We all knew, in this circle, that it was beyond repair and that we had to find a different way.... Generally speaking we came to the Round Table without any clear strategy.... Solidarność came with a very clear strategy. They knew what they wanted – they were by far better prepared than we were.[37]

Stanisław Ciosek argues that PZPR negotiators understood what the impact of relegalizing Solidarność would be and rejects the notion that communism collapsed in Poland because of the party's misperceived strategies at the Round Table:

Everyone in my opinion was realizing that the relegalizing of Solidarność is the effective end of the leading role and sole ruling of the party. That's why there was discussion and opposition in the party to making the trade union legal because it was such an important step...there were great political battles on this topic. Remember the famous Tenth Plenum where Jaruzelski threatened to resign. So this was a conscious decision – large sections were against the issue of legalizing the union.[38]

Grażyna Staniszewska who was a Solidarność representative at the subtable on the economy is sceptical about Ciosek's view that 'everyone' understood the significance of the decision to relegalize Solidarność:

Now Ciosek says that the decision about the relegalization of Solidarność was taken by the party before the Round Table. I was very distrustful of this – I was sure it was a trap. It was a trap to get us to the Round Table. So I was surprised that the party had agreed to relegalize the union and it was done very quickly at the early part of the Round Table, nearly immediately.[39]

Mieczysław Rakowski was a party reformer and the last PZPR prime minister of Poland. He admits that he did not anticipate the effect of relegalization. He expected that Solidarność 'would function as a trade union. Nothing more! Of course now we can say that we lacked imagination or anticipation! But talking sincerely, Solidarność also didn't anticipate!'[40]

In a Polish Situation Report written for *Radio Free Europe* published on the day the Round Table talks commenced, Louisa Vinton discussed how the aims of Solidarność and the PZPR 'are ultimately at odds':[41]

> Solidarność's chief goal, as Lech Wałęsa has put it, is to 'break the [party's] monopoly' over politics, the economy, and public organizations. The party, on the other hand, is determined to maintain its primacy in public life; its willingness to contemplate the legalization of Solidarność seems to stem from the realization that a failure to make changes now may pose a greater threat than the risks entailed in negotiating with Solidarność. As Politburo member Marian Orzechowski has said, 'the PZPR will not surrender its leading role, but it does not wish to and can not implement this role as it has in the past'.[42]

The office of president and an upper house

The issue of the creation of the office of the president was the central plank of the PZPR's strategy both before and during the Round Table negotiations. The PZPR hierarchy who envisaged Jaruzelski, or some other party nominee, filling the post, regarded the presidential office as a guarantee of continuity.[43] The report of a PZPR interdepartmental team, which analysed the institutional changes envisaged in the context of the Round Table, provides a fascinating insight into the strategic goals of the party elite. Entitled 'Concept of Changes', the document, which was prepared in September 1988, begins with the following statement: 'The "round table" should constitute a bridge for establishing a Council of National Agreement, which would unite all social forces committed to cooperation on the basis of the constitutional order of the PRL (Polish People's Republic).'[44]

The reference to the 'constitutional order of the PRL'[45] is informative. In a later part of this document the writer notes that 'Extremist organizations...pronouncing themselves against the constitutional order in force (anti-socialist groups, PPS [Polish Socialist Party] not accepting the leading role of the PZPR etc.) should be excluded.'[46]

Clearly, none of the institutional changes envisaged in the context of this document at least anticipated any tampering with the PZPR's institutional hegemony. In other words, the leading role of the party would not be challenged. In a later section entitled 'Outline Concept of Changes in Institutions of State Authorities', the writer explains the purpose and function of the establishment of a second House of Parliament and the office of the president of the PRL. The document notes that the establishment of the office of the president and formation of a second house was driven by the necessity to do away with the institution of the Council of State:

> It is a majority opinion that the second House should not be autonomous (presidents of the regional national councils etc.) but should create opportunities for people of independent views, widely respected by society (people from cultural and scientific circles) and for people associated with the opposition's activities or activities of lay groups associated with religious organizations or associations, to get involved in political activities. This House, by tradition, can be called the Senate.
>
> Selection of the II House should not be done through general election since it would give it too strong a position *vis-à-vis* the I House, but for example one-third would be nominated by the President of the PRL and two-thirds would be designated by prominent public organizations named and authorized to do so by the *Sejm*. II House should have classic rights such as the right to participate in legislative work, the right to defer the coming into force of certain laws and resolutions passed by the Parliament or decisions made by the President. In short, it should have advisory and representative functions, and, to a limited extent, decision making ones without, however, any legislative initiative.
>
> In such a concept, the block of ruling parties does not have to have a qualified majority. More places (e.g. 50 per cent) could be allocated to the centre and opposition because it would not threaten the interests of parties in the government coalition. In such a construction, the Senate and not the *Sejm* would be the main place for the opposition. However, in order to hold the power and to ensure operational efficiency, PZPR, ZSL and SD[47] need a majority in the *Sejm*.
>
> The President of the PRL would be the highest institution of state authority with legislative and executive powers.
>
> The President would be elected in a secret vote of the National Assembly (I and II House of the Parliament plus the president of WRN and people prominent in the state, e.g. President of the Supreme Court, President of the Academy of Science, President of the Constitutional Tribunal etc.). The term of office would be seven years with the possibility of election for two terms. There was no tradition of general presidential elections in Poland. The last president of the Polish Republic was also elected by the National Assembly. The President should always come from members of the PZPR. In this situation, the office of vice-president should not be established, and it should be accepted that, in the absence of the President, the role of the head of the state should be temporarily taken over by the president of the *Sejm*. A different election system can be provided for, e.g. through locally selected electors.
>
> Given such profound changes in the structure of the main institution of state, enabling the opposition to participate in them, presidential power must be strong. Constitutionally the President should be equipped among others

with the following powers:

1 he is a head of the Armed Forces of the PRL,
2 he appoints and dismisses the Government with consent of the *Sejm*,
3 he has right to dissolve the *Sejm* and call new elections,
4 he is entitled to issue independent legal acts,
5 he has right, if he wishes to do so, to chair meetings of Council of Ministers (Cabinet).[48]

It is clear from a perusal of this document that the Senate was designed as a means of co-opting non-party people into the institutions of government. It is also clear, however, that the selection of such people was to be strictly controlled by the party, which would control both the *Sejm* (which would authorize the nominating organizations) and the president (who would nominate a one-third of senators). Even then, its powers were to be purely advisory and representative. A key phrase in this document is the reference to the fact that in order to 'hold the power and to ensure operational efficiency',[49] the PZPR and its coalition partners 'need a majority in the *Sejm*'.[50] Furthermore, the document notes that because of the 'profound changes in the structure of the main institutions of state...presidential power must be strong'.[51] Crucially, the president must always be a party member.

While the document quoted earlier may serve to create the impression that the PZPR had a precise view of the role of the president, constitutional lawyer, Professor Stanisław Gebethner has argued that at the outset of the Round Table discussions there was no clearly specified conception of the sphere of presidential powers or of the president's position in a new constitutional order.[52] The outline of the presidential role worked out at the PZPR KC in September 1988 was, in general terms, a copy of the 1935 constitutional position. So while PZPR negotiators may have had an idea about how the presidency would act as an important institutional power base for the party, the big problem was that there had been no resolution of how the existing Council of State would operate if the office of the president were established.

Professor Stanisław Gebethner represented the coalition side at the subtable on Political Reforms: 'It would appear that nobody, apart from specialists in constitutional law, had realized that the mechanical replacement of the Council of State by the presidency was simply impossible.'[53]

These are by no means the nit-picking points of a constitutional lawyer. The PZPR's lack of specificity in relation to its proposal for the establishment of the new presidency provided bargaining opportunities for the opposition. At the second meeting of the Round Table subcommittee on Political Reforms held on 18 February (two weeks after the commencement of the Round Table), constitutional expert Piotr Winczorek of the Democratic Party, representing the government coalition, presented the proposal to establish the office of president of the PRL:

1 The president would be the authority and the arbiter in social conflicts.
2 The president would be accountable before the State's Tribunal.

3 In the area of international affairs:

a) represents the country to the outside world;
b) ratifies and dissolves international agreements;
c) appoints and recalls authorized representatives of Poland to other countries;
d) accepts letters of credence and letters of recall from the representatives of other countries.

4 In relation to internal affairs:

a) appoints to civilian and military posts, referred to in existing legislation;
b) awards decorations and medals of honour;
c) uses the right of clemency.

5 In relation to the *Sejm*:

a) orders elections to *Sejm* to be held;
b) summons its sessions;
c) dissolves the *Sejm* before its term of office in situations described by the legislation.

6 The president carries out the function of the Chief Commander of the military forces and the Chairman of the National Defence Committee.
7 In situations of great urgency, introduces a state of emergency in a part or in the entire territory of the state.
8 The president shall have the right to legislative initiative, which at present belongs to the Cabinet, and also the right to put forward to the Constitutional Tribunal a legal question in relation to the conformity of legislation with the Constitution.
9 Presents to the *Sejm* the initiative of holding national referenda.
10 Has the right to present to the *Sejm* the candidate for the Chairman of the Cabinet and to appoint ministers proposed by the Prime Minister.
11 The method of electing the President:

a) The President shall be elected by the *Sejm* or by the *Sejm* and representatives of local administration organs;
b) The President shall be elected by way of general elections. (The Government leaves this matter open to discussion).

12 The designation of a candidate for the office of President shall be done by the *Sejm* or alternatively by the elected National Agreement Council (Rada Porozumienia Narodowego).
13 The term of office shall be between 4 and 7 years with the possibility of one re-election.
14 The adoption of constitutional legislation on the office of the President should be carried out during the present term of the *Sejm*.[54]

It is clear from a comparison with the September 1988 interdepartmental team document that the PZPR's conception of the presidency had changed somewhat. It is difficult to determine whether or not this change can be explained by the simple fact that the matter was being handled at the Round Table by an expert from its nominally independent coalition partner or whether it was simply the case that the PZPR's real interest had to be disguised under the glaring lights of the Round Table. Either way, there are significant differences between the bluntly stated conception of the advantages of a strong presidency in the PZPR's internal document and the initial draft opened by Professor Winczorek at the Round Table. In particular, it is notable that in the Winczorek document, the issue of how the president should be elected is left open for discussion while the PZPR memo stipulates a mechanism that would have allowed the party to retain effective control of the office. The Solidarność-opposition side was unimpressed with the Winczorek proposal when it was presented at the Round Table subcommittee table on Political Reforms on 18 February:

> Following the presentation by the opposition of a significant number of objections and reservations in relation to this concept, which could be reduced to concerns and even fear of the strengthening of the state's executive power, Bronisław Geremek made a statement, in which he concluded that 'we think that at present there are no grounds for making even an initial political decision in relation to this point of the agenda.' Therefore, the government's proposal was not even discussed.[55]

Another factor that influenced the presidential issue was internal differences within the PZPR over whether the office of first secretary and president of PRL should be held by the same incumbent. There was a clash between those who wanted Jaruzelski to remain as party leader as a guarantee of continuity with 'the constellation of political forces'[56] and those who wanted Jaruzelski to resign the party leadership. This confusion and lack of clarity became publicly manifest when the PZPR press spokesman Jerzy Urban denounced the presidential proposal as an SD (Democratic Party) initiative. While Urban may have thought he could get away with this statement given the fact that it was an SD member, Piotr Winczorek, who had introduced the proposal at the Round Table, the incident further highlights the PZPR's hesitation and lack of resolution on this key issue.

The constitutional lawyer, Professor Piotr Winczorek, was a member of the Democratic Party and negotiated on behalf of the government-coalition side at the Political Reforms table at the Round Table. Professor Piotr Winczorek remembers the meeting of the coalition side's negotiating team which took place prior to the Round Table subtable on Political Reforms on 18 February. He makes the point that while the PZPR had a preference for a strong president they did not articulate this overtly:

> I remember a funny moment. We were talking about presidential powers. It had not been said publicly, but everybody knew that Mr Jaruzelski would be the president.... So the powers were very important. This day the

governmental party was sitting on the second floor while the Solidarność side waited for us on the first floor. We were late and there was no idea about what powers could be given to the future president. There was no paper available and we had taken napkins – so the proposals were being written on napkins. As we went down to meet them some experts were rewriting their proposals on the napkins. It's an indication of how little preparation there was. Such an important thing could be decided in such a way.

I was just one of the experts, but if the leaders decided to restore the presidential office they should have had an idea about what this president should be. But nothing! They didn't know. They wanted a member of the Democratic Party to present this idea because we had always been in favour of this idea. They wanted to profit from this. It was me who presented the idea but only the general idea. The idea was that the Council of State would be removed and be replaced by the president with this same power. The first election was to be made by the National Assembly and the second by general election. The problem was what presidential decisions should be countersigned by the Prime Minister? It is a crucial decision because the president was not responsible to the *Sejm*. The problem was that the politicians had no idea and it was left to be decided at a later date. It was not resolved until the passing of the so-called Small Constitution (1992).[57]

In his assessment of the PZPR's aims and understanding of the impact of the introduction of the office of president, Stanisław Gebethner agrees with the characterization of the party's proposals as incoherent and haphazard as outlined by Professor Winczorek:

The problems of introducing the office of president into the constitutional order were clearly dealt with as a functional response to circumstances. No deeper discussions concerning the conceptions of socio-political change were held; in general it was not realized that changes such as the establishment of the office of President would inevitably have such far-reaching consequences for the functioning of the whole political system and constitutional order.[58]

The Senate

It was noted earlier that a very limited role is envisaged for the proposed new Senate in the PZPR interdepartmental team report 'Concept of Changes in the Political System of the Polish People's Republic'.[59] So the question arises as to how a chamber that was conceived as a tool to co-opt the opposition and whose membership the party would effectively control was transformed into the vehicle that precipitated the untimely collapse of the PZPR's power.

Stanisław Gebethner produced a research report during the course of the Round Table which had been commissioned by the Council of State working party on constitutional change. This report indicated that the idea of establishing a Senate was anachronistic.[60] Significantly, Gebethner says that the chair of the Council of State, the PZPR deputy prime minister, Kazimierz Barcikowski, shared this opinion:

> What is most striking and significant is the fact that this occurred two days before the meeting in Magdalenka at which the government-coalition side submitted the proposal for establishing a Senate based on the election of two Senators for every province.[61]

Gebethner does not regard this apparent change in the PZPR's conception of the Senate as a sign of division within the leadership but as confirmation of the absence of any cohesive and fully worked out conception of the reform of the political system. MP Professor Jerzy Wiatr recalls:

> That part of the story I remember very well – because I was involved in this. I was not at Magdelenka when Kwaśniewski[62] made this proposal and it was accepted. That was a Saturday night. Sunday morning Reykowski called me – we had a conversation on the phone. He was jubilant and told me about this. I told him it was going to be a disaster. We will lose the election for the Senate and that would be a disaster because we will show to everybody how weak our side is.[63]

Janusz Reykowski throws interesting light on how Aleksander Kwaśniewski's suggestion that the Senate be elected in a totally free general election came to be known beyond the private arena of the Magdalenka palace:

> Jerzy Urban [PZPR spokesman] revealed to the press that the completely free Senate had been proposed.... It had been discussed in a very small group and the group was split on the issue. Kwaśniewski had said that Urban had not been given permission to mention it publicly. Jaruzelski had not said anything definite, but said that the final decision would be made at the Politburo meeting on Tuesday and this debate had been on Saturday. So it was to be a secret until Tuesday. But on Sunday, Urban leaked it to the international media.... So he leaked it and the major media in the west announced that there would be a free election in Poland for the Senate. So on Tuesday when the Politburo got together it was already an international fact. Everybody knows that there is going to be a free election in Poland and so the Politburo has its hands tied.... I don't know whether he did it by himself or whether Jaruzelski gave him the go ahead. Jaruzelski was always playing very secretly.[64]

Professor Jerzy Wiatr remembers that the Kwaśniewski proposal emerged in the context of bargaining over the contractual *Sejm* and presidency:

> The Senate came in the middle of the Round Table as a way to pay Solidarność for its acceptance of this contractual division of seats in the *Sejm*. And also – and this was not fully clear – for the agreement not to contest the presidential

election! When it all started the original idea was that Solidarność would be co-opted into the existing system in such a way that Solidarność candidates would be given a certain share of seats in the *Sejm* without changing the system of election. The system of election as used before practically guaranteed the election of candidates put on the top of the list. It was the List system combined with majority vote – an unusual system. You had a list of candidates longer than the number of seats. You technically had the right to delete any candidate. If you did not delete anybody your vote was cast for the top candidates in the number of seats in the constituency. Practically speaking this meant that people put on the safe places were elected. So the original idea was that we would simply divide the cake giving Solidarność a certain number of seats on this list – had Solidarność accepted this, the election would not have been a test of strength between the party and Solidarność. But Solidarność rejected this altogether and it started to propose various concepts. One, I remember was proposed by Janina Zakrzewska [opposition electoral adviser] that the *Sejm* would be divided into two parts. Fifty per cent would be elected from the national list that Solidarność would not contest. In other words the party and its allies gets 50 per cent free. The remaining 50 per cent is contested in competitive one-seat constituencies. On face value it looked like guaranteeing the party a majority because it was unthinkable at this stage that the party would lose all 230 seats in this contest. It was rejected for obvious reasons because it would expose the weakness of the party altogether. There was a stalemate with various ideas and then there was this idea of the division of seats but where each would be contested – but various political forces would have the monopoly for nominating candidates. The idea was separate lists of candidates for each seat. This way the party candidate would not compete with the Solidarność candidate. But party candidates would compete between themselves for each of the party seats. That was not good enough for Solidarność, and then you got Kwaśniewski with his proposal of the fully free Senate. And that was enough, as I understand, to make Solidarność happy with the outcome.[65]

Stanisław Gebethner says that the participants in the Round Table Group on Questions of Political Reform on the government-coalition side were told of Kwaśniewski's suggestion at Magdalenka on the following day (2 March). He points out that at this stage, the conception of the future constitutional position of the Senate was 'more than a little hazy'.[66] Gebethner argues that the party reformers wanted to use the Senate to co-opt the 'constructive opposition' into the political system, while the free election of the Senate would, in turn, help to legitimate the election of the president. The unspoken assumption was that the opposition would gain a majority in the Senate. The third premise was the hope that the Senate would provide the possibility for a greater numerical representation of the opposition in parliament. The fourth idea, according to Gebethner, was the desire to mobilize the PZPR provincial organizations into more energetic activity in the hope that they would engage in a genuinely competitive electoral struggle.

A detailed analysis of the PZPR's choice of voting systems and electoral rules and of how these choices precipitated the collapse of the party's power following the June 1989 elections will be presented in Chapter 6. As a result I will not deal in any depth at this point with the issue of the PZPR's expectations in relation to the outcome of the Senate election. However, it is clear from Stanisław Ciosek's remarks quoted later that, in his view at least, the newly created upper chamber would not be a forum where the opposition would exercise power:

> The effect of Senate result was a huge demonstration. But our assumption was that the Senate was being given to Solidarność, and so I was not shocked by the result! In my mind, it was not very important whether they [Solidarność] got 51 per cent or 98 per cent of the Senate – I mean in the sense of the mechanism of this whole agreement.[67]

The mechanisms put in place by the PZPR, including the contractual *Sejm* and strong presidency, were intended as the linchpins of the party's continued hold on the reins of power.

While affirming his oft-stated view that party reformers, such as himself, saw the Round Table process as a mechanism designed to create the conditions of change in Poland, President Aleksander Kwaśniewski is in no doubt that had the PZPR anticipated the electoral defeat in the free election to the Senate no such election would have taken place:[68]

> I did not have any doubts that at the Round Table we initiated our path to democracy. This was not a coincidence and it did not come out of a whim that I proposed freely contested elections to the Senate during a discussion on our strategy of talks with Solidarność at our closed Party-Government sessions. My colleagues justified this idea with me being young. But I tried to explain to them that one could not build a system, which was supposed to be completely different from the previous one, and, at the same time, to make only incremental changes, to defend the position of the Party and not to allow, even partial, political verification.
>
> At last, freely contested elections to the Senate were accepted. It must be appreciated and at the same time one must acknowledge – none of us expected that the elections would result in such a serious defeat of the Party. If one had said then, that the Party would have one senator out of 100, and on the top of this Henryk Stokłosa would be the one, and that the result would be 99 to 1 to the benefit of Solidarność, I am quite sure – we wouldn't have had freely contested elections. Fortunately, our belief in a miracle was stronger than common sense or a political calculation.

Conclusion

This chapter sets out to examine the relative merits of the Przeworski and Colomer hypotheses in the context of the Round Table bargaining over the relegalization of Solidarność, the PZPR's preference for a strong presidency and the decision to establish a freely elected Senate. We now return to the observable implications that flow from these hypotheses in order to assess what the evidence says about these conflicting expectations.

The relegalization of Solidarność

It appears clear from an analysis of the data that there were different conceptions within the PZPR hierarchy of the impact of relegalizing Solidarność. Reykowski emphasizes that, on the one hand, the move was seen as a trade-off for Solidarność's agreement to participate in the semi-free election, while for other PZPR negotiators, including Kwaśniewski and Ciosek, relegalization was part of a broader process of system transformation. So straight away we can see that there is evidence to support both Przeworski and Colomer on the question of whether PZPR actors are short-sighted or non-myopic in motivation. Reykowski concedes that there were many situations where people did not 'think clearly'[69] about the potential impact on one-party rule if Solidarność were relegalized. So, if this analysis is true, then it cannot be claimed that actors were evaluating the relative strength of the players or updating information about how relegalization might affect the party's power.

Reykowski points out that there were those within the party who did regard the opening up of talks and the agreement to relegalize as having the potential to bring about the collapse of the party. However, he argues that the 'dominant thinking'[70] within the party did not anticipate the end of communist power as a result of the move. If Reykowski is right, it follows that Przeworski is also right. Wiatr saw relegalization as part of an offer to share power with Solidarność, but it was the 'weakest elaborated part of the (PZPR's) strategy'[71] and he says that the party was 'fundamentally' unprepared for the new situation. Again, Wiatr's evidence tends to support the short-term and mistakes hypothesis of Przeworski, as does that of former prime minister Rakowski who argues that he did not expect Solidarność's relegalization to have any impact beyond its functioning as a 'trade union. Nothing more.'[72] As we have seen, Stanisław Ciosek disagrees. He asserts 'everyone in my opinion was realizing that the relegalizing of Solidarność was the effective end of the leading role and sole ruling of the party'.[73]

The closest we are likely to come to an understanding of the lack of coherence surrounding the decision to relegalize the union is evident in the remarks of Politburo member, Marian Orzechowski, when he announced that the 'PZPR will not surrender its leading role, but does not wish to and can not implement this role as it has in the past'.[74] This lack of a specific conception of how the party would retain and implement its leading role while, at the same time, conceding the relegalization of Solidarność appears to confirm the fact that the PZPR was not acting in a coherent manner in relation to this particular institutional choice. There is no indication of coherent pooling or updating of information concerning the impact of relegalization and, yet, the move was conceded at a very early stage of the Round Table talks. While it is arguable that the bulk of the evidence indicates that party negotiators saw the move as part of a strategy that would help secure the PZPR's hold on power and that as a result it is plausible to claim that the PZPR's behaviour conforms to Przeworski's expectations, there is clearly conflicting evidence on this issue. Given this fundamental disagreement about the meaning and impact of the decision to relegalize Solidarność, it is not possible to conclusively confirm one or other hypotheses.

The presidency

It has been argued earlier that the PZPR envisaged the new office of president as being the guarantee of the party's continuity and political control following the Round Table process. An examination of the party's September 1988 'Concept of Changes' document clearly shows that the PZPR did not anticipate any diminution in its political hegemony arising out of the proposed institutional changes.[75] According to the document, 'The President of the PRL would be the highest institution of state authority with legislative and executive powers'[76] and, crucially, the president would always be a party member. In this case, the evidence supports Przeworski's hypothesis. The creation of the office of president was part of a strategy designed to retain political control in what would be a 'broadened dictatorship'. However, when PZPR negotiators presented the proposal at the Round Table, they did so on the basis of a document produced by Democratic Party member Piotr Winczorek and not on the basis of the earlier document.

As we have seen, there are major differences between the conceptions of the strong presidency outlined in the PZPR's September 1988 document and the Winczorek proposal. One crucial difference between the two proposals is the fact that Winczorek leaves open the issue of how the president should be elected, while the PZPR's September document stipulates a mechanism that would have allowed the party to retain effective control of the office. Gebethner argues that the problem of introducing the office of the president into the constitutional order was dealt with as a functional response to circumstances. Party negotiators did not fully appraise themselves of the socio-political change that would result from the move, nor was it realized that the introduction of the new office would have far-reaching consequences for the functioning of the whole political and constitutional order.[77] This tends to support Przeworski's expectation that regime actors will make mistakes.

Clearly, informational deficits and flawed evaluations led party negotiators to negotiate on the basis of the wrong document. As part of a plan to legitimize the election of the president, the PZPR conceded free elections to the Senate without fully assessing the potential impact of this move. Given this failure to evaluate potential effects, to react and counter-react to moves or to update information, it seems clear that Przeworski's hypothesis is confirmed in the case of the PZPR's bargaining over the presidency.

The Senate

It has been shown that the PZPR's concession of a freely elected Senate is inextricably linked with its bargaining over the semi-free parliamentary elections and its desire to introduce a strong presidency. Interviews with PZPR negotiators and an examination of the September 1988 'Concept of Changes' document shows that at the outset of the process only a very limited role was envisaged for the Senate and that it was regarded as little more than a talking shop for the opposition prior to Aleksander Kwaśniewski's bombshell at Magdalenka. The evidence indicates that the PZPR negotiators lacked a cohesive or fully worked out conception of how the various institutional pieces they were conceding would fit into the institutional jigsaw. As Gebethner points out, even after Kwaśniewski's proposal was made public, the PZPR's ideas concerning the future constitutional role of the Senate were 'more than a little hazy'.[78]

Clearly, if the Senate was conceded as part of the plan to get Solidarność's agreement to the contractual elections and in response to the PZPR's desire for a strong presidency, then, at least in intent, the Senate can be regarded as supporting Przeworski's 'broadened dictatorship' argument. However, the PZPR could clearly not have expected to control the Senate, if, as we anticipate following Przeworski that liberalizers only create institutions they can hope to do well from. Ciosek's analysis tends to support Przeworski. He made the point that the concession of the Senate was not a mistake because the PZPR viewed it as a talking shop for the opposition. This flawed evaluation of the potential impact of the Senate is clear proof that there was little evidence of players reacting and counter-reacting in this particular case. While PZPR actors may or may not have conceded the Senate on the basis of an evaluation of the relative strength of the two sides, there is no convincing evidence of far-sighted motivation in relation to this institutional choice. As in the case of the negotiations over the office of president, we see a difference between the PZPR's initial conception of an institution and the reality that emerges as a result of the Round Table dynamic.

6 Strategies and outcomes

Part 2 – the PZPR's choice of electoral system and voting formulae

Olson has asserted that the electoral system that resulted from the Round Table process was not designed as a competition for power as neither the ruling party nor Solidarność were willing to act as competitive political parties at that stage in the transition.[1] But if Olson is correct, then what was the PZPR's aim in its negotiations over the complex institutional arrangements put in place for the elections to the Upper and Lower Houses to be held in June 1989? If the communist party did not regard the electoral system as designed for political competition, then what was the point of the elaborate 'compartmentalized' set of electoral institutions negotiated at the Round Table? If these institutions were not designed to secure the continuance of PZPR power in freely contested or contractual elections, then what was their purpose and how did the PZPR perceive this purpose? It is to this issue that we now turn our attention.

We will evaluate the PZPR's choice of electoral system and voting formulae in light of the Przeworski and Colomer hypotheses. In the context of the Przeworski hypothesis, we do not expect the PZPR to pay much attention to electoral formulae because in so far as its goal is a broadened dictatorship this end will be achieved by other institutional strategies it will seek to put in place. As we have already seen, the PZPR considered the establishment of a strong presidency to be its safeguard in the context of a reformulation of the rules of the game. We do expect that the PZPR will focus its attention on the preservation of the balance of power within parliament as well as its ability to dominate the legislative process. We expect the party to try and institutionalize its legislative dominance and control. However, it also follows, given Przeworski's analysis, that the PZPR will make flawed evaluations in the context of the dynamic of the bargaining at the Round Table. In the context of Colomer's hypothesis of far-sightedness, we expect the PZPR to regard the choice of electoral system as an important choice en route to an intermediate regime. We expect PZPR negotiators to evaluate the relative merits of voting formulae and to update their information about the differential impact of voting systems.

PZPR social support

This section uses Politburo documents, Magdalenka transcripts and author interviews with negotiators from both the PZPR and Solidarność concerning party perceptions of its social support prior to the Round Table.

It has been argued that the biggest mistake made by the PZPR at the Round Table was its bargaining over the electoral law.[2] In simple terms, the question is why PZPR negotiators agreed to the adoption of the least advantageous electoral system from its point of view. While some PZPR negotiators now claim that they did not expect to win the contractual elections agreed at the Round Table,[3] many key figures within the party, not to mention its lower echelons, were shocked by the party's electoral collapse on 4 June. So, given the fact that many senior PZPR negotiators did not contemplate the notion of an electoral defeat,[4] the question is on what basis was this positive assessment of the party's future electoral performance formulated?

A CBOS poll conducted between 21 and 24 January 1989 asked respondents: 'Does the PZPR activity serve society well and is it in agreement with society's interests?'[5] A 'Yes' answer was given by 3.9 per cent, and a further 22.3 per cent answered 'rather yes'. A 'rather no' answer was given by 29 per cent and a further 24.8 per cent said 'No', while 19.9 per cent had no opinion. Combining the 'yes' and 'rather yes' figures give a total of 26.2 per cent. This figure is boosted further when adjusted for the 'no opinion' category to over 32 per cent.[6] It is interesting to note that by 10 April 1989, just after the Round Table had concluded, only 15 per cent of those who were prepared to declare themselves in a CBOS poll said that they would vote for the government coalition.[7]

Interviews with key players such as General W. Jaruzelski and Mieczysław Rakowski highlight the fact that a form of doublethink appears to have influenced the cognitive processes of many party negotiators. This doublethink appears to have had a fatal impact on the PZPR's evaluation of the information at its disposal. Marek Kamiński has shown that the communist party estimated their level of political support from unadjusted 'confidence polls'.[8] He has argued that such polls were doomed to paint an overly optimistic picture of social support for the PZPR. The CBOS 'confidence polls' of the 1980s, though carefully conducted, were flawed in many respects.

There were three fundamental problems with the surveys that led the PZPR to rely on a skewed picture of likely electoral support. First, 30 per cent of respondents on average refused to complete the surveys in the late 1980s.[9] The major cause of the increase of refusals can be attributed to a reluctance of many Solidarność supporters to interact with communist institutions. A second systematic factor was the fear among the respondents who agreed to answer the questions. In simple terms, people did not believe that the polls were secret and, therefore, did not always express their true preferences. Piotr Kwiatowski has shown that polls undertaken in universities consistently produced results that were not as favourable to the communists as were those undertaken by CBOS researchers.[10] Given the fact that many high-ranking academics[11] were also senior party members, the question is why such information was not evaluated within the party. Another key factor was the party's control of the mass media. This asymmetric access to the mass media cannot be overestimated as factor in the assessment of confidence polls:

> Combined, these three systematic factors produced a picture of public opinion that was systematically and seriously distorted. Revealed ratings slowly shifted against the communists in 1987. The first serious jump in the ratings

occurred in December 1988 and the second one in April–May 1989. This 'revealed' a decrease in support that probably was not only due to the drop of real support, attributable to an economic decline, but also to the weakening influence of the three biasing factors described above. When this influence disappeared completely, which occurred in the final eight weeks of the campaign, the ratings changed dramatically.[12]

The analysis of interviews conducted with both General W. Jaruzelski and Mieczysław Rakowski shows clear evidence of some form of cognitive dissonance in their evaluation of the opinion poll information they had at their disposal both during and immediately after the Round Table.

During the course of a number of interviews Mieczysław Rakowski has never changed his explanation of his and the party's failure to foresee the 4 June election result:[13]

> In May after the end of the Round Table the opinion polls showed that fourteen per cent of the electorate would vote for us and the Peasants,[14] while forty per cent said they'd vote for Solidarność. The rest had no opinion. Till now I don't know why we thought that the rest would vote for us. We were prisoners of our past, when the elections weren't free. It just didn't register that the 'don't knows' wouldn't vote for us.[15]

General Jaruzelski was at an even greater loss than Rakowski to explain the PZPR's failure to appreciate its true levels of electoral support:

> We were used to winning the election no matter what! We did have strong propaganda – the Rakowski government was getting good results. So we thought that there was no big danger.... We were used to winning no matter what![16]

Lech Kaczyński was adviser to Lech Wałęsa and Solidarność negotiator at the Round Table subtable on trade union pluralism. He argues that the PZPR did not foresee defeat in the elections for a variety of reasons:

> Officially, they didn't anticipate because their culture didn't include the possibility. They were distributing false information within the party. I know what it was like in Gdańsk. They were sending questionnaires (about local support) to party leaders in institutions and these people were filling in the answers 'from the ceiling' as we say here. And this was the basis for some calculations. These people had a false perception – even within the party – of what was going on.[17]

The notion of the 'party's' perception of the process it was engaged in and its level of social support is problematic on a number of levels. As one of the key players on the Solidarność side, Lech Kaczyński had many opportunities to observe the conflicting impulses and motivations within the PZPR. He argues that it is facile to talk about the concept of the 'party' when talking about PZPR Round Table strategies and goals:

> Definitely – you cannot say 'party' because people thought about it differently. Some took part because they had to – because they had lost the battle to stop the Round Table. Maybe this group hoped that things would return to normal in Russia and that they would be able to control the opposition in Poland. The second group really did believe in a new reformed system. They thought that people who were legitimated by Solidarność would be able to get the reforms though and then there would be free election in four years. Then the third group thought that the system was finished and wanted to find a boat to sail into the new system. Jaruzelski thought he could keep the role of guarantor. I thought it was like that. This second group controlled the political and army apparatus. That was the guarantee of Jaruzelski's power. This all became clear at the Tenth Plenum. Our main opponent was in this first group. The betrayers, I call them. The second group was the old communists and then there were the young ones like [Aleksander] Kwaśniewski [president of Poland] and [Józef] Oleksy [now a prominent member of the post-communist SLD] who wanted to get rid of the old communists and they did it in one year. Whether these young communists had the conception of transforming the PZPR into the SdRP, I don't know. It is hard to examine it.[18]

Clearly, this diversity of interest and goals within the PZPR had a profound effect on the negotiating process. But it was also the cause, or maybe the effect, of the differing perceptions of the party's social support. The Politburo member, Stanisław Ciosek, has always claimed that he was under no illusions about the party's social support at the time of the Round Table.[19] The PZPR ideologue, Professor Jerzy Wiatr, and his son, Sławomir Wiatr (founder member of the post-communist SdRP), have also asserted that they understood what the results would be in a freely contested election.[20] However, as we shall see, the predominant conception of the party's support did not reflect that held by Ciosek and Wiatr, senior and junior. Lech Kaczyński was a key participant in the 'secret' Magdalenka meetings and remembers well the diversity of opinion within PZPR ranks:

> In Magdalenka, he [Stanisław Ciosek] kept saying that they would lose [the election]. He said that they couldn't agree to fully free elections to the Senate because they would lose. I remember it. However, a young Central Committee secretary, an optimist [Capt. Jerzy Kretkowski] kept worrying about the opposition in his reports. He was worried that they [Solidarność] would lose too much. The central polling agency was also optimistic for the party. I asked [Józef] Oleksy after the election at the meeting of the commission if they had put Kretkowski in jail. He said they hadn't but that they should have.[21]

Professor Janusz Reykowski maintains that the PZPR's assessment of the support ratio between itself and Solidarność played an important part in the decision to negotiate with the opposition:

> This was an important factor. From the data I had... a number of sociological studies from the Institute of Sociology and Philosophy... it was clear that towards the end of the eighties it was assessed that 25–30 per cent of the population supported the... regime. It was thought to be relatively strong support. Clear support for Solidarność was similar – also between 25–30 per cent. There was a large group in the middle who did not declare themselves! Another aspect was that there was a decline in the support for Solidarność leadership towards the end of the eighties. Towards the end of 1988 support for the main Solidarność leadership was quite meagre. As a matter of fact it was one of the arguments for negotiation because some people in the party leadership were afraid that if Wałęsa and his leadership lost his authority, there would be a new generation of leadership with much less political experience and much less political responsibility.
>
> There were two things that happened in the autumn of 1988. One was an interview with Wałęsa in Polityka. The other was more obvious – a debate between Wałęsa and Miodowicz.[22] This debate presented Wałęsa, not only to the public, but also to the leadership in a very different light. In general, the Solidarność leadership was regarded as quite seasoned politicians in comparison to these young strike leaders in 1988 who were very radical, simple-minded and dangerous. So this decline in support for the Solidarność leadership was not a decline in oppositional atmosphere, it was a decline in the authority of the Solidarność opposition. So it was also one argument for speeding up of negotiations with the Solidarność leadership as a real partner in comparison to others. It also had an impact on strategies during election to the Senate. It was expected that the party could get around 30 per cent but there were also some indications that various personalities had higher support than the party itself. So the whole campaign was set to personalities and not to parties. And as you remember from the data it was approximately true. It was between 25–30 per cent of the electoral votes that was collected by the regime and some persons got higher numbers but less than Solidarność. It turned out that latent support for Solidarność was quite strong![23]

Claiming to have always anticipated the possibility of the PZPR losing the election, Stanisław Ciosek says that the party had 'precise research'[24] before and during the Round Table process. He says that as he understood it in early 1989, a '50:50 outcome'[25] was being predicted by the polls:

> We saw that there was no clear winner. So we knew there was a risk. But at some stage the polls were showing a bad outcome, but the process had started and we could not withdraw. I was at a meeting when the church side warned us that we would lose – so the church had better information than the secret

police! But the good will to change was so big that we took the risk. We were the slaves of the dynamic of change and once it had started – it was hard to stop. To withdraw – it would mean to lose face, honour, and it would be cowardly not to stand in the election. I did not believe it was possible to withdraw. Of course, we believed it was a good agreement and that we had our own guarantees that we would not be out manoeuvred.[26]

Professor Andrzej Werblan warned the party hierarchy of the potential electoral disaster if it proceeded with its plan to employ a majoritarian electoral system in the proposed free Senate election.[27] While not actively involved in the Round Table process, Professor Werblan was a former Politburo member and was in contact with many of the key participants. He argues that senior members of the PZPR 'overestimated their own chances'[28] in their evaluation of the electoral outcome:

They never thought that they would have a third of the votes. They counted on having 50–60 per cent. The majoritarian system would have been good in this context. It was not a question of being uninformed or of there being a lack of knowledge – this was a question of the estimation of the state of public opinion. Every government makes these kinds of mistakes. The opinion polls were not objective and they were not conducted properly. They were corrected – the results were corrected. Jaruzelski was surrounded by people who were not giving him credible information. This was a dictatorship.... [Jaruzelski] estimated the situation as being better than it actually was. People in power have the tendency to wishful thinking. One of Mr Jaruzelski's closest associates, Józef Czyrek, in charge of foreign affairs – said at a number of meetings that the party would have to be careful not to do too well so as not to marginalize Solidarność. It was funny, but true. I think he really thought this way. That's why the election was a kind of a shock.... It resulted from the information that they were getting from the apparatchiks. They believed in strange things. They believed that if they put popular people on the (election) list – neutral people – that these people will [sic] gain support. They put the director of one of the Zoo's on the list, for instance, and people from the radio, and they thought it would help. The elections had the character of a plebiscite. People either voted for the government side or Solidarność – the faces didn't matter. If a donkey had been photographed with Wałęsa – he would have been elected. The top level of the PZPR did not take this into account before the election. They were expecting that the opposition would have one-third of the votes. They thought about a division of power and that there would be a long period of coexistence and power sharing.[29]

The electoral system and voting formulae

This section uses Politburo documents, Magdalenka transcripts and interviews with PZPR and Solidarność negotiators concerning party perceptions of the choice of electoral system and voting formulae.

Kamiński's investigation of the PZPR's choice of electoral system supports the analysis on which this discussion is based. Kamiński's counterfactual discussion of the 1989 election results has shown that apart from the fact that the PZPR's consent to the elections was founded on an overly optimistic estimate of its popular support, that an alternative electoral law, the STV, would have been mutually acceptable to both Solidarność and the party.[30] STV would have produced a much better electoral outcome for the communists. The crucial point is that had the result been less dramatic and the party's actual seat share been more commensurate with their vote, then the contractual power-sharing arrangement agreed at the Round Table may well have remained in place. In a nutshell, it is argued that the Solidarność coalition government may not have been formed and the communist party might not have been dissolved.

The communist side proposed single-member district majority run-off as their preferred electoral law at the Round Table. This gave them worse outcomes than STV or PR Party List systems would have produced. Both STV and PR would have been acceptable to Solidarność. Kamiński attributes this mistake to the complexity of the decision-making environment, the lack of technical knowledge about electoral rules and their properties and, finally, the fact that, under communist estimates about the distribution of voter preferences, alternative laws produced similar outcomes.[31]

The point is that there was nothing inevitable about Solidarność's victory. In terms of popular support, the results were far less impressive than might be understood on a cursory examination of seat share. Solidarność took around 70 per cent of the votes cast in the *Sejm* and Senate elections while the PZPR got about 25 per cent. The majority run-off system converted Solidarność's support into 100 per cent of the freely elected *Sejm* seats and also gave the union 99 per cent of the Senate seats. Kamiński has shown that with districts of a typical magnitude of three to four seats, and with an allocation formula friendly to small parties, practically any PR scheme would have resulted in a division of seats roughly proportional to popular votes, regardless of the further details of the electoral law. The essential point is that had PR been used, the outcome of the elections would have been very different.

Kamiński makes the point that an indication of how little awareness there was, within the PZPR, of the impact of electoral systems can be seen in the fact that STV was not even proposed at the Round Table negotiations. It is worth noting that there is no mention of voting rules in an otherwise detailed Politburo memo concerning the 'non-confrontational but competitive election'[32] sent to PZPR regional secretaries on 15 February 1989.[33] It appears that the various methods of vote aggregation was not a matter that overly troubled PZPR leaders used, as General Jaruzelski puts it, to 'winning the election no matter what'.[34]

Former Interior Minister C. Kiszczak could barely control his anger when asked about the choice of voting rules! 'We could have had any election rule. Not this stupid majority one! Any other election rule would have guaranteed victory for the party. The electoral rules were a huge mistake!'[35]

General Jaruzelski was even more candid than Kiszczak!

> The electoral regulations – when the party were in power for 40 years – not democratically of course – it is not easy to see the small print of the rules. What version to choose – not easy to decide which version to choose – it is not easy to make such a conscious decision. We were used to winning the election no matter what! We did have strong propaganda – the Rakowski government was getting good results. So we thought that there was no big danger. It was naïve that we chose the majority system – where the stronger comes through – and not the proportional one. If the rules were changed in the Senate, for example, instead of 99 for Solidarność, it would be closer to 70. So this was a psychological knockout. But it would be different if it was 70 and not 99 to 1.[36]

Before moving on to a detailed analysis of the individual components of the electoral system and voting formula, it is interesting to note General Jaruzelski's recollection of his mindset just after the Round Table in April 1989. This recollection emphasizes the fact that Jaruzelski regarded the non-electoral institutional mechanisms negotiated at the Round Table as guarantor of both his and the party's power:

> The [electoral] regulations that were adopted were negotiated in a really tough and tedious process. And both sides were realistic. The Soviets were still around – the bloc was there. [This was] one of the strongest limitations when I was making decisions. I was keeping it in mind that I must not hamper Gorbachev. I knew he was in a tough situation.... On the 27 April 1989, I was in Moscow for two days talking about cooperation between Polish and Soviet youth – that's why Kwaśniewski was there. He was Minister in charge of Youth affairs.... We were also having solid talks with Gorbachev. We were explaining to Gorbachev that what we were doing in Poland was not going to lead to the fall of socialism. We...talked about the guarantees including the 65 per cent and me being the president – for Gorbachev, these assurances were important because he was under pressure from the conservative forces in Russia. Poland was always central to the reforms in the bloc and Gorbachev admitted that. He was looking at Poland as an example. If the putsch against Gorbachev had happened in 1989 and not 1991, it could have been much worse. We did not want to give the impression that we were giving away power. Even after losing the election – we were always reassuring the Russians. My role as the president and the master of the military was important in terms of reassuring the Russians that everything was okay.... This was used against the Russian marshals who were against Gorbachev...that in Poland, it is possible to carry out reforms so that, on one hand there is opposition, but still the good people are in control.[37]

Election to the new Senate using the majoritarian system

Olson has observed that the essence of the Polish compartmentalized election system was seven separate segments of electoral competition where each compartment consists of a defined set of participants with a defined type of competition with its own rules.[38] In the election, the Senate district system and vote-counting methods swamped the PZPR and all but one of the non-Solidarność independent candidates. As has been discussed earlier, a proportional representation election method would have aggregated votes from around the country to give the PZPR at least some small share of Senate seats. Both Kamiński and Olson have observed that using a proportional system would have required a formal acceptance by the PZPR that rival organized political parties existed, thus compromising the leading role of the communist party. Kamiński and Olson emphasize the PZPR's unwillingness to acknowledge Solidarność as a political party as being the main reason for their failure to even consider the use of a proportional system. However, interviews with PZPR negotiators highlight the fact that they were more interested in the ratio of seats in the contractual *Sejm* and the institution of the presidency as a guarantee of the party's post-Round Table power.

> The decision about the free election to the Senate was made during a critical debate within the narrow leadership – 10–12 people. The argument was used that the party is a bureaucratic structure that executes power and such a party cannot survive in a democratic environment. So if it is to survive, it must learn new rules of democratic policy and this new agreement, that is being discussed, gives it [PZPR] a chance of reconstruction. It was expected that it was politically secure because 65 per cent [of seats in the *Sejm* were reserved for the PZPR] of votes are predetermined and . . . in this basic political security or safety it is possible to initiate a political game where the party may try to attain a new competence. But it was being formulated in conditional terms. They were not saying – the party will learn a political game, but it has a chance to learn the political game . . . . It was seen that there are some chances to improve the situation by this political game.[39]

Stanisław Ciosek argues that foreknowledge about the actual election result would not have changed any of the specifics of the electoral package agreed at the Round Table.

> It would not change too much even with this information . . . . I was the author of this conception the 35–65 per cent arrangement for the *Sejm*. So, in the *Sejm*, we needed two-thirds of a majority to deal with the presidential veto and the Senate . . . . But two-thirds is not 65 per cent but 67 per cent, so we were minus 2 per cent. Thirty-five per cent is not one-third, so the real fight [at the Round Table] was about this 2 per cent. The backbone of the offer to Solidarność was that they could win this 2 per cent. We were saying that a lot of Solidarność members were, in fact, in the party. But on the other hand, I was saying to the party that they could have more than the 65 per cent because they take a few per cent from Solidarność during the election because there are party members in Solidarność . . . . So the sides were

deliberating and they took – deliberately – the risk of fighting over this 2 per cent. It was not too much. The Senate – which was 100 per cent free, was not considered important. It was a sort of demonstration, but not practically important. Because in this conception, the majority in the Senate was held by Solidarność, and so the Senate can veto, but the President is able to veto also. The most important element of the bargain was the *Sejm* and who controls this 67 per cent of votes.... Both sides chose to gamble. I was writing the same thing to both sides and I was the author of this idea.... This system was guaranteeing stability, so I was not so worried about winning. I was always sure that we would always be able to organize a majority for particular events or topics such as the bill of laws... so this conception was very sensible at that time. It was sincere.[40]

Information concerning private talks between Solidarność and PZPR negotiators at Magdalenka provided by General Czesław Kiszczak at the Politburo meeting of the PZPR held on 14 March 1989:

The fifth issue that was discussed in a stormy and, at times, dramatic manner, was the package of political reforms concerning the office of the President and the Senate.

Solidarność and the opposition have analysed especially closely proposals, which were presented by us, focusing their attention on presidential powers, which could be used in situations of extreme political conflict. The issue here is the possibility of dissolving Parliament. They also tried to widen significantly the competency of the Senate, aiming at the concept of the Senate as an alternative to the *Sejm*. This was based on a belief that the opposition has a chance to monopolize the composition of the Senate.

It seems that with the progress of the debate on this subject, the position of the other side became more rational and realistic. In the end, at the last working meeting in Magdalenka, there was only one disputable question left regarding the Senate – the retention by the Senate of the right to veto, used to block any legislation; this would require two-thirds vote majority in the *Sejm* to force it through. Our proposal is the majority of three-fifths.

It should be explained that three-fifths means 60 per cent of votes in the *Sejm* – the exact number guaranteed by the political contract for the coalition of the three parties. However, two-thirds votes represents 67 per cent, i.e. 2 per cent more than the guaranteed in the contract 65 per cent of seats for the entire PRON coalition.

The dispute, therefore, is for the 2 per cent of votes in the *Sejm*, but, in fact, it is a principal question for us, as it requires the avoidance of the danger of a parliamentary crisis, which could paralyse the functioning of the authorities and the state. These 2 per cent could mean the possibility of a kind of 'liberum veto' for the opposition.

We think that there has been enough of learning on one's own mistakes and experimenting on a living organism. We are saying openly to Solidarność and the opposition that – on the basis of the Polish historical experience and the experience of many other countries – we stand for strong power, because weak power was always the source of disasters and misfortune.[41]

It seems clear from the accounts of Ciosek, Reykowski and Kiszczak's report to the Politburo that the party's share of seats in the contractual *Sejm* was the central focus of PZPR bargaining. Arguably, this focus affected PZPR negotiators' perceptions of the significance of other segments of the electoral bargaining.

It has been already noted that Professor Jerzy Wiatr was horrified when he became aware of the Magdalenka deal that provided for a free election to the Senate. Aleksander Kwaśniewski had introduced the idea of the free Senate without prior consultation with other negotiators. Wiatr heard of the proposal in a telephone call from Professor Janusz Reykowski who was delighted with the development. Having told Reykowski that the free election would be a 'disaster' for the party, Wiatr suggested a voting rule that would have given the PZPR some chance of getting its candidates elected in a free election:

> I proposed a small modification to the system of election. Each voter would have only one vote – not two or three – and then the candidates will be declared elected by the order of votes received. The implication of this is that in a typical voivodship were two Senators were elected – the first – the frontrunner would have been a Solidarność candidate. But unless Solidarność was ... powerful the second place would go to a candidate of the party or its allies. Andrzej Werblan made a similar proposal, but going further. He proposed formally that the Senate should be elected by a proportional system and argued quite correctly that that would give the government side about 30 per cent of the seats in the Senate, which is exactly what would have happened. Both these proposals were rejected. And I know from Reykowski that the most important factor in rejecting these proposals was Jaruzelski himself. Now they hoped – Jaruzelski's people – hoped that Solidarność's weakness in rural Poland would compensate in the election for the Senate for its strength in the urban conglomeration. They thought that the backward provinces would give the seats to the party and also they did not anticipate that the Catholic Church would engage itself in the election. But it did, and that was a critical factor. These weak provinces, from Solidarność's point of view, were also the most Catholic. So Solidarność was weak but the Church was strong so the outcome was that these provinces became even worse from the party point of view than provinces like Warsaw and Katowice.[42]

Professor Stanisław Gebethner was a participant in two Round Table working parties appointed to prepare changes in the electoral law and to amend the constitution. He provides a fascinating account of the PZPR hierarchy's failure to inform itself about the differential impact of voting rules.[43] According to Gebethner, the proposal for establishing the freely elected Senate was almost universally criticized at a meeting of negotiators for the government-coalition side. Gebethner argues that everybody pointed to the real risk of a PZPR defeat in a Senate election carried out in two-seat constituencies on the majority vote principle:[44]

> I elaborated a short report, but very detailed, and proposed a proportional representation system with 13 big constituencies and elections on 3 lists – Party, PRON and the opposition. They would be allocated proportionally in three elections according to d'Hondt. I presented this paper to Professor Reykowski[45] and there was no response. I then had a conversation with Mr Czyrek[46] about my proposal and he said that it is interesting academically and an interesting project. But it is the opinion of the voivodship secretaries that they will win in the majoritarian system and we will have to act on the basis of the political instinct of the secretaries. Józef Czyrek was a Politburo member and party secretary and formally charged with these negotiations. I reported this conversation to my friends and they were laughing. When the elections brought such total defeat in the Senate election, Professor Reykowski sent for this report because he was blamed for the result as well as the electoral system. But he said that they [the party] had Gebethner's project and the party rejected it.[47]

Professor Gebethner has no doubt that his electoral advice was available to the highest levels of the PZPR. He argues that the level of knowledge within the party of the differential impact of voting formula was extremely low, but that this lacuna was exacerbated by a huge degree of 'self-confidence'. So, here, we see two different mistakes. The PZPR made a mistake in relation to the selection of electoral rule and voting formula, a mistake that was made worse by the party's failure to base their evaluation on a correct assessment of support for the party.

Gebethner was not alone in fearing the impact of a freely and proportionally elected Senate. Professor Janusz Reykowski remembers being approached by a former member of the Politburo, Professor Andrzej Werblan, who had produced a document predicting electoral defeat if the majority run-off system was used in the Senate election:

> When the free election to the Senate was announced I got a visit from Professor Werblan who brought me a special document that predicted the complete collapse of the party at the election. But the decision-making groups who were debating the issue finally decided that this outcome was not very likely. This was probably 15 March 1989. It was thought that this prediction of Werblan's was not very likely. Not everybody disagreed with Werblan but the majority of decision-makers, the few people who made the decisions, felt it was too Cassandric to believe it. Werblan's idea was to negotiate another electoral law instead of the majority system and to use a proportional law. Of course the composition of the Senate would change if there was a proportional system but it was rejected. They thought that there was no need to change it. So in March the majority [in this decision-making group within the party] did not expect defeat. But some expected it![48]

Professor Werblan took the precaution of sending his document to Prime Minister Mieczysław Rakowski on 17 March.[49] Rakowski subsequently published the letter in an edited volume of his own correspondence.[50]

Professor Andrzej Werblan stated that

> There was no discussion within the party. The matter came up all of a sudden during the talks at Magdalenka.... Primarily it was planned to make only the *Sejm* a contractual arrangement, and later, because Solidarność wanted some element of free election, Kwaśniewski got the idea of free elections to the Senate. The idea was the same as the United States – two Senators from each voivodship. I think it was the idea of aparatchiks who thought that in the small, rural voivodships it would be easier to get the seats. I wasn't in power at the time, but I was observing what was going on. When I heard about the concept of the Senate elections on TV, I rang Rakowski and told him that God was punishing him and that he had had his brain removed. I told him that, with this system, he wouldn't have a single mandate in the Senate. It would be more reasonable to have the pre-war proportional electoral system to the Senate. Solidarność would have 70 places and the party would have had 30. There would have been a proportion between the *Sejm* and the Senate. The *Sejm* was contractual, and so the opposition would have one-third there. In the Senate, it would have been the opposite. The headquarters of the party was so sure that it would not lose the election to the Senate that they felt they would have 64 of the 100 seats. That's why they stayed with this majoritarian system.
>
> After the telephone call, I wrote a letter to him in which I mentioned the old pre-war electoral system.... Rakowski gave the letter to Jaruzelski and Barcikowski. Later Rakowski published the letter in a book called 'Letters to me'.... I didn't even have to think of anything new. In Poland, the elections were made three times before the war using the proportional system.... There were large districts – five, six, seven mandates. The voting was on numbered lists, not on names. So number 3 was the Polish Socialists, etc. We used d'Hondt. It was purely proportional system.... The party did not take my propositions into consideration. They thought that the majoritarian system would give them a better chance. They overestimated their own chances.[51]

Again, we see the point being made that the PZPR made two separate mistakes. They chose the wrong voting rule and they expected more support than they had. Werblan is emphatic, as are Gebethner and Wiatr that the PZPR hierarchy was made aware of the potentially disastrous consequences of a free election to the Senate conducted under a majoritarian system. He rejects any suggestion that the PZPR lacked the knowledge to evaluate the differential impact of voting formulae:

> They did have expertise. I told them. It wasn't a lack of knowledge that played the decisive role. It was wishful thinking. They were sure of a better

result – they were very confident. The result wasn't that bad taken into consideration the free elections to the Senate. In these elections the coalition got about 25–30 per cent of votes depending on the district. But after 45 years of dictatorship – at least 10 as a totalitarian regime and 10 after martial law – if the party gets 25 per cent of votes – it is quite an achievement. If you take into account that 36 per cent of people did not take part, then I claim that the government side did not have such bad results – it wasn't a catastrophe. Four years later – they won the elections.[52]

The collapse of the national list

While the PZPR's collapse in the Senate election had a huge demonstration effect, the collapse of its national or country list was also a devastating blow given the fact that the party's elite was simply crossed off this list by the electorate. The question is why the PZPR retained this negative form of voting; was there any awareness of the potential dangers of crossing off when voters had non-party candidates to choose from?

Olson provides this account of how the system actually worked when a person went to vote:

> The usual communist system election rule was retained whereby each candidate must obtain an absolute majority of all votes cast .... Voters had no easy task to express their intentions at the polling place, a marked departure from previous practice. Voters were presented with one large white ballot, one pink ballot, and several small white ballots. The large white ballot, uniform throughout the entire country, contained the 35 names on the national list. The pink ballot listed the names of the candidates for the two or three Senate seats within each province. The voter was also presented with as many small white ballots as the district had seats (two to five per district).
>
> The names on each ballot were listed in alphabetical order, without any designation. Not only were the parties unlisted on the Senate ballot, even the *Sejm* district ballot design helps account for the PZPR's emphasis in the names of candidates. The same design, however, also accounts for the Solidarność strategy of emphasizing a negative vote against all but its own few designated candidates .... The vote was cast by crossing out the names of the candidates for whom the voter did not wish to vote, leaving unmarked the names of the candidates whom the voter wished to support. The Solidarność appeal was simple: cross out all names but our few candidates in all compartments.[53]

Professor Stanisław Gebethner points out that the PZPR should have learned from the experience of the elections in the Soviet Union, prior to the Round Table, where official candidates had been crossed off. Gebethner campaigned against negative voting all through the 1980s and produced a paper arguing against the use of the system in Poland. Gebethner recalls discussing the issue with a party secretary who rejected his arguments:

> This idea of crossing out was an aggressive way of voting. It was better to vote positively, but it was impossible to convince them, but I told them. I remember a conversation with Mr Szmajdziński, who was secretary of the parliamentary club. He rejected my view. I said, 'Look at the results in the Soviet Union.' There had been the results of the first semi-free elections in the Soviet Union and the official candidates had been crossed out by the same method. During the TV time for Solidarność, people were told to cross out the names of the party names on the national list. The national list collapsed because they constructed the list in the way they did and Solidarność refused to cooperate with it.[54]

Zoltan Barany and Louisa Vinton note that the large number of candidates registered meant that voting was inevitably a taxing procedure. In Warsaw, for example, voters had to cross out 29 of 32 candidates on the Senate ballot to cast a valid vote.[55] Again, the question arises as to why PZPR negotiators did not anticipate the possibility that the people would simply cross off the names of party candidates.

Professor Andrzej Werblan said that

> They expected more loyalty from Solidarność! They didn't expect that Solidarność would agitate against the country list. They didn't expect Solidarność to instruct people to cross off the whole list. Solidarność used their TV time to show people how to cross off. I don't think it was with Wałęsa's permission. He wanted to stop it, but the majority of the leaders supported it. The government did not expect it! But I also think that Solidarność did not expect that it would cause the collapse of the list. Their aim was to reduce the votes because they knew that the collapse of the list meant breaking the agreement. That's why, after this, they were rather embarrassed and were looking for a way out. But the way out was unconstitutional. They changed the electoral rule midstream before the second round.[56]

Werblan was equally scathing about the party's failure to look at alternative methods of voting for the national list:

> No – only the Senate system was discussed. The press was not free enough to have such a discussion in public. The government didn't feel the need to discuss it. I started the Senate discussion privately because I knew Reykowski and Rakowski. If I hadn't known them, then there would have been no discussion. You have to understand this mechanism of a closed society.... Such a possibility [losing the election] could not be openly discussed. Big circles of the apparat were against cooperation or compromise with Solidarność. In these circles, it was argued that power was being given away. It was not because they anticipated what happened, but because they thought that even sharing power means losing. They cannot imagine anything other

than monopolistic power, and for this reason, anyone who starts a conversation about the method of compromise or which method would retain long or short-term power would be seen as a supporter of the hardline.[57]

Werblan argues that because of the opposition to the changes being envisaged by the reformist elite this core group[58] had to move

> in some kind of conspiracy. It was impossible to have an open discussion – it had to be in a tight group.... In this narrow group, they were thinking about my arguments, but they were not convinced and there was no wider discussion. Even people from the Politburo were not involved. They were considered hardliners.[59]

The use of the crossing-off formula devastated the PZPR's nationalist list and precipitated a crisis for both the PZPR and the opposition. There was no run-off arrangement for the 35-person national list, so the party was faced with the reality that its key people had failed to enter the *Sejm*.[60]

MP Professor Jerzy Wiatr:

> I don't think that all the consequences of this electoral system were realized! For instance, there is an obvious sign that people did not realize how vulner-able the national list for the *Sejm* was.... Because otherwise people like Rakowski should have run from the districts. Had Rakowski run...from a district where the seat was reserved for the candidates, he would have been elected. And the same about all the other people on the national list! Instead they believed that the national list was a safe vehicle – which it was not.... I think that in the case of the national list – they underestimated the strength of the negative vote. This list was defeated by a purely negative vote.... They underestimated the strength of the negative vote and thought that mostly when people are confronted with a kind of vote, which is not a choice but a confirmation that many who are passive would say yes.... In fact, they were partly true because the proportion of those who voted for the national list was higher than the percentage of those who, in contested elections, voted for the party candidates for the Senate. But it was not high enough to have the national list elected. This is a proof that these people did not fully understand all the implications of the electoral system.[61]

As Michael Laver points out this is yet another kind of electoral error or misuse of the chosen system.[62]

Candidate selection procedures

The PZPR selected nearly 700 candidates for its 156 seats in the contractual *Sejm*, while Solidarność sponsored only 161 candidates for the 161 seats it was contesting. Likewise for the Senate, 186 candidates were PZPR affiliated, while Solidarność nominated 100 candidates for the 100 seats. The Solidarność tactic of endorsing only one candidate for each of its eligible seats proved as effective against independent challengers in the *Sejm* as against PZPR candidates to the Senate.

Again the question arises as to why the PZPR ran so many candidates. Andrzej Werblan provides a harsh assessment of his former colleagues: 'Because of stupidity! These people had no experience of the mechanism of free elections.'[63]

As Millard notes in a majoritarian second-ballot system, a high number of candidates reduces the chance of electing a candidate on the first ballot.[64] In many *Sejm* constituencies, as many as seven or eight PZPR candidates competed, while in the Senate contest, the party 'allowed its own vote to be split, one case seventeen ways'.[65]

PZPR's expectation of rural support

PZPR negotiators believed that they could win the Senate election in at least 30 rural provinces.

Professor Stanisław Gebethner thought that

> This calculation was based on the general assumption that provinces with a majority rural population were pro-government. At any rate such a conclusion was drawn from the higher rates in voting turnout previously noted in these regions. Hence the PZPR fell into its own trap. For many years a single individual was allowed to vote for a whole family in the countryside, in order to increase the numbers of voters in the electoral statistics. Officials were often encouraged directly in such practices. As a consequence it was believed that the countryside continued to support the existing system and that it would elect coalition, and not opposition candidates. This belief was strengthened further by a mistaken interpretation of one of Lech Wałęsa's responses that Solidarność was supported in 19 urbanized and industrialized provinces. The conclusion drawn from this was that the PZPR, or the coalition as a whole, had the support of the majority of the electorate in the remaining 30 or so provinces.[66]

Professor Andrzej Werblan said that

> They did think they would do well in the rural areas. I don't know why. Two things misled the party! First, the secretaries of the voivodships who guaranteed them victory and said it was in their pockets, and secondly, the church. The church was misleading. The PZPR did not expect the church to openly support Solidarność.[67] This had a big impact on village society. People there were ready to listen to the priests.[68]

Heyns and Białecki analysed the election returns as published in *Gazeta Wyborcza*.[69] The major conclusion from the aggregate election data was that the strongest relative support for Solidarność was concentrated in poor, rural areas and not in the traditional strongholds of the urban working class. We will return to the issue of the PZPR's expectation of support in rural constituencies in Chapter 7.

The PZPR bargaining

The PZPR bargaining over the contractual election to the *Sejm* leaves the party without an overall majority except with the support of its coalition partners.

The PZPR's failure to retain an overall majority without the support of its coalition partners is one of the strangest of all Round Table outcomes. Each of the four political forces within the government coalition was allocated a share of seats within the 65 per cent of reserved seats. Zubek describes the decision as the PZPR's 'Trojan horse'. He argues that the Polish transition might well have had a somewhat different character if, at the time, the party had made the decision to rid itself of the coalition. However, the decision to persist with this arrangement proved to be a 'pathetically misguided attempt designed to strengthen those parties by allotting them a solid share of the pre-divided *Sejm* seats'.[70]

Gebethner notes that the PZPR displayed 'arrogance' in relation to their coalition partners.[71] However, once the election was over and the bargaining over the new government began, the ZSL (Peasant Party) and the SD abandoned their coalition arrangement, joining forces with Solidarność in August and thus removing the party's apparently secure majority. As Millard points out, PZPR leaders assumed the stability of the government coalition.[72] Millard quotes Jacek Kuroń, the veteran dissident, who noted in March 1989 that a guaranteed majority for the coalition 'does not mean a majority for the Communist Party, since the other coalition partners are beginning to come to life'.[73]

Conclusion

This chapter sets out to examine PZPR's choice of electoral system and voting formulae in the context of the Przeworski and Colomer hypotheses. We noted that it followed from Przeworski's hypothesis of short-sightedness that PZPR negotiators would not pay much attention to electoral formulae given their preoccupation with other institutional safeguards designed to facilitate their desired goal of a broadened dictatorship. We also expected that PZPR negotiators would focus on strategies that would ensure the preservation of their legislative veto. However, we also expected to see strategic mistakes as a result of the PZPR's failure to evaluate or update its knowledge of the differential impact of electoral formulae. In the context of Colomer's hypothesis of far-sightedness, we expected the opposite kind of behaviour from PZPR actors. We expected them to value the choice of electoral system as a step on the road to an intermediate regime. It follows that if this hypothesis is to be confirmed, the PZPR should have chosen an electoral system and voting formula that maximized the party's seat share. Furthermore, negotiators should have updated their information on the differential impact of voting formulae during the course of the negotiations. With these expectations in mind, we examined a number of institutional choices or scenarios to assess whether they conformed to the predictions of either hypothesis.

Three categories of error

The PZPR's erroneous estimation of its support is, arguably, the root cause of the party's collapse at the 4 June election. Of the three categories of mistakes made in relation to the election, the flawed evaluation of the party's actual support was the most fundamentally damaging. Had party negotiators really believed that they were in danger of electoral annihilation, it seems unimaginable that they would not have taken a keener interest in the differential impact of alternative voting rules. Had party negotiators appreciated their true support levels, they might not have made a mistake in choosing the voting rules. It follows that, if the party was operating on the basis of an accurate estimation of social support, its decision-makers might not have made strategic mistakes such as splitting the vote by running too many candidates.

Confidence polls

It seems clear that this error of estimation was rooted in the fact that the party was, as General Jaruzelski pointed out, 'used to winning – no matter what'.[74] The material examined in this chapter reveals that many of the party's senior players did not behave rationally when considering the level of support for the PZPR. Kamiński's analysis of the adjusted confidence polls taken throughout the 1980s clearly indicates that it was not rational for the PZPR to rely on these polls for an accurate estimate of support.[75] He identified three fundamental problems that led the PZPR to rely on a skewed and favourable estimate of their social support. The analysis of interviews with Jaruzelski and Rakowski, in particular, shows that a form of doublethink appears to have prevented these senior figures from understanding the evidence at their disposal and led them to expect higher levels of social support than even the adjusted polls indicated. As Lech Kaczyński remarked, the PZPR did not anticipate the likelihood of defeat 'because their culture didn't include the possibility'.[76] That said, it is clear from interviews with Stanisław Ciosek, Jerzy Wiatr and Sławomir Wiatr, as well as interviews with Solidarność negotiator Lech Kaczyński, that not all the PZPR Round Table players held this optimistic view of party support. However, at the end of the day, the predominant view of likely support was, as Politburo member Andrzej Werblan argues, based on the false information being supplied by the apparatchiks.

In this instance, it seems clear that many key PZPR figures failed at the most rudimentary level to ensure that they were estimating their support on the basis of reliable information. It is also clear that there was a failure at the most senior level of the PZPR to update or seek out accurate information that would have enabled a more reliable estimate of the likely impact of differential voting rules. The PZPR's behaviour in relation to the estimation of its support confirms Przeworski's analysis. PZPR decision-makers did not evaluate their next choice or move on the basis of the relative strengths of the two sides because they did not know these relative strengths.

Majoritarian voting rules

The evidence in relation to the PZPR's choice of voting rules makes it absolutely clear that party negotiators chose voting rules that resulted in a worse outcome than would have resulted from almost any other voting system. While Kamiński has argued that an indication of how little awareness there was within the PZPR of the differential impact of electoral systems was the fact that STV was not even proposed at the Round Table negotiations, this analysis has produced evidence which proves that senior negotiators were made aware of the damaging impact of using a majoritarian system in the Senate election.

Politburo member Andrzej Werblan advised Round Table co-chair Janusz Reykowski that a proportional system should be adopted for the Senate, and later wrote to Prime Minister M. Rakowski outlining the plan. Jerzy Wiatr has confirmed that he advised Janusz Reykowski of the disastrous consequences of choosing a majoritarian system. He also says that he understands that it was General Jaruzelski who rejected both sets of proposals. Stanisław Gebethner also confirms the fact that the notion of electing the Senate on the majority principle was 'almost universally criticized'[77] at a meeting of the government coalition group at the Round Table. He also produced a report outlining the merits of a proportional system. Gebethner's advice also was ignored. Gebethner says that a senior Politburo member, Józef Czyrek, told him 'it was the opinion of the voivodship secretaries that they will win in the majoritarian system and we will have to act on the basis of the political instinct of the secretaries'.[78]

On the basis of this evidence, it is clear that senior PZPR players not only failed to update their knowledge of the differential impact of voting systems, but also ignored the advice of three experts, two of whom were from within the party's own ranks. It, therefore, follows that the PZPR's behaviour in relation to the choice of voting rules supports Przeworski's hypothesis.

Crossing-off and the collapse of the national list

The evidence here is clear: had the PZPR been updating its information, it should have responded to the experience in the Soviet Union where voters had crossed off official candidates in the first semi-free election there. Again, there was information advising against the use of this negative form of voting available to the party. Stanisław Gebethner had written papers arguing against the use of the system and describes himself as having campaigned against the crossing-off system throughout the 1980s. Again, the PZPR's behaviour confirms Przeworski's expectation that 'misperceptions lead liberalization to transition'.[79]

Candidate selection

The PZPR's decision to run 700 candidates for its 156 seats in the contractual *Sejm* and another 186 for the Senate election falls into the category of an error of strategy. In a majoritarian second-ballot system, a high number of candidates reduces the chances of electing a candidate on the first ballot. In this case, the PZPR once again failed to understand the implications of allowing multiple candidates to stand, given the use of the majoritarian voting rule. Again, the PZPR's behaviour confirms Przeworski's hypothesis.

PZPR reliance on its satellite coalition partners

The PZPR made a strategic error when it assumed the stability of the government coalition and failed to anticipate that its satellite partners might cease to support the party at a future date. This assumption, which was central to the PZPR's bargaining over the contractual *Sejm*, seriously undermines the notion of party negotiators as far-sighted actors. The failure to protect the PZPR's dominance in the negotiations for the contractual *Sejm* struck at the heart of the party's most important goal, that is, its legislative veto. Here we see that the party's aim in negotiating the contractual *Sejm* was subverted by hubris. It wrongly assumed that the support of its satellite coalition partners was unconditional. Again, evidence of flawed evaluation and a failure to find out the most basic intentions of its coalition partners supports Przeworski's analysis.

7 The election campaign

If PZPR actors were the strategic far-sighted players posited by Colomer, we would expect them to have engaged in a vigorous election campaign designed to ensure the maximum seat share it could reap under the terms of the electoral deal agreed at the Round Table. Specifically, we would expect the PZPR to use its superior financial and organizational resources to get its election campaign off to an early start with selection conventions and registration of candidates completed ahead of the opposition; we would expect that PZPR strategists would have used the party's control of the media to promote its candidates and to dominate the campaign agenda; if PZPR strategists were alerted to tactical mistakes made at the Round Table, we would expect to see them attempting to rectify those mistakes where possible. In other words, we would expect them to react and counter-react to the moves in the game.

If, however, we look to what flows from Przeworski's analysis we do not expect to see PZPR actors engaging in an active campaign. The party's main strategic focus was on securing its legislative veto in the contractual *Sejm* and the establishment of a strong presidency, both of which were expected to ensure the PZPR's continued control in, what was envisaged as, a broadened dictatorship. In reality, the campaign turned out to be of crucial importance to the PZPR precisely because of its failure to ensure the effectiveness of its legislative, inbuilt, majority in the contractual *Sejm*. However, given Przeworski's hypothesis and the expectations that flow from it, we do not expect that PZPR decision-makers would have re-evaluated the electoral agreements and strategies that emerged at the Round Table in the hope of being able to maximize the party's performance.

The PZPR'S campaign

In a commentary written just a few months after the election, Paul Lewis notes that the PZPR did not appear to have embraced the election campaign with any degree of enthusiasm.[1] Following the election some commentators said that the PZPR had given up the ghost even before the campaign had started and that much of the coalition's election literature remained in party offices because no one had bothered to distribute it. Lewis points out that the campaign was later criticized by reformists within the party's leadership for being slow and old fashioned, and many members were said to be bitter about the way the whole election had been conceived, planned and executed.[2] Lewis does not find this behaviour surprising:

> The post-war Polish party had never been concerned with establishing political dominance by relying purely on its own resources and had had little need to perpetuate its position through elections. The primary interests of its staff, activists and supporters had certainly not lain in this area, and it was hardly surprising that the new atmosphere of political competition did not uncover much enthusiasm or aptitude for it.... Given the agreement on the distribution of seats, it was probably not immediately evident to the ruling party that it needed to contest the elections in quite the same way as the recently legalized opposition.[3]

While Lewis may be correct in arguing that the PZPR was not naturally equipped to fight election campaigns and that many of the party's hierarchy may have assumed that there was no danger given the distribution of seats, what concerns us here is the admission that reformist elements within the party were unhappy about the way the campaign was run. It is clear from interviews with senior PZPR activists that this concern was voiced,[4] so the question is why this concern did not generate positive action. David M. Olson argues that the PZPR did not seem to know how to campaign.[5] As we have seen in earlier chapters, some senior party members were sceptical about PZPR election prospects, but Olson points out that confidence played a role in the party's catastrophic election campaign. He argues that the PZPR thought it would win about one-third of the Senate seats and that non-Solidarność candidates would win about a third of the independent seats in the *Sejm*.

Olson's view that the PZPR thought itself well protected by the ratios among the electoral compartments is supported by the views expressed by senior PZPR Round Table negotiators interviewed in the course of research for this book.[6] Olson talks of an assumption among party leaders that they did not need to campaign. When it became apparent that there was a real danger that party candidates were going to lose, Olson claims that both opposition and party elites interpreted the PZPR's inaction as stemming from a perceived lack of options and a sense of desperation, rather than from any deliberate strategy. According to Olson 'the party presented a severe case of trained incapacity'.[7] PZPR party spokesman Jan Bisztyga remarked at the height of the campaign that the 'party is not accustomed to election battles like this'.[8]

The PZPR's inbuilt campaign trap

Voytek Zubek points out that the PZPR's own ideological platform contributed to the creation of a campaign trap that ensnared the party in a debate over the least ideologically advantageous issues from its perspective.[9] The problem arose as a direct consequence of the changes to the party leadership and hierarchy, which was a *sine qua non* for the initiation of the Round Table process. The struggle between the reformers and the old guard had been accompanied by ideological reassessments and condemnation of past mistakes.

However, as Zubek points out, while the ideological debate proved to be a most effective means of defeating the conservative wing, it also added fuel to a debate over the negative role of the PZPR in Poland. Party reformers perceived themselves as being radically different from the conservative wing and expected to be seen as a completely different breed from their party opponents.[10] However, up until the end of the campaign, most of the Solidarność leadership refused to acknowledge the distinction between the PZPR's contemporary reformist leadership and its past. By refusing to acknowledge differences between the reformers and the conservatives, and by acting as if very little had changed in the party, Solidarność manoeuvred the PZPR into a most uncomfortable campaign position.

On the one hand, party reformers spoke of the battles they had fought to bring about the Round Table, while Solidarność both spoke and acted as if the reformist leadership and its policies were just the most recent wave of crafty gimmicks unleashed by the hard-pressed vanguard party. Solidarność operated a simple campaign strategy. It characterized the party as the embodiment of all that was evil in Poland, which had the effect of trapping both reformers and conservatives alike in a hopelessly damaging debate over the definition of the degree of the PZPR's historical guilt.

The PZPR's reforms

> The casual approach to the campaign reflected a deep underlying misconception of the relationship between rulers and ruled. Senior party and government officials believed that the party would reap credit for its inauguration of the reform process.[11]

Frances Millard points out that PZPR strategists wrongly assumed that they would be rewarded for their role in initiating the Round Table process.[12] This view was corroborated many times in the course of interviews with senior PZPR Round Table negotiators, General Czesław Kiszczak among them:

> I consider myself the father of the Round Table – I take responsibility for the pluses and the minuses. The Round Table was the most important event to help Poland change politically without killing people. The shops are full now and people have full freedom. It was a detonator for the rest of the bloc, and it brought about the end of the Imperium. The Round Table should have been given a Nobel Prize. The creators of the Round Table from the government side are hated. In that regard, the first place of honour goes to Kiszczak, and the second place goes to Jaruzelski. Solidarność and the Church have hijacked the Round Table.[13]

It is not difficult to understand how this expectation of public gratitude led the party into a series of interconnected traps. Starting from the position that the reformers expected to be thanked for having won out in the battle against the conservative wing of the party, they then went a step further and wanted recognition for having allowed Solidarność to join, albeit in a limited fashion, the political process. Basing their campaign on these two fundamentally flawed assumptions, party strategists then proceeded to tell the exhausted Polish electorate that they would have to be ready for the austerity necessary to get the Round Table bargain off the ground. As George Sanford argues, there was considerable confusion during the government-coalition's badly organized electoral campaign. It emphasized the socially unwelcome message that the public had to shoulder the burden of the massive cost of implementing the Round Table Agreement, estimated at 5 billion zlotys (US$ 1.5 billion).[14]

As the campaign wore on, party strategists became frustrated by their inability to engage the Solidarność's leadership in a focused, detailed debate concerning economic reform. Given the fact that the imperative of economic reform was the driving force behind the initiation of the Round Table talks in the first place,[15] it is not surprising that reform scenarios were key components of the PZPR's electoral platform since the party leadership had come to consist almost exclusively of reformers, notwithstanding the only very recent conversion of some to their reformist views. As Zubek quite rightly argues, the party hoped that, if Solidarność were to engage in a debate on the actual detail of the reform measures, then the superiority of the party's experience would impress many voters.[16] However, what the party failed to anticipate was the Solidarność leadership's tactic of ignoring the PZPR challenge and its ability to adhere to its own campaign message. Another example of the party's inability to set the campaign agenda was its failed attempt to play the foreign policy card against Solidarność, who might have been perceived, by the public, to lack experience in this arena. Solidarność anticipated this problem and simply refused to engage in a debate about Poland's foreign policy commitments and relationships in the post-Round Table context.

The television debate between Miodowicz and Wałęsa

While the election campaign proper did not commence until after the completion of the Round Table in April 1989, it is arguable that the real campaign began in November 1988 in the context of the television debate between the leader of the party's trade union, Alfred Miodowicz, and Solidarność leader Lech Wałęsa. A number of facts surrounding how this debate occurred, expectations of its effect on the PZPR's public support as well as the details of the actual sanctioning of the encounter, provide support for the view that the party operated on the basis of false assumptions and misperceived strategies. The debate itself took place on 30 November and was watched by some 20 million viewers.[17] Amazingly, those involved in the affair from the PZPR's side expected that it would lead to an increase in support for the party. This assumption could not have been further from reality. As Marek Kamiński argues, whereas some rise in support of the communists was expected, the 30 November televised debate resulted in significant falls in CBOS confidence indicators.

Kamiński points out that the debate was intended to cautiously sound public reaction to the first television appearance of Wałęsa and help communist rulers gauge the strength of its opposition.[18] In fact, subsequent polls showed that 63.8 per cent of respondents thought that Wałęsa had won the debate, while only 1.3 per cent believed that Miodowicz had won.[19] Apart from the 'surprise' of Wałęsa's approval ratings, the debate also produced another unexpected result. A substantial attitude change towards the relegalization of Solidarność was also detected. But in August, the difference in respondents supporting and opposing relegalization was over 12 per cent, the figure jumped to over 32.4 per cent following the encounter between the two trade union leaders.[20]

While it is hard enough to believe that those PZPR members involved in arranging the debate between Wałęsa and Miodowicz expected an increase in party support to result, it is even more surprising to learn that the encounter went ahead without the prior knowledge or approval of General Jaruzelski and the KC PZPR. Evidence to support this claim is to be found in the minutes of a stormy meeting of the Secretariat of the KC PZPR and its trade union ally, the OPZZ, in early February 1989:

> Com. Jaruzelski summarizing the debate expressed his hope that this meeting between the Secretariat of the CC (KC) and the AATU [OPZZ or PZPR affiliated trade union] leadership will clear the atmosphere and will make people aware of common dangers . . . .
>
> Some issues emerged in the course of this debate that are worrying. AATU comrades' consciousness is burdened with a view that 'the party betrayed us.' We never used any argument against unions. The party went through deep self-criticism. The unions were not criticized apart from polemics between coms. Rakowski and Miodowicz. The party leadership is politically and morally entitled to criticism. AATU comrades say that 'the party betrayed', but this charge can be turned round [interview with Com. Miodowicz in ˙Perspektywy']. We weren't informed about your contacts with 'S' [Solidarność]. We didn't surprise anybody with the 'round table'. We took this decision faced with increasing danger of strikes, possibility of Wałęsa getting ahead of us, and the need to play for time.
>
> It was neither surprise nor betrayal. It was us who were taken by surprise by com. Miodowicz's initiative to have debate with Wałęsa on television. This public debate raised Wałęsa's status. Further developments stemmed from there. Up to that point we defended a formula that there would be no 'Solidarność', that conditions/grounds for it must evolve in future. Was that class attitude?[21]

By the autumn of 1988, the interests of the reformist wing of the PZPR and the party's trade union ally, the OPZZ, were clearly diverging. However, given the sensitivity and complexity of what Jaruzelski and his coterie were attempting, it is surprising, given the party's control of the media, that Miodowicz was able to take a decision to take part in a public television debate with Lech Wałęsa without the matter being considered by either Jaruzelski or the Politburo. However, that is exactly what appears to have happened.

Pełczyński and Kowalski argue that the electoral campaign showed not only a fundamental lack of symmetry between the government side and the Solidarność opposition, but also a basic difference in approach.[22] Even though the governmental coalition had overwhelming advantage in access to mass media and means of expenditure, it did not capitalize on this asset:

> Solidarność was allowed to start a mass circulation daily paper and some weeklies and had the support of some independent (mostly Catholic) weeklies. It had only 7 minutes a day on television (to the government coalition's 23 minutes) and very limited share of radio time. But it received tremendous support from Polish language foreign radio stations, especially Radio Free Europe, which was frankly partisan in its comments. It made up its lack of other opportunities by the massive and imaginative use of posters, stickers and leaflets which dominated Polish streets during the campaign. They were financed by individual contributions to the election fund but also by foreign aid, much criticized by the Communist press (like outside broadcasting) as 'foreign interference' although it was not against the law. The Solidarność-organized election meetings were far more numerous and better attended; the government coalition candidates were scarcely visible in public.[23]

This sense of the PZPR's almost frozen inertia at a time when decisive action was required is visible in exchanges between a disgruntled team of OPZZ leaders at a meeting with the Secretariat of the KC PZPR in February 1989. The exchanges highlight how unprepared many elements of the party were for the impact of Solidarność's new-gained access to the media. Widespread concern and disapproval of that media access was expressed at this meeting, while many leading figures voiced worries about the effect of the end of censorship.

It is clear, in the context of accusations, that the PZPR strategists behind the Round Table project were selective with information about the extent of its contacts with Solidarność, that even the reformist dominated leadership was divided on how the new relationship with Solidarność should be managed. The meeting took place on 9 February, a day after a meeting of the Round Table's subtable on the economy. The OPZZ delegation, which was led by Alfred Miodowicz, was clearly angered by the television coverage of the subtable, in particular, by the manner in which the OPZZ statements were edited. The minutes note that the vice-president of the OPZZ, Com. Wacław Martyniuk, was present at the Round Table subtable on 8 February:

> Having been present at yesterday's meeting of the economy group [I] had the impression that it was a great seminar for economy professors. [The] Opposition partners were perfectly prepared. After six statements and a declaration read by Bugaj [Solidarność representative] our side was only clarifying, we were not aggressive.... The director completely ignored our unions.... The television transmits the full text of Bugaj's declaration and only one-third of mine. This is a manipulation of our unions.[24]

A Politburo spokesman, Com. Franciszek Ciemny, offered the view that the PZPR side was ineffective at the Round Table meeting on the economy:

> Our side lacked firing power. There was none of it in Professor Kaczmarek's statement. We should have determined people in all the groups, fighters. ready to defend socialism. The opposition acts with arrogance, does not abstain from sharp criticism, caddish behaviour, scoffing. We keep quiet, we don't retort. Why are our representatives so poorly prepared; only the AATU [official trade union] people defend the agreed position.[25]

Prime Minister Mieczysław Rakowski was not concerned by Solidarność's strong and televised performance at the economic table meeting. Rakowski threw cold water over concerns that the PZPR negotiators lacked vibrancy and dismissed Solidarność negotiator Ryszard Bugaj's analysis of the economic crisis in Poland as nothing new. He also implies that Deputy Prime Minister Sekuła's non-attendance at the meeting was tactical. Clearly, Rakowski is confident that the PZPR had the situation under control:

> The comrades are excited by yesterday's meeting of the economy group. Too early. It's only the beginning. The declaration read by Bugaj indicates that 'the emperor is naked'. Everybody was talking about it as far as the beginning of the eighties. Deputy Prime Minister Sekuła purposely did not appear yesterday. In spite of shortcomings of our economic programme nobody will get anything more by some magic trick. If we want to fit the opposition into shared responsibility we have to give up something, preserving however unity in our camp. We have no illusions as to ideological nature of the opposition including the constructive side.[26]

Registration and candidate selection

Given the internal battles within the PZPR between reformers and hardliners, it is perhaps not surprising in retrospect that the party's main focus after the Round Table should be on selling the agreement to its own members. Lewis observes that the communists took less note of the election campaign and were more concerned with the National Conference of PZPR delegates which met early in May.[27] Even so, it is somewhat surprising that the PZPR manifesto was not published until 29 May, less than a week before polling day. Pełczyński and Kowalski argue that the Solidarność leadership was initially pessimistic about its campaign prospects, given the party's many advantages in terms of resources and organization.[28] However, that perception began to change.

In terms of election preparedness, Solidarność began to show its organizational efficiency. Almost a month before the party submitted its list of candidates for registration to run in the election, Solidarność had its complete list of candidates ready. As if hitting the ground limping and late, rather than early and running was not bad enough, the PZPR used the suicidal tactic of fielding numerous candidates in the seats assigned to them. As Sanford notes, this tactic 'divided up what proved to be their low vote in the equivalent of primaries without doing much to enhance their democratic credentials'.[29] In terms of strategy and tactics, Solidarność played a masterstroke by selecting 100 candidates for the 100-seat Senate election and endorsing a limited and, in many cases, single candidate in the seats it was allowed to contest in the *Sejm* election. Sanford's résumé of the list of registered candidates is illuminating and, once again, highlights the PZPR's gaffe prone approach to fighting election campaigns:

> The final number of 558 registered candidates for the 100 Senate seats was made up as follows: 186 PZPR (whittled down from an original total of about 500 nominations), 90 ZSL [Peasant Party], 69 SD [Democratic Party], 10 PAX [Catholic Groups], 73 non-party, 100 Solidarność and 21 other opposition groups (including 5 KPN, one Union of Real Politics and even one Orange Alternative!). As far as the *Sejm* was concerned the PZPR had a participation explosion which it could not handle; it started off with 1,200 individuals vying for nomination for its 156 non-National List seats, the ZSL with 217 for its 67 seats, the SD with 78 for its 27 seats. The PZPR ended up with generally between three and six candidates competing for each of their assigned *Sejm* seats. These figures compared very badly with the almost total [Solidarność] Civic Committee discipline in endorsing a limited, or even single number of candidates per seat despite one or two local conflicts.[30]

Personality-first strategy

> The political establishment has designed its election campaign to blur distinctions between official candidates and those on the Solidarność ticket. The Solidarność Citizens' Committee is determined to keep these distinctions clear, and to make the elections a contest between the tested Solidarność team, with its evolutionary program to change the system, and the defenders of the status quo masquerading as independents.[31]

Writing in May 1989, *Radio Free Europe*'s Louisa Vinton notes that, cognizant of its own lack of popularity, the communist party establishment decided to run a strangely apolitical campaign whose main aim was to increase the confusion of voters in elections whose rules are already extremely complicated.[32] 'Qualifications not Affiliations' was the theme of the party conference while the PZPR campaign slogan was 'Choose according to ability not affiliation'.[33] As the journalist Krzysztof Wolicki remarked on a Solidarność Citizens' Committee radio programme, 'Finding a candidate from the communist party who will admit that he is a candidate from the communist party is an enormously difficult task'.[34] Olson concurs with Vinton's view.[35] He argues that the PZPR had no leading personality, unlike Solidarność, who branded their candidate list as Lech's team.

All Solidarność candidates had their photograph taken with Lech Wałęsa and that was the only picture that appeared on hoardings throughout the campaign.

The PZPR adopted the opposite tactic and did not endorse its own candidates in the *Sejm* or the Senate elections. There were no advertisements in the party's name. Olson argues that according to participants on both sides, the party's abstention from the visible campaign seemed to stem from the fact that there was a conscious decision to shift the emphasis away from both the party organization and its symbols:

> Its candidates stressed their personal accomplishments rather than their party ties or the party's record and platform.... One leading party figure said, 'We did not use organizational symbols.... We wanted the talented people of the party to win and not the party symbol or its organizational seal'.[36]

Solidarność shrewdly adopted the opposite tactic and argued that what mattered was the organization that nominated people. Voters were invited to treat the election as a plebiscite for Solidarność or for 'really existing socialism'.[37] In order to highlight the rejection of the communist system and to prevent the electorate being sidetracked by personalities running for the communist party, voters were asked to strike out all but the Solidarność candidates on the ballot paper. As we have seen earlier, the PZPR's national list fell foul of this call with only 2 of the 35 names nominated by the party gaining more than the required 50 per cent of the popular vote on the first round.

Speaking with his political scientist's hat on, Professor Jerzy Wiatr believes that it is arguable that if the PZPR had run a more personalized campaign around the personality and record of General Jaruzelski, the campaign result might well have been affected:

> Then there is another factor, which has never been tested – Jaruzelski's personal popularity! The election was never run as Jaruzelski's team versus Wałęsa's team. It was Wałęsa's team versus the conglomerate of the old timers, with Jaruzelski keeping a kind of a distance and being earmarked for the next president.... This is a factor that was never investigated... but considering the fact that Jaruzelski was far more popular than the party or any of its leaders – the fact that he put himself out of the picture – helped Solidarność. If it had been more Jaruzelski versus Wałęsa and had the game been played earlier... and if Wałęsa had pictures showing him with the various candidates... had Jaruzelski pictures with his people – the result might have been better for Jaruzelski's people![38]

Crossing off PZPR candidates

The catastrophic impact of the retention of the crossing-off system of voting has been discussed in Chapter 5. As was noted earlier, the PZPR's 35-candidate national or country list was almost totally wiped out as a result of the crossing-off formula. We also saw how PZPR negotiators were advised against the retention of the system both before and during the Round Table negotiations, but chose to ignore this

advice. At the PZPR's election convention on 4 and 5 May, two delegates voiced the
fear that was probably at the back of most delegate's minds: that voters could cross
out all the PZPR candidates on the ballot. Vinton reminds her readers that the PZPR
insisted at the Round Table that candidates would be listed alphabetically on the
ballot and that no information about them except their name would appear.[39]
According to Vinton, the 'authorities quite rightly fear that many voters will
automatically cross out candidates whom they identify with the communist party':[40]

> Although it may be tactically shrewd, the political establishment's wager on
> 'personalities' in an election campaign designed to convince the public that
> political affiliation is unimportant could backfire. The attempt to suggest that
> the official coalition's candidates share all of Solidarność's good points and
> that the party's program could be mistaken for Solidarność's constitutes a
> remarkably compromising admission that the official coalition has nothing
> of its own to offer. In this situation, voters could easily decide that they pre-
> ferred the genuine article. In addition...should the official coalition's media
> campaign continue to conceal the political orientation of candidates appear-
> ing on the ballots reserved for the establishment, voters might decide it was
> impossible to distinguish among them and simply cross them all out.[41]

There can be no doubt that if *Radio Free Europe*'s Warsaw correspondent was
able to predict the possibility that PZPR candidates would be crossed off by voters, party hierarchy was also aware of this possibility. The party's failure to
respond to fears about the possibility of its candidates being crossed off is yet
another example of it not attempting to rectify mistakes or suboptimal choices
made at the Round Table. Writing on the eve of the election, Louisa Vinton noted
that the most obvious and important feature of the campaign had been the
political collapse of the Communist party with some of its leaders facing the real
possibility of a humiliating public rejection:[42]

> The key problem here is that the names of these establishment leaders were
> put on the so-called national list: the people on this list are running unop-
> posed for seats in the *Sejm*. The list was designed to ensure that the leaders
> of the party and its political allies retained their seats in the country's main
> legislative body; the lack of opposition appeared to guarantee that outcome.
> As a result of a possible oversight, however, the certainty that the party leaders
> will be elected has been undermined by a general provision that all
> candidates must win at least 50 per cent of the votes cast in the first round in
> order to win seats in parliament. This requirement applies to the candidates
> on the national list but, because they face no opposition at all, they cannot
> run in the second round. This opportunity has been spotted by both the oppo-
> sition and the public, and it is quite likely that some prominent political per-
> sonalities may struggle to be elected. This situation may reflect carelessness
> or overconfidence on the part of the establishment's campaign organizers. It
> also suggests, however, disarray within the establishment, a factor that could

have major political consequences if the party leaders were defeated in the election. This disarray has been noticeable for some time and has been openly admitted by various activists and officials. The campaign has brought it into the open. Many observers think that the political eclipse of the current establishment, particularly the party, is inevitable.[43]

'Intricate election mechanisms, simple choices'[44]

Ultimately, the PZPR's strategy of confusing the electorate was a self-defeating mechanism. As Louisa Vinton noted on 2 June, two days before the election: 'The mechanics of the elections to the *Sejm* and the Senate are very complicated. This design was intentional and reflects the authorities' general effort to confuse voters as to who represents them.'[45]

Confusing and complicated as the multiple ballots were, Solidarność was able to ride roughshod over the party's tactic with a very simple instruction to voters to cross off all names except those of the Solidarność candidates. This was made simple by Solidarność's other strategic decision to limit the number of candidates running in each electoral compartment. In contrast, PZPR supporters would have had the much more difficult task of identifying their candidates, given the decision not to include party credentials on the ballot. Furthermore, the 'explosion' of PZPR candidates from which voters were forced to choose, exacerbated the problem. Solidarność's Citizens' Committees all over Poland sent supporters out to train Poles how to mark the ballots and, on election day, its supporters sat outside polling stations under eye-catching Solidarność banners advising voters to cross off all but the Solidarność names.[46] Solidarność's new election gazette, *Gazeta Wyborcza*, devoted a daily column to explaining electoral procedures, while local Citizens' Committees published 'crib sheets', small leaflets with all the names of the Citizens' Committees' candidates, for a particular region so that voters could carry them with them into the voting booth. One inventive Citizens' Committee in Poznań told would-be voters that its crib sheets would be valid as a raffle ticket, if turned in at election booths on polling day.[47]

It is hard to conceive of the PZPR doing itself any more electoral harm than it managed during the election campaign between April and June 1989. Despite having control of the media and huge organizational resources, the PZPR fell at every campaign hurdle. Solidarność got its campaign off to a much earlier start having registered its candidates a full month ahead of the party. The PZPR defeated the possibility of retaining its core vote by its personality-first policy. This tactic also allowed Solidarność to pursue a very simple campaign agenda, that is, to invite the electorate to regard the election as a simple plebiscite on the role of the communist party in Poland. By failing to limit the number of its candidates running in each electoral compartment, it confused the electorate and provided Solidarność with the opportunity to exhort voters to make the simple choice of voting for the Solidarność candidate – singular not plural. By deliberately making voting a complicated procedure, it also created the opportunity for Solidarność to legitimately call for its supporters to cross off the party's candidates.

Apart from all of these errors, the party set out under the false assumption that it would reap the benefit of having initiated the process of reform. This assumption was compounded by the fact that the reformist wing, which had pushed for the Round Table, assumed that it would receive differential treatment and respect from the public, who would recognize that the party reformers were not the same as hardliners. This assumption allowed Solidarność to set the campaign agenda and thwarted the reformists who hoped to show that they were a different and more deserving breed than their hardline colleagues. Finally, it is clear that the party simply ignored the warnings, from both within its ranks and from other sources that its national list could potentially collapse as a result of voters crossing off its candidates. In a word, the PZPR failed to update its information or rectify strategic mistakes made at the Round Table.

The PZPR and the Catholic Church

'They drank a sea of vodka with Ciosek and the others'.[48]
Stanisław Ciosek explained that

> We started to talk to the church about the need for social dialogue almost immediately after martial law [December 1981]. One important thought. For obvious reasons – the structure of the party – hierarchical and stable – it was easier for the party to talk to a similar structure in terms of hierarchy.... It was easier to believe what the church was doing because of certain similarities and credibility. Those two structures were able to understand each other quite well. It was easier for the party than talking to this new wild Solidarność movement! The Solidarność movement was unpredictable – the party was talking to the church very regularly in the 1980s. The church was the advocate of Solidarność but we felt that it understood the party. The role of the church was gigantic. The Round Table agreement would be impossible to achieve without the church mediation. And that's very specific to Poland.[49]

In retrospect, it might appear counter-intuitive to argue that the PZPR made the fatal error of expecting its apparent enemy, the Catholic Church, to remain neutral during the election campaign. However, the fact that this was the case is not so difficult to comprehend if one looks at the issue from the perspective of those party negotiators who had the closest contact with the Church throughout the 1980s. In the context of tracking the gap over a range of issues between the PZPR's expectations of strategies or relationships and actual outcomes, perhaps its most fatal error was its failure to fully understand the nature of its relationship with the Catholic hierarchy.

As is clear from Stanisław Ciosek's remarks quoted earlier, the PZPR thought of the Catholic Church as an organization very similar to the party. Implicit in Ciosek's remarks is the view that the church was not 'wild' like Solidarność. It perceived the church as reliable and predictable; it understood the party and they could speak the common language of power. In a word, Ciosek thought he could do business with the church, and as is clear from Bishop Orszulik's memoirs which are cited later, the church thought it could do business with the party. Ultimately, however, while the bishops might have 'drunk a sea of vodka with Ciosek', the Polish hierarchy never lost sight of what side it was on.

Bishop Alojzy Orszulik was one of the key figures in the contacts between the Catholic Church and the PZPR:

> The Church initiated the talks.... What induced the Church to adopt this position? The late archbishop Dąbrowski once said: 'At a time when the society was disposed of its subjectivity and voice, out of necessity, the Church had to take its place and, at the same time, paved the way for a socio-political dialogue.' The Church looked for peaceful solutions – reached through dialogue. It saw its role in reconciling two opponents: on the one side those ruling, on the other an embittered society. The Church initiatives did not mean that it was willing to compromise with the authorities to the disadvantage of the society, as some dissidents claimed. The Church defended the opposition; this is why it was accused by the communists of anti-State activities.
>
> Despite the communists' critical attitude towards the Church, they welcomed the idea of talks on the social accord. Why?
>
> First, the desperation of the society was such that there was a risk of extreme upheaval. The authorities realized that they would not be able to suppress riots, even with the use of force.
>
> Second, they could not find a partner for talks among opposition circles. According to the communists, the Lech Wałęsa-led hierarchy of Solidarność was too radical because its main aim was to deprive the communists of power. There was no common ground for bargaining. On the other hand, they realized that the social order could not be restored unless there was cooperation with Solidarność.
>
> Thus, the Church initiative enhanced prospects of getting out of a deadlock. The communist authorities hoped that the Church would have beneficial influence on Wałęsa and his advisers.[50]

After martial law, the party was in desperate need of an interlocutor. The church was the obvious and, from the PZPR's perspective, the safest and only choice. Arguably, the church was at its strongest during this time. The party was dangerously at odds with the very workers it claimed to embody. In showing financial generosity and tolerance to the church, the party sought to ease the steam from the pressure cooker and, by doing so, retain a line of communication with society.

Church historian Peter Raina argues

> There is no denying the fact that for the authorities the Church became the only partner for dialogue. Moreover, through Church mediation, the authorities sought contacts with the society, which was indispensable for solving contentious issues. This was confirmed by secret talks between the authorities and the Church.[51]

This Orszulik/Raina account of the Secretary of the Episcopate – Archbishop Dąbrowski's discussions with internal affairs minister, General Czesław Kiszczak clearly indicates that the PZPR expected that the church authorities would reciprocate its 'kindness':[52]

> We are concerned about the deterioration of Church–State relations. The form and contents of the 204th Press Conference of the Episcopate upset us. Bishops want to exacerbate the situation. This gives both your enemies and our enemies' grounds for attack. The Episcopate's memorial from this conference is ruthless and unpleasant. In the communiqué of the Press Office as well as that of the Primate, there shouldn't be any such notions. They are dangerous endeavours – one more step and we will face a confrontation....
>
> Is any confrontation necessary? Who needs it? At present, the Church enjoys privileges. For example: seminaries are full; the financial situation of priests is very good – they pay symbolic taxes; the building of sacral premises is proceeding; and the churches are full of worshippers who are not disturbed. We do not object to continuation of church-going practices because we realize the positive role of the Church. Now, when losses are not to be recovered due to a severe winter, priests empoison people's mind against the authorities. After all, the authorities do everything for the people to live better lives. Nobody starves, nobody feels cold, and people have clothes to put on. For the good of the people, the Church should support the authorities.
>
> Does the Church help us? Yes, in churches 'Our Lord, Free Motherland, gives us back' is sung, as during tsar's or Hitler's times. A conclusion is simple – one does not work for the oppressor but boycotts it. Wałęsa identifies himself with the underground. The Church sides with Wałęsa – consequently, it supports the underground too....
>
> We need each other – we depend on each other. We won't escape from that. We must search for an agreement and not look for the confrontation.[53]

This perception that the PZPR and the Catholic hierarchy were mutually dependent is a constantly reiterated motif in the exchanges between party negotiators and church representatives throughout the 1980s.[54] It is also clear that Stanisław Ciosek, who conducted most of the negotiations with the hierarchy, believed himself to be doing a deal with the Church. The church's role throughout the 1980s, especially during the Round Table, is a complex one, and while the church was indeed wielding enormous power, it could not be seen to be visibly attempting to control Solidarność or the opposition. Leaving aside whatever aspirations the Catholic hierarchy might have harboured, Solidarność was no monolith; it was made up of a wide range of disparate influences. Solidarność was a broad church ranging from atheistic Marxists to Catholic fundamentalists with would-be Thatcherites in the wings. The Catholic hierarchy was too shrewd to allow itself to overtly assume the role of speaking for the opposition.

In September 1988, during the intense series of meetings prior to the start of the Round Table, Bishop Orszulik, once again, reminded Ciosek that, if there was to be an agreement, it must be concluded with the workers and not with the hierarchy:

> On 13 September 1988, Stanisław Ciosek met Father Orszulik for a longer conversation. Ciosek was talking about discontent among the party members owing to Kiszczak's meeting with Wałęsa and objections towards Jaruzelski's 'inconsistency and weakness'. Ciosek counted on the Church to exert a calming pressure on Wałęsa's postulates. Father Orszulik did not see it happening. He expressed his opinion that the sooner Solidarność became legalized the better for the welfare of the country. Moreover, he said that the issue of trade union pluralism should be discussed directly with competent people [i.e. the union].[55]

Later in the same note from Orszulik's diary, the bishop draws attention to Ciosek's belief that he was doing a deal with the church:

> 'The authorities hope to reach an agreement with the Church', Ciosek added.
>   I said that I had stated many times that with regard to workers the authorities should reach an agreement with the workers rather than the Church hierarchy.[56]

Despite being regularly reminded that the church's role was that of go-between rather than dealmaker, the PZPR, and Stanisław Ciosek, in particular, continued to believe that they were doing a deal with the hierarchy. This perception of doing a deal and the long period of close contact led many senior party figures to believe that the church would not intervene to directly support Solidarność in the course of the election campaign. Politburo member Andrzej Werblan explains that the PZPR expected that the church would remain neutral during the election campaign because of its self-perceived generous treatment of the church in the early 1980s:

WERBLAN: [The party expected that the church would remain neutral in the campaign]...because of the fact that the relationship between the church and the party – during martial law – had been perfect. The government made a lot of conciliatory moves towards the church.
HAYDEN: And they expected payback?
WERBLAN: Of course! The party had supported the building of churches. There were more churches built during martial law than during the previous 400 years.... The government thought that the church would not want to enable or facilitate dramatic political change, but this was a mistake. But the priests felt it was possible to go further. So the question is: did direct relationships between the party and the bishops affect things? Of course it did. Today, bishops don't want to say that this is true but they drank a sea of vodka with Ciosek and the others.[57]

Professor Janusz Reykowski was the PZPR's co-chair of the subtable on Political Reform at the Round Table:

> One thing that was under evaluated – it was believed that Solidarność did not have an appropriate logistic for organizing its campaign. The argument against this was that the church would help Solidarność, and it will make up for the lack of a political structure. Some very influential members of the leadership claimed that it would not happen – that the church would be neutral except a few priests. The church, as an institution, would remain neutral. I think it was in the last years of the 1980s when the relationship between the church and party officials was very good and cordial – the church does not like to hear it now. It is politically incorrect to say it now. But at that time, the party leadership tended to believe that they had real friends in the church [laughing]. I remember very positive statements from General Jaruzelski about Cardinal Glemp and his attitudes. And as we know, it was the very opposite. The church gave a structure for Solidarność...I didn't think anything – I had no experience. I didn't know church people. So I simply accepted what I was told. These people have so much contact with the church for so long. So probably they know what they say. In my initial document [anticipating the campaign] was the expectation that the church would be a sort of infrastructure for Solidarność, but they said no – so I thought maybe they know![58]

This belief that the church would remain neutral during the campaign led to an overestimation of the electoral outcome in rural constituencies where the PZPR wrongly assumed that Solidarność would do poorly. Party strategists were calculating on the basis that Solidarność was a largely urban phenomenon with no organization or appeal in rural constituencies. Whatever the right or wrongs of this calculation, the PZPR's failure to factor in the powerful role that would be played by rural priests meant that it completely miscalculated its support in rural areas. Jerzy Wiatr argued, as recorded earlier, that senior PZPR strategists hoped that Solidarność's weakness in rural Poland would compensate in the election for the Senate for its strength in the urban conglomeration.[59] Wiatr argued that it was thought that the backward provinces would give the seats to the party. However, while these provinces were weak from Solidarność's point of view, they were also the most Catholic. So, while Solidarność was weak, the Church was strong, and the party's failure to anticipate the role the church would play in supporting the union meant that the outcome in these provinces was even worse from the party's point of view than provinces like Warsaw and Katowice (where the party expected to do badly).

While calculating the differential impact of the Catholic Church on urban and rural voting patterns in the June 1989 election is something of a gargantuan task, analysis of the actual results shows that the strongest relative support for Solidarność was concentrated in poor, rural areas and not in the traditional strongholds of the urban working class.[60] Heyns and Białecki's study of the Polish election results was based on election returns published in the summer of 1989 in *Gazeta Wyborcza* and in *Tygodnik Solidarność*, as well as statistical data available from the voivodships and survey results from the 1987 Social Structure and Mobility Project sponsored by the Polish Academy of Sciences. Heyns and Białecki acknowledge that aggregate data provide a meagre basis for testing the effects of specific social characteristics on voting behaviour. While individual-level voting data was not available, the authors claim that the models that support their conclusions are quite robust irrespective of the measures used.[61] In 23 of the 49 voivodships, the estimated number of votes for Solidarność cast by independent farmers exceeded the number cast by workers, despite the fact that workers outnumber peasants in Poland as a whole.[62]

According to Heyns and Białecki, even with other individual characteristics controlled, there are strong residual differences between the workers and the peasants. Polish peasants in 1987 were more hostile to the system of government and more supportive of change than were workers who claimed to have been members of Solidarność in 1981.[63] In describing support for Solidarność, Heyns and Białecki argue that the single variable most significantly and consistently related to aggregate voting behaviour is location in one of the rural south-eastern voivodships.[64] Polish sociologists have provided a number of potential explanations for the strength of Solidarność's support in the south-eastern part of the country. First, the region had experienced substantial emigration, but little immigration since the Second World War. Second, collective farms were virtually nonexistent, and, third, the population was reputedly the most traditional and the most committed to Catholicism in the country.[65] In the context of the south-eastern part of Poland, Heyns and Białecki point out that

> In the countryside, it is difficult to exaggerate the importance of the local parish for communication and mobilization. Under the leadership of Bishop Tokarczuk, who has the reputation of being very sympathetic to opposition organizations, the church was crucial in facilitating the organization of civic committees in this region.[66]

It seems clear that the PZPR made three fundamental errors in relation to their estimation of support in rural constituencies. First, they wrongly assumed that Solidarność would not penetrate the rural vote because they perceived the union as an urban voice. Second, they ignored the fact that there is a long-standing tradition of political opposition in the south-east of Poland. The PZPR's own political scientist, Jerzy Wiatr, had shown that these voivodships were more likely to abstain from voting or strike out names of state candidates in the elections held in the 1950s.[67] Finally, the PZPR simply did not calculate on a rational basis when it failed to consider the potential impact of the Catholic clergy actively supporting Solidarność in the election campaign.

Conclusion: 'the party is not accustomed to election battles like this'[68]

If ever there was a time when the PZPR could have displayed strategic, far-sighted behaviour, it would have been during the electoral campaign. This was a period when party far-sighted strategists would have evaluated the outcome of the Round Table dialogue and agreement in order to assess what needed to be done in the context of the new arena of competition. As we have seen, warnings about the upcoming electoral contest came from both within and outside the party. However, as we have also seen in the foregoing pages, there is no evidence that PZPR negotiators attempted to rectify any of the strategic errors made at the Round Table. In fact, while warnings might have been voiced they were simply ignored by the relevant actors. The campaign did not matter to strategists who understood the new game in terms of the legislative veto they had secured with the 65–35 division of seats in the contractual *Sejm*. The PZPR's political hegemony was secured because of its inbuilt legislative dominance and its control of the presidency.

It is arguable that the PZPR's election campaign did not collapse, as such, because it never really began. Party spokesman Jan Bisztyga's comment that the party was not accustomed to election battles seems like a case of stating the blindingly obvious. In so far as there was a PZPR campaign, it was based on two fundamentally flawed assumptions. PZPR reformers wrongly assumed that there would be a payback for their defeat of the hardliners within the party. Furthermore, they expected to be able to use this victory as a persuasive campaign argument. It was also assumed that, as well as rewarding party reformers for initiating the reform process, the Polish public would be happy to make the necessary sacrifices in order to facilitate the implementation of the economic reform package agreed at the Round Table. Clearly, these actors had become so engrossed in their own internal political struggles that they were not responsive to the atmosphere and feelings within society. In simple terms, the PZPR expected a return, but did not base this expectation on a rational or informed analysis of the public mood.

The evidence in relation to the conduct of the campaign is clear: the PZPR did not put its logistical and financial superiority to good use. Solidarność beat the party hands down with a fraction of the funds and resources. The analysis of the discussions at the KC PZPR meetings at the start of the Round Table indicates that the party was clearly not prepared for the impact Solidarity would make when it was given access to the media. The fact that the OPZZ's Alfred Miodowicz arranged to engage with Lech Wałęsa in a televised debate without the prior knowledge of General Jaruzelski is astonishing and, once again, confirms the fact that PZPR players were not coherently evaluating the impact of moves. They were not reacting and counter-reacting but were being dragged along by the tide of change they had unleashed.

The personality-first strategy left the PZPR dangerously exposed to Solidarność's instruction to voters to cross off all but the union's candidates. Designed as a way of convincing the electorate that organization or party membership did not matter, the strategy allowed Solidarność to argue the opposite. The union told the electorate that there was only one campaign issue – the historical record of the PZPR. Again, it is clear that the party embarked on an ill-informed strategy based on the false assumption that society would distinguish between

Polish communism and Polish communists. In conclusion, it seems clear that the PZPR's election campaign is best understood as a series of strategic mistakes that resulted from poor information, short-sighted interests and an inability to play the game on a new pitch. It follows that the PZPR's conduct of the electoral campaign supports Przeworski's analysis.

Strategic friendships

The relationship between the PZPR and the Catholic Church deserves far greater treatment than it has received here. The brevity is justified, however, as the only issue we are concerned with here is whether or not the PZPR was strategic in its expectations of that relationship. It has been clearly demonstrated that the expectation of some PZPR actors that the church would remain neutral during the election campaign was neither rational nor supported by the behaviour of the church. Clearly, the opinion of the party's chief church contact, Stanisław Ciosek, is crucial here. Arguably, he became too close to his church contacts, most especially Father Alojzy Orszulik. This closeness was not confined to Ciosek alone; General Jaruzelski was known to be an admirer of the Polish Primate Cardinal Glemp. Janusz Reykowski testifies to this in the interviews analysed here.

The rejection of Reykowski's assessment that the church would support Solidarity in the election campaign is further confirmation of the repeated failure of senior PZPR negotiators to listen to their own advisers. It is also evidence of some sort of wishful thinking that seemed to dog the PZPR's ability to make rational evaluations about expected behaviour even when they were dealing with an avowed enemy. This expectation that the church would support the party in the election campaign was as unfounded as Rakowski's expectation that the 'don't knows' would vote for the PZPR or as inexplicable as its assessment of its social support prior to the Round Table. The view that the church would remain neutral in the campaign, combined with the PZPR's wrong assessment of its chances in rural areas, proved devastating for the party. Heyns and Białecki's analysis of the pattern of support for Solidarność clearly demonstrates the degree to which the party's assessments and expectations were wrong.[69] It is also clear that there was information available to the party, such as Wiatr's work on patterns of abstention and crossing off, which shows that the party, once again, acted on the basis of misinformation. It, therefore, follows that the PZPR's conduct of its relationship with the Catholic hierarchy is further evidence of a repeated pattern of flawed evaluations, failure or indeed refusal to update information which places the PZPR's relationship with the Catholic Church into a category of behaviour best understood or explained by Przeworski's hypothesis.

8 Discussion and conclusion

This analysis set out to discover why the Polish communist party lost power in Poland over the summer of 1989. Given the fact that neither the PZPR nor Solidarność anticipated the fall of communism at the outset of the Round Table process, the question addressed was what factors best explain the collapse of the party's hegemony so shortly after its negotiators had concluded a deal they hoped would enable the government to carry out its economic reform programme. The question is an important one because, prior to the collection of data, it was intuitively apparent that PZPR negotiators appeared to have adopted positions and strategies during the Round Table process that led to suboptimal institutional outcomes for the party. So if it is assumed that the PZPR were rational actors and did not deliberately decide to hand power over to the Solidarność-led opposition. what explains the behaviour and strategic choices that brought about the collapse of the party's power? The question is, therefore, significant from two perspectives. First, political scientists failed to predict the possibility of the collapse of communism in the Soviet Union and Eastern Europe in the later 1980s. It is consequently important to attempt to construct an analysis with the potential to highlight the factors that might have given an intimation of the impending collapse. The issue is also important because, superficially at least, it seems to cast doubt on the validity of the assumption that PZPR negotiators were rational actors.

While it is not necessary to repeat the discussion in Chapter 2, this volume is a direct response to the debate between Przeworski and Colomer who take opposing views on the issue of whether well-informed regime actors will promote processes that lead to democratization. Two key issues arise out of the Colomer and Przeworski debate. The first is the question of whether actors will operate on the basis of a 'farsighted criterion of choice'[1] during periods of regime crisis given the long-term consequences for the rules of the game, while the second issue is whether transition results from the mistakes of regime liberalizers as Przeworski hypothesizes.[2] These two issues were directly addressed in the course of this volume. Colomer's argument in relation to far-sighted time horizons is a central plank of his analysis of the process of democratic transition in Eastern Europe. It is also an important part of his rejection of Przeworski's contention that 'broadened dictatorship' is the only outcome where actors are rational and well informed at moments of regime crisis. It was noted earlier that, while it is hard not to agree wholeheartedly with Colomer's attack on structuralist scholarship, which failed to predict the collapse of communism, his rejection of Przeworski's contention that democratic transition could only be the outcome of 'misinformed or miscalculated strategies' is more problematic.

It is important to bear in mind that Colomer makes no claims about the behaviour of regime actors once the decision to negotiate or not negotiate with the opposition has been made.[3] Furthermore, Colomer would argue that the focus of both his and Przeworski's analysis is on the period when this initial decision is made and that the subsequent rounds of bargaining are not relevant to this argument. In this analysis, it has been argued that this leaves the problem of how to characterize the subsequent behaviour of regime actors who have made the initial decision and entered into negotiation with the opposition. In particular, in the case of the PZPR, how do we characterize the behaviour of actors who had, arguably, taken the 'far-sighted' decision to negotiate with the opposition? Bearing in mind Colomer's reservations about the application of his hypothesis to the negotiations that follow on from the initial regime decision, this analysis set out to provide a process-driven account of a range of bargaining scenarios at the Polish Round Table in order to track the gap between the communist party's expectations and the actual institutional outcome. In doing so, it was intended to evaluate the relative merits of the conflicting hypotheses of Przeworski and Colomer.

At the heart of the matter is the question of whether or not the transactions between the PZPR and Solidarność produced their anticipated outcomes or whether the collapse of communism was an unintended consequence and precipitated by the strategic misperception of PZPR Round Table negotiators. In particular, we have paid close attention to the issue of whether PZPR actors behaved rationally in the sense that their decision-making was underpinned by available information and reasonable expectation as Colomer posits. It should be emphasized that available information is not perfect information and that perfect information is not a necessary condition for a rational decision. It, therefore, follows that the central focus of this analysis has been how PZPR actors treated the available information at their disposal during the bargaining process. With this in mind, and in order to provide a rigorous analysis of the PZPR's Round Table bargaining, the party's institutional choices were analysed in the context of the expectations or observable implications that flow from the respective hypotheses of Przeworski and Colomer. In doing so, it was possible to differentiate between the intentions of PZPR negotiators and their institutional follow-through or outcome.

Following Bates *et al.*, it was argued that to construct a coherent and valid rational choice account, scholars must 'soak and poke' and acquire the same depth of understanding as that achieved by those who offer 'thick' descriptions.[4] In exploring a concrete historical case, such as the Round Table process and the collapse of communism in Poland, it was noted that we are examining the choices of individuals embedded in specific settings. In examining such choices, it is necessary to unpack and trace the sequence of actions, decisions and responses that generated events and outcomes.[5] In employing the analytic narrative approach, we seek to account for outcomes by identifying the mechanisms that generate them. In doing so, this analytic narrative method employs rational choice theory and 'thin' reasoning to produce tightly constrained accounts based on rigorous deductive reasoning grounded on close attention to empirical detail. Finally, it was argued that analytic narratives are 'disciplined by both logic and the empirical record'.[6]

Controlled and incremental political change

Before embarking on an analysis of each of the Round Table bargaining scenarios, it was argued that it was necessary to establish that PZPR players had not simply decided to hand power to Solidarność. While the notion appears intuitively unlikely, formally establishing the intention of party actors was an important initial step for a number of reasons. First, if it had been established that the PZPR had decided to relinquish power then clearly the notion of strategic misperception would be nullified. Second, the entire logic of the research project depends on being able to establish the intention of the key party players. Clearly, establishing the nature of the intention of PZPR Round Table negotiators makes a contribution to the literature on this topic. Finally, in analysing the data it has been possible to expose the wide range of conceptions of that intention within the party elite who promoted the Round Table process. Laying bare the range of PZPR conceptions of the purpose of the Round Table makes a contribution to political science. It does so because it has provided us with the opportunity to evaluate whether or not the real life behaviour of political actors conforms to the expectations posited by rational choice theory. This analysis also makes a contribution because it has attempted to discover which of the two conflicting versions of rationality posited by Colomer and Przeworski provides the greatest leverage in explaining the actual outcome.

While this form of analysis is always open to charges that the findings are trivial, or not significant, because they are intuitively obvious, establishing the intention of PZPR Round Table actors is the first and most fundamental brick in the logical structure of this research project. It would not have been logically possible to analyse the PZPR's bargaining strategies if its primary intention had not been established first.

Interviews with key players such as General Jaruzelski, General Kiszczak, Mieczysław Rakowski, Stanisław Ciosek, Janusz Reykowski and Jerzy Wiatr have confirmed the fact that fear of economic collapse was the key motivating factor in the party's decision to initiate talks with the opposition.[7] Solidarność's weakness, internal power battles and its poor showing in the spring and summer strikes across Poland in 1988 convinced many senior PZPR players, including Stanisław Ciosek, that this was the party's opportunity to drive a hard bargain for the union's support for the government's economic reform package. The fact that General Jaruzelski intended to control the process of reform is confirmed in the Prague document.[8] In this document, Jaruzelski talks of the need to 'neutralize' Solidarność while Poland 'passes through a difficult period of 1–2 years'.[9] Clearly, Jaruzelski did not intend to relinquish power. In this case, it has been clearly shown that the *ancien regime* did not simply decide to give up. While the analysis of interviews with key party players highlights a variety of ideas about how the process of change would be handled, these interviews confirm the fact that it was not intended to hand power over to Solidaność. General Kiszczak speaks of wanting to 'loosen the straightjacket' but is emphatic that 'we didn't aim to give power to the opposition'.[10] Stanisław Ciosek, who characterized himself as being involved in a 'deliberate attempt to change the system'[11] in Poland, emphasizes the limits of the PZPR's plans at the start of the Round Table: 'It was a democratization process – a fuzzy democracy'.[12]

In the context of the conflicting hypotheses of Przeworski and Colomer, the evidence is somewhat equivocal. The assessment of General Jaruzelski, General Kiszczak, Prime Minister Rakowski and Janusz Reykowski tends to support Przeworski's view that regime liberalizers will only seek broadened dictatorship.[13] The Prague document could not be more explicit on the short-term interest that was to be served by the initiation of talks between the PZPR and Solidarność.[14] Analysis of other documents including the PZPR's Interdepartmental Team report clearly shows that, in September 1988, party strategists were thinking in terms of the creation of institutions, which would assist in the retention of the party's political hegemony in any new institutional arrangement. Specifically, it has been shown that the presidential office was to act as the party's guarantee of continued power. The Orszulik memoirs also confirm the fact that, as late as November 1988, the party hierarchy did not envisage the idea of free elections. Bishop Orszulik refers to Stanisław Ciosek's anger at hearing Solidarność spokesman Janusz Onyszkiewicz's demand for free elections. Clearly, in the months prior to the start of the Round Table, PZPR strategists thought they were initiating a process of incremental and controllable change. However, other PZPR actors, including Stanisław Ciosek, father and son, Jerzy and Sławomir Wiatr, provide a perspective that supports Colomer's hypothesis of far-sightedness. Jerzy Wiatr talks about the aim having been the creation of a 'form of contractual democracy'.[15] The more long-term goal was the democratization of the system. This supports Colomer's contention that liberalizers will seek to create an intermediate regime as they extricate from authoritarianism. The actions and behaviour of the younger members of the PZPR, including Aleksander Kwaśniewski and Sławomir Wiatr, conform to Colomer's expectations. These players were non-myopic and believed that they would achieve 'important positions in the new system'.[16]

The relegalization of Solidarność

The PZPR sought the creation of institutions it could realistically hope to control.

Next we turn to the question of the institutional choices agreed to by PZPR nego-tiators at the Round Table. In Chapter 5, we examined the PZPR's perception of the potential outcome of its agreement to the relegalization of Solidarność. The data clearly shows that there were widely varying perceptions concerning the purpose and potential impact of relegalizing Solidarność. In some sections of the party hierarchy, the move was seen as a trade-off for Solidarność's agreement to participate in the semi-free election, while other sections, including the group around Kwaśniewski and Ciosek, saw relegalization as part of a broader and far-sighted process of systemic change. While some party players, including Stanisław Ciosek, did regard the commencement of talks with Solidarność as the beginning of the end of one-party rule, and the decision to relegalize the union as a move that could bring about the collapse of the party, the evidence clearly confirms that this was not the dominant thinking within the PZPR hierarchy. Reykowski emphasized in his interview with the author that the prevailing wisdom did not anticipate that the relegalization of the union would precipitate the collapse of communism.

Relegalization was a means to an end: the end being the incorporation of Solidarność into the government coalition for the purpose of implementing economic reform. As Prime Minister Rakowski observed, relegalization would have no impact beyond the union being able to function as a 'trade union. Nothing more!'[17] As has been shown, there is no indication of organized pooling or updating of information concerning the impact of relegalization and there was no agreed perception of the meaning and impact of the decision to relegalize Solidarność. Thus, there is evidence of both non-myopic and short-term motivation thereby lending support for the hypotheses of both Colomer and Przeworski.

The new office of president

As we have already seen, the PZPR's intention in relation to the introduction of the office of president was entirely rational and office seeking. The PZPR's September 1988 'Concept of Changes' document clearly shows that the PZPR did not expect any diminution in its political hegemony arising out of the proposed institutional changes.[18] In fact, the aim was to retain control in the new order by controlling the mechanism through which the president would be elected and by endowing the office with extensive executive powers. It was envisaged that the president would be the 'highest institution of state authority with legislative and executive powers'[19] and, crucially, the president would always be a party member. So the evidence here supports Przeworski's broadened dictatorship hypothesis. Furthermore, PZPR negotiators did not negotiate on the basis of the September 1988 conception of the office, but on the basis of a proposal produced by Democratic Party member Piotr Winczorek.

There are many differences between the party's initial formulation and the Winczorek document. The most important of these differences is the fact that the Winczorek proposal was silent on the crucial issue of the election of the president, while the PZPR's September document stipulates a mechanism that would have allowed the party to retain effective control of the office. So, here again, we have evidence of a mistake that had the potential to negate the PZPR's main purpose in pursuing its presidential strategy. We have seen from the evidence, and that of Gebethner in particular, that PZPR negotiators did not fully apprise themselves of the consequences of introducing the office.[20] Winczorek points out that PZPR negotiators hoped to legitimize the idea of the new office by presenting the proposal to the Round Table as a Democratic Party idea. However, in accepting the Winczorek document as a basis for the bargaining over the office, PZPR negotiators left a number of hostages to fortune.

The evidence of Gebethner is clear on the fact that PZPR negotiators did not update information in the course of the bargaining over this institution. Having started with a perfectly rational conception of how the presidential office might benefit the party, PZPR negotiators failed to keep the proposal on track or ensure that the consequences of concessions made to gain support for the office did not result in unforeseen outcomes. As we have seen, Kwaśniewski's proposal, that a new and freely elected Senate should be introduced, was regarded as a means of legitimizing the presidency; however, the potential impact of this move was not assessed. Misperceived strategic choices led to outcomes that had not been anticipated by PZPR negotiators in their bargaining over the office of the president and hence this bargaining confirms Przeworski's hypothesis.

The new Senate

The PZPR's concession of a freely elected Senate was one of its greatest strategic errors at the Round Table. As we have seen, negotiators such as Stanisław Ciosek, still maintain that the concession of the free Senate was not important because it was not envisaged that the chamber would have any power; in crude terms, it was to be a talking shop for the opposition. However, Solidarność's crushing victory in the election, taking all but one of the hundred Senate seats, served as a massive symbolic rejection of the party. As we have seen, the Senate concession was inextricably linked with the party's bargaining over the contractual parliamentary elections and its desire to introduce a strong presidency. It is clear from the analysis of both the interviews and the September 1988 document that the Senate was not perceived as having substantial power in the initial formulation. However, because party negotiators were responding to a dynamic offer and counter-offer at the Round Table, and because they lacked a cohesive or fully worked out conception of how the various institutional pieces they were conceding would fit into the institutional jigsaw, they failed to anticipate the potential consequences of the decision to concede a freely elected Senate. Gebethner highlights this lack of regard for the consequences of institutional choices when he points out that even after Kwaśniewski's proposal was made public, the PZPR's ideas concerning the future constitutional role of the Senate were 'more than a little hazy'.[21]

As in the case of the negotiations over the office of president, we saw a difference between the PZPR's initial conception of the institution and the reality that emerges as a result of the Round Table dynamic. We saw that, at least in intent, the concession of the Senate supports Przeworski's broadened dictatorship hypothesis, given the fact that the idea was part of a strategy designed to get Solidarność's agreement to the contractual election and the presidency. However, the PZPR could not have rationally expected to control this freely elected institution. Stanisław Ciosek's contention that the concession of the Senate was not a mistake because it was not deemed to be an arena of importance clearly supports

Przeworski's analysis. This flawed evaluation of the potential impact of a freely elected Senate is clear evidence that the PZPR was not engaged in reacting and counter-reacting in a far-sighted manner in its negotiations over the presidency and Senate. So while the evidence supports the contention that party strategists were rational in their deliberations over the Senate prior to the start of the Round Table, they subsequently failed to fully assess or evaluate information that might have led negotiators to seek a different bargain in this case. Specifically, these actors did not negotiate on the basis of the available information and thus we must, therefore, conclude that PZPR negotiators were not far-sighted and strategic in their decision-making over the concession of the Senate.

The electoral system and voting rules

If PZPR negotiators were far-sighted, as Colomer posits, we would expect them to choose an electoral system and voting formula that maximized the party's seat share. We would expect them to regard the choice of an electoral system as an important step on the road to an intermediate regime. We would also expect negotiators to have updated their information on the differential impact of voting formulae during the course of the Round Table negotiations. In this regard, we have identified three categories of error in the way PZPR strategists responded to the issue of voting rules for the contractual election.

The first mistake is an error of estimation. Before party strategists could evaluate the differential impact of voting rules, it would be necessary to have reliable information about social support for the PZPR. The analysis is clear on this point. Many of the party's senior players did not behave rationally when considering the level of support for the PZPR. Kamiński's analysis of the adjusted confidence polls taken throughout the 1980s clearly indicates that it was not rational for the PZPR to rely on these polls for an accurate estimate of support.[22] Three fundamental problems with the conduct of opinion polling in the relevant period led the PZPR to rely on a skewed and over-favourable estimate of their social support. It appears incontrovertible that a form of cognitive dissonance affected senior PZPR players such as Jaruzelski and Rakowski. This led them to expect higher levels of social support than even the adjusted polls indicated.

However, it is clear from interviews with Stanisław Ciosek, Jerzy Wiatr and Sławomir Wiatr as well as interviews with the Solidarność negotiator, Lech Kaczyński, that not all of the PZPR Round Table players held this optimistic view of party support. That said, the evidence that emerges from the interview material and the work of other scholars supports the contention that the predominant estimate of the party's support was informed by the false information being supplied by the apparatchiks. It, therefore, follows that many key PZPR figures failed to ensure that they were estimating their support on the basis of reliable information. It is also clear that there was a failure at the most senior level of the PZPR to update or seek out accurate information that would have enabled a more reliable estimate of the likely impact of differential voting rules. This first category of error clearly confirms Przeworski's expectations.

The second category of error relates to the choice of voting rules. Kamiński has shown that the PZPR chose voting rules that resulted in a worse outcome than would have resulted from almost any other voting system.[23] However, in this volume, evidence has been presented that demonstrates that not only did negotiators make a bad choice but they also ignored advice that would have prevented the party's electoral defeat had the advice been taken. It has been shown that senior negotiators were made aware of the damaging impact of using a majoritarian system in the Senate election.

Three well-known academics, two of whom were members or former members of the Politburo, advised against the majoritarian system of voting. Andrzej Werblan advised Round Table co-chair Janusz Reykowski that a proportional system should be adopted for the Senate election and later wrote to Prime Minister M. Rakowski outlining his analysis. Jerzy Wiatr has confirmed that he advised Janusz Reykowski of the disastrous consequences of choosing a majoritarian system. Wiatr also claims that the decision to reject both sets of proposals came from General Jaruzelski. Gebethner cites two instances where advice was ignored. He points out that the idea of electing the Senate on a majority basis was 'almost universally criticized'[24] at a meeting of the government coalition group at the Round Table. Gebethner also produced a report in support of the use of a proportional system. PZPR strategists also ignored this report.

It, therefore, follows, in the context of this stunning failure to take on board the advice of a number of sympathetic 'experts', that the PZPR's behaviour in relation to the choice of voting rules supports Przeworski's hypothesis.

The decision to retain the crossing-off method of voting proved disastrous for the PZPR. Had PZPR strategists been updating their knowledge and information, they should have responded to the experience in the Soviet Union, where voters had crossed off official candidates in the first semi-free election held there. Again, there was information advising against the use of this negative form of voting available to the party. We have seen that Stanisław Gebethner had written papers arguing against the use of the system and that this advice was ignored.

Two other serious mistakes, which fall into the category of strategic error, complete this litany of misperceived electoral strategies. The PZPR's decision to run 700 candidates for its 156 seats in the contractual *Sejm* and another 186 for the Senate election is almost inexplicable. But again we see that the PZPR failed to understand the rules of the game they were playing. In this case they failed to understand the implications of allowing multiple candidates to stand, given the use of the majoritarian voting rule where in the second-ballot system a high number of candidates reduces the chances of electing a candidate on the first ballot.

At the end of the day, it is perhaps the assumption of the continued support of its coalition allies that highlights the enormity of the irrationality that drove the party's bargaining in this area. In failing to secure its own overall majority in the *Sejm* without the support of its coalition allies, PZPR strategists contemptuously failed to anticipate even the possibility of their allies changing sides. This assumption, which was central to the PZPR's bargaining over the contractual *Sejm*, seriously undermines the notion of party negotiators as far-sighted. As we have seen, the PZPR's failure to protect its own parliamentary majority struck at the heart of its most important goal, the retention of its legislative veto in the *Sejm*. The assumption that its satellite coalition partners would continue to support the PZPR no matter what the circumstances smacks of enormous hubris. The fact that PZPR negotiators did not even bother to ascertain the likelihood of the continued support of its partners emphasizes that, once again, we see party negotiators failing to seek basic information or making flawed evaluations that lead to strategic mistakes. In particular, we have demonstrated that PZPR negotiators disregarded information that was available to them and that as a consequence they acted on the basis of unreasonable expectations, which contravenes the rationality requirement as understood by Colomer and other scholars.

The PZPR's relationship with the Catholic hierarchy

Moving on to the conduct of the party's election campaign and its negotiators' relationship with the Catholic hierarchy, we see the same pattern of false assumptions, as well as a failure to rectify earlier strategic errors. In our earlier discussion of the campaign, we saw that it was based on two fundamentally flawed assumptions. First, key Round Table negotiators who were predominantly drawn from the reform wing of the PZPR expected that the Polish public would differentiate between their role and that of the hardliners who had opposed reform. These reformers expected electoral support on the basis that they had defeated the hardline element within the party and initiated the process of contacts that resulted in the Round Table agreement. The reformers further assumed that this victory would be a persuasive campaign argument.

Because these players had been involved in, what was for them, an all-consuming battle, they failed to appreciate that the issue was not afforded the same degree of significance by the Polish public. The assumption that party reformers would be rewarded for initiating the reform process led to the false view that the Polish public would be prepared to embrace austerity in order to ensure the economic reform package agreed at the Round Table. Again, we see expectations and strategies that were not based on a rational appraisal of the data available to the PZPR. We saw earlier that key players, such as Rakowski, acknowledged the poor showing in the polls in the month prior to the election, but for some inexplicable reason, expected the 'don't know' category to vote for the party. This cognitive dissonance clearly affected many elements of the reform wing of the party, and while we have seen that players, such as Stanisław Ciosek and the group around Aleksander Kwaśniewski, held more realistic estimates of likely support it remains the case that the campaign was fundamentally flawed by the expectation of support that was not based on a rational or informed analysis of the public mood.

Given the party's superior financial and logistical resources it was to be expected that the PZPR campaign would be more effective than Solidarność's. However, the reverse was the case. The PZPR did not put its logistical and financial superiority to good use. Solidarność consistently out-performed the PZPR with considerably less resources. It is clear from the analysis of the discussions at the KC PZPR meetings that many party players were horrified and unprepared for Solidarność's effective use of its television time. The decision to give the union access to television and the media was discussed in the context of the establishment of the Round Table, but the tenor of the discussion at the KC highlights the fact that the impact Solidarność made during the transmitted elements of the Round Table was not anticipated. However, even more surprising is the fact that the OPZZ's Alfred Miodowicz arranged to engage with Lech Wałęsa in a televised debate without the prior knowledge of General Jaruzelski. As we have seen, this debate was won hands down by Lech Wałęsa, who effectively used the debate to launch his campaign platform with the establishment of the Citizens' Committees. This debate played a crucial part in the further destabilizing of the PZPR. The fact that it was arranged without the knowledge of General Jaruzelski is astonishing and, once again, confirms the fact that PZPR players were not behaving either coherently or rationally.

The PZPR's personality-first strategy should be understood in the context of the assumption that reformers expected payback for their defeat of the hardliners. These reformers assumed that if they disassociated themselves from the PZPR's historical legacy, voters would assess the personal, as opposed to the party, profile of each candidate. Again, this was a false assumption and left the PZPR danger-ously exposed to Solidarność's instruction to voters to cross off all but the union's candidates. While the strategy was designed as a way of convincing the electorate that party membership was unimportant, it allowed Solidarność to argue that association with the party was the only issue. Solidarność turned the election into a plebiscite on the party's record. So, once again, we see that the reformers embarked on an ill-informed strategy based on the false assumption that society would distinguish between Polish communism and Polish communists. The party's conduct of the campaign confirms Przeworski's analysis.

It has already been noted that the relationship between the PZPR and the Catholic Church deserves far greater treatment than it has received here. However, we are only concerned here with whether or not PZPR actors were rational in their expectations of that relationship. The central issue was the PZPR's expectation that the church would remain neutral during the election campaign. It has been demonstrated that this expectation was neither rational nor supported by the behaviour of the church. Stanisław Ciosek was the party's main contact with the church. The tenor of Ciosek's remarks, as outlined in the memoirs of Bishop Alojzy Orszulik, clearly shows that this was a personally warm relationship. This closeness was not confined to Ciosek. General Jaruzelski was known to be an admirer of Polish Primate Glemp and as was argued earlier, Janusz Reykowski testifies to this in the interviews analysed here. Clearly Ciosek, and perhaps even Jaruzelski, confused the personal regard they entertained for individual members of the Polish hierarchy with their rational assessment of the church's behaviour during the campaign.

Janusz Reykowski's assessment that the church was likely to be of considerable use to the Solidarity campaign was rejected and is further confirmation of the repeated failure of senior PZPR negotiators to listen to its own advisers. This mistaken assumption that the church would remain neutral, combined with the PZPR's flawed assessment of the support it would receive in rural areas, proved devastating for the party. So while there might have been some basis for the party's assumption that Solidarność might not perform as well in the country as they would in urban areas, there was no basis for their view of the church's role. The church proved to be an active and persuasive pro-Solidarność campaigner and nowhere was this support more effective than in rural areas. Heyns and Białecki's analysis of the pattern of support for Solidarność clearly demonstrates the degree to which the party's assessments and expectations were wrong.[25] Again, we see that the party failed to update its information. PZPR member Jerzy Wiatr's work on patterns of abstention and crossing-off in Poland should have alerted party strategists to the fact that they were in danger in some rural regions. In describing support for Solidarność, Heyns and Białecki argue that the single variable most significantly and consistently related to aggregate voting behaviour is location in one of the rural south-eastern voivodships.[26] Furthermore, they have shown that, in this region, the population was reputedly the most traditional and the most committed to Catholicism in the country.

This example of the devastating impact of the PZPR's failure to anticipate the impact of the Catholic Church's pro-Solidarność campaigning is just one demonstrable example of how this falsely perceived relationship misled PZPR strategists. As has been stated earlier, the Catholic Church played a huge role in the emergence, sustenance and eventual victory of Solidarność; that PZPR actors could get that role so badly wrong is conclusive evidence in support of Przeworski's hypothesis. It has already been noted that Colomer regards his hypothesis as providing the most explanatory leverage when it is applied to the initial decision to negotiate or not to negotiate. In this volume, we have examined Colomer's behavioural expectations in the context of the subsequent bargaining of regime actors. However, given the importance of the role and influence of the Catholic Church in the PZPR's initial decision to negotiate with Solidarność, the fact that key party actors clearly misunderstood the nature of their relationship with the church tends to weaken our earlier conclusion that this decision can be characterized as far-sighted and thus conforming to Colomer's expectations.[27]

Implications for the study of regime change and democratic transition

As has already been noted, this analysis is a response to Przeworski's request that his analytical framework and hypotheses be tested empirically.[28] In this case we have examined a case of regime change in what became a dual transition to democracy and a market economy. However, the analytical framework and hypotheses utilized here could be used, albeit in differing form, in cases where both or just one kind of transition is being examined. The key heuristic device employed here is the ability to track a complex process or set of events in the context of what is expected given one hypothesis or another. In simple terms, we can match the events of the real world with the expectations that flow from the hypotheses. In doing so, we are enabled to reach conclusions and characterizations which are soundly based in scientific method and thus are reliable and not ad hoc.

Given the emphasis in this type of analysis on the gap between the expectations of actors and the actual institutional outcome, it provides a most useful basis on which to commence the examination of the potential trajectory of a process of transition. Because this type of approach allows us to understand what regime actors hoped to achieve when they initiated the dialogue with the opposition, it follows that we can learn much in the course of our research about the preferred institutional outcomes of these actors. Given the path-dependent nature of transition and the view that the mode of transition has a major impact of the success of the democratization process, it follows that an understanding of the institutional preferences of the elites who negotiate the initial regime change is crucial if we are to predict the trajectory of transitional countries.[29] Josep Colomer's analysis of the Spanish transition is one example of the successful use of formal modelling.[30] In the case of the present analysis, informal tools were used and proved as successful in tracking the gap between expectation and outcome and exposing the underlying dynamic of the Polish process of regime change. It seems clear that this approach and method could be used to examine other cases of regime change or transition. In particular, it seems clear that the approach would be useful to researchers examining cases of negotiated transition such as occurred in Hungary or, indeed, Bulgaria where communist party elites attempted preventative reform so as to control the process of change.

Theoretical implications of the foregoing analysis

The foregoing analysis of the PZPR's strategic intentions and expectations gives rise to a number of theoretical implications for the study of regime change and democratic transition. First, at a very fundamental level, previous structural explanations would have ignored the preferences of regime actors and, thus, would have missed this rich vein of predictive analysis. Purely structural accounts ignored the factors that precipitated changes in political and institutional equilibrium and, thus, failed to identify the conditions that changed the relative costs of the preferences of regime actors. Given the fact that none or very few of the structural preconditions normally associated with democratic transition existed in 1989, it is not surprising that political scientists, conditioned in this view, failed to identify the possibility of regime change. On the basis of the findings of this analysis, it is clear that structural accounts alone do not provide the explanatory power required to offer a coherent account of why some regimes fall and others survive.

Elite theory, which focused on elite settlements and elite convergence, has proved a more useful tool in the analysis of transition, as has the idea of analysing new institutions as bargains among self-interested politicians. However, perhaps the most important insight highlighted in this analysis has been the confirmation of the view that scholars must not assume the motivation and goals of elites. If actor-based approaches are to provide explanatory leverage, they must be underpinned by theoretical assumptions and testable hypotheses. It was assumed that PZPR reformers were behaving as political entrepreneurs anticipating the twin reward of retaining power by shaping the way the new rules of the political game were formulated, as well as the possibility of economic benefits that would derive from the introduction of economic reform. This process-driven examination, based on a clearly defined set of observable implications which flowed from the conflicting hypotheses of Przeworski's and Colomer's seminal work, allowed for a tractable and explicit analysis of the intentions and strategic behaviour of PZPR negotiators. This approach prevents the use of ad hoc explanations for particular scenarios and outcomes. Crucially, it separates intention from actual behaviour and, by applying a rigorous standard of rationality, makes it possible to identify where the outcome was not the one intended by actors.

In this case, the application of a theory-driven analysis has shown conclusively that party reformers were rational in intent when they initiated the talks process with the Solidarność-led opposition. The evidence shows that negotiators did not perceive themselves to be relinquishing power:

> Communist leaders wanted to maintain their control of public life and the stability of the system, particularly its Socialist character and its membership in the Warsaw Pact, by increasing its inclusiveness and limited pluralism with the voice of the moderate wing of the opposition in parliament.[31]

It is also clear that this rational intent predisposed party reformers to prefer a 'broadened dictatorship', as outlined by Przeworski,[32] or an 'intermediate regime', as specified by Colomer,[33] but not an immediate transition to democracy. While it is evident in many of the interviews in this volume that some PZPR players foresaw that the chronology of events might be faster than the competitive elections planned for 1993, the dominant view was that the deal represented a breathing space in which the party could prepare itself for competitive politics in the future.

Throughout this analysis we have seen evidence to support Colomer's claim that a far-sighted criterion of choice induces non-myopic equilibria.[34] None of the reformers around General Jaruzelski had any desire to repeat the experience of martial law when Pole was forced to shoot Pole. Significantly, many party negotiators referred to the perception that Lech Wałęsa was losing control of the union in the late 1980s and that more radical elements might soon take over. The union's weakness was the party's opportunity to reach an agreement that would retain maximum incumbent power. This is an important finding from the perspective of Colomer's hypothesis and is consistent with his own research focus on the initial decision to negotiate or not to negotiate. Specifically, this research has confirmed Colomer's hypothesis in the context of the arena in which he has claimed it has the most explanatory leverage. It follows that Colomer is right when he claims that the bargaining that proceeds from the initial decision to negotiate is not an appropriate milieu in which to expect non-myopic behaviour. However, it is important to remember that a null hypothesis is as valid and important a finding as a positive result. In this case, it has allowed us to track the gap between the formal prerequisites of rationality as understood in conflicting interpretations of rational choice and the perceptions of human beings making decisions they assume to be in their best interests.

While the analysis confirms the fact that PZPR negotiators were rational in intent prior to the start of the Round Table, it has conclusively shown that they made mistakes in the conduct of the bargaining over institutions. The consistent failure to update information, and the quite remarkable ignoring of the expert advice of Werblan, Gebethner and others, tends to confirm Przeworski's conception of how transition follows the mistakes made by regime liberalizers who seek broadened dictatorship. This process-driven account relied on a thin conception of rationality to track the gap between ideal, formally rational behaviour and the historical reality of the PZPR's behaviour during the course of its Round Table negotiations. It has proved a useful heuristic device in the analysis of a complex set of events where elite actors engaged in a round of bargaining that created its own dynamic.

The combination of this 'soak and poke' approach and the application of the observable implications that flow from the hypotheses of Przeworski and Colomer has conclusively shown that over a range of bargains and scenarios the PZPR's strategies produced unanticipated outcomes. It is clear that many of these outcomes could have been predicted had party negotiators relied on the available information at their disposal. Making decisions on the basis of available information is a minimal requirement of a rational actor; however, we might also expect that rational actors would have updated their information and knowledge over a range of institutional choices and listened to the advice of sympathetic advisers. Not only is it the case that the PZPR's misperceived strategies produced an unexpected outcome, but it is also arguable that the failure to act on the available information is the key to any explanation of the collapse of communist power in Poland in 1989. In conclusion, it is a plausible hypothesis that rationally intentioned PZPR actors who updated their available information would not have negotiated the suboptimal institutional bargains agreed at the Round Table. Perfect information had the potential to change the course of the history of both Poland and the rest of Central and Eastern Europe.

Appendix 1

The concept of the system of election to *Sejm*, based on the formula of non-confrontational but competitive elections, held on the basis of agreed principles

Annex 1

16 February 1989

Confidential

[Rectangular stamp: At the request of Com. K. Cypryniak. Sent to the secretaries of Regional Committees, 15.02.1989; ref. no. KS/195/89]

This concise formula: non-confrontational, but competitive elections held on the basis of agreed principles, demands an explanation and a more detailed definition.

I. The competitiveness would in this form mean, that:

   1) In every constituency and for every seat there will be more than one candidate with equal rights – this should be the competitiveness at a personal level;

   2) In every constituency (both two- and five-seat ones) one or two seats would be sought after by candidates of various political persuasions, from both the coalition in government, and from the opposition groups, on the basis of various electoral programs and without excluding competition between candidates from PZPR and ZSL, PZPR and SD, or SD and ZSL – that would mean competitiveness at the program level.

II. Non-confrontational character should mean in this case that: the participants in the elections, i.e. candidates and parties and their allied organizations and opposition groups which put forward their candidates, undertake to refrain during the entire election campaign from:

   1) Any attacks on the principles of the political system, defined in the Section I of the Polish Constitution (that is the leading role of the PZPR, constitutional basis of the three-party coalition and the alliance with USSR);

   2) Attacks on the origin of the Polish People's Republic, discussions concerning the responsibility for the mistakes of the past (such as accusations

of totalitarianism or statements about the country being taken over by the communists, etc.), responsibility for the 1981 conflicts and the martial law, or propagating a total negation of achievements of the past 40 years.

III. The formula of elections held on the basis of agreed principles would mean that:

1) There would be an agreed declaration on the subject of an agreement of the Poles as to overriding interests and objectives of the Nation, which would have to be respected by all those participating in the elections throughout the entire election process;

2) The right to putting candidates forward will have political parties, agreed categories of organizations, including the recognized opposition groups which have been described in the legislation (in the electoral law or in a separate legislation); and also groups of citizens consisting of four thousand to five thousand people. Five per cent of voters [added in handwriting].

3) Generally established exit proportions will be observed as to the division of seats, including the selection of seats for direct competition between parties and groups.

The question of guarantees as to the observance of these conditions, which ensure the non-confrontational character of elections to *Sejm* and also that they would be held within the agreed principles, is outlined below.

Firstly, however, one must present the essence of a system, which would meet such a formula of elections that are non-confrontational but competitive and organized on the basis of earlier agreed principles.

This would look as follows:

Sejm [Parliament] has so far 460 members. In two- and five-seat constituencies 430 members would be elected. However, 30 members of Parliament shall be selected from the general or 'country' list.

In each constituency there will be any number of candidates put forward for each separate mandate. At least two candidates must run for each seat.

Sixty-nine free seats [added in handwriting] would have a free number of candidates of various orientations and political parties registered. However, as for the remaining seats, candidates would be registered only from that party or that political orientation, which on the basis of an agreed understanding is the 'disposer' of such a place.

This means that 69 [numeral 138 is crossed out and numeral 69 written by hand] members of Parliament, i.e. 15 per cent of candidates [30 per cent crossed out and 15 per cent written by hand] of the Parliament will be selected on the basis of 'free competition'. As a result of this, the final political division of those 69 [written by hand] seats is absolutely and fully the result of free election by citizens participating in elections.

However, 78 per cent [63.5 per cent crossed out and 78.5 per cent written by hand] seats, i.e. 361 votes [292 crossed out and 361 written by hand] shall be initially, on the basis of the agreed by way of negotiations agreement, divided as follows:

PZPR	176	i.e. 38.3%
ZSL	76	i.e. 16.5%
SD	25	i.e. 5.4%
PAX, UChS		
PZKS	15	i.e. 3.2%
Opposition	69	i.e. 15.0% [written by hand]

Thirty members of Parliament, i.e. 6.5 per cent of all elected, will be put forward from the 'country' list. The political composition of candidates for MPs on the 'country' list will match the political composition of candidates for MPs who are being elected in constituencies. Based on this principal, seats on the 'country' list shall be divided as follows:

PZPR	11
ZSL	5
SD	2
PAX	1
UChS	1
PZKS	1
Independent	5
and	
Opposition	4

[numeral 9 for jointly: the independent and opposition – crossed out and written by hand – 5 for independent and 4 for the opposition].

Assuming, that free seats in various constituencies (69) [written by hand] are won by the non-party candidates (independent and opposition), the political composition in the *Sejm* will be as follows (total seats in various constituencies and those on the 'country' list):

PZPR	187 seats	40.7%
ZSL	81 seats	17.6%
SD	27 seats	5.9%
Total	295 seats	64.2%
PAX	8 seats	1.7%
UchS	6 seats	1.3%
PZKS	4 seats	0.9%
Free seats	74 seats	16.0%
Opposition	73 seats	15.9%

[31.9% for the joint independent-opposition group, crossed out and replaced with a hand-written note: free seats 74 (16%), opposition 73 (15.9%)].

IV. Final comments and conclusions:

1) It is proposed that the election be held in two stages. The first stage on 11 June. The second stage on 25 June.

In the first stage, candidates from the 'country' list and from the 'constituencies' lists will participate in elections to select members of Parliament; they would receive 50 per cent of all valid votes plus one vote.

In the second stage, two candidates, who received the largest number of votes in the first stage, should contest each seat. The candidate with the largest number of votes shall be elected.

The elimination from the electoral procedure of 'convention'-type institutions, whose objective was to eliminate the surplus of candidates, would be an enormous step towards the inclusion of a wider society in the joint governance. It would fundamentally change the existing character of elections. [It would] start totally new motivations amongst the candidates and the electorate.

With the acceptance of this mechanism of putting forward, selecting and electing candidates for parliamentary seats, one has to take into consideration, that the social composition in the *Sejm* will be representative of selections made by the electorate.

2) Elections held in this manner will be fully competitive at a personal level, and in relation to 15 per cent [30 per cent crossed out and 15 per cent written in its place by hand] of seats, also confrontational on the level of issues. Because of that, it would be possible, without a threat of loosing power, to study the composition of forces amongst the electorate; processes would also be created, which would encourage the emergence of a new generation of activists within both our party and other forces.

3) Assuming, that the 69 free seats [138 crossed out and 69 written by hand] will be won by non-party candidates, the following set-up of power should emerge:

   a) PZPR, having 40.7 per cent of seats, will not be able to pass any resolution by itself. This would create a totally new basis for building coalitions. However, It would be able to block any legislation that requires two thirds of all votes, i.e. the Constitution;

   b) PZPR, ZSL and SD, having 64.2 per cent of seats, will not be able to pass any legislation, that requires two thirds of all votes (for example, the Constitution). Therefore, in such situations they would have to seek the support of at least PAX and UChS or other groups;

   c) PZPR and ZSL, having 58.3 per cent of seats, could pass any legislation which do not require qualified majority;

   d) the creation of a block consisting of ZSL, SD, independent members of Parliament and the opposition, gives a majority which is adequate for the creation of a coalition government.

4) The creation of the above set-up in the *Sejm* should serve as a guarantee for all sides taking part in the agreement. This would be evidence that the party takes elections seriously, having the awareness, that in an extreme situation it could be eliminated from the government.

5) If the elections were to be held on the above dates (11 and 25 June of this year), it would be necessary to introduce by 8 March amendments to the legislation on electoral regulations and a draft constitutional legislation, requiring a shorter working period of the *Sejm*.

Warsaw, 14.02.1989

Appendix 2

Werblan's letter

Dear Mietek,

1. The idea of setting up the senate as an upper chamber with powers that are not too far reaching, seems to be very wise for the transitional period to normal political democracy. Wise and at the same time courageous, is also the idea of selecting the senate in contesting elections, i.e. with the participation of rival (competing) sides.

2. Unfortunately, the idea of implementing the majority electoral ordinance in the Senate is totally reckless (from the point of view of the need to ensure an evolutionary and peaceful process in the transition to this democracy), and even hypocritical (resembling a referendum and the second stage of the reform). Something has failed here, either the imagination or knowledge, or both.

3. The majority ordinances, typical for English-speaking countries, favour decisively the party, which obtained the majority of votes. Having received 60% of votes, [such a party] takes 80–90 per cent of seats, and in conditions of low political stability, even more. This system aims to ensure that the winning party has an appropriate and lasting advantage, and to eliminate smaller parties, in fact, all of them, but two. The Conservative party in Great Britain, having recently obtained 53 per cent of votes (I recall this from memory – and so I might possibly be mistaken) received nearly 70 per cent of seats, while the liberals – for a dozen or so percent of votes received only a couple of seats. And all this despite the existence of super stable constituencies, i.e. those, where the electorate for a hundred years gave the majority of their votes to the candidate of a particular party. Today, in Poland, the majority-based system (i.e. one-seat constituencies and the election by a majority of votes) promises the opposition 100 per cent or nearly that number of seats with 65–70 per cent of votes received.

4. Political consequences of such total defeat of the government camp could be unpredictable. One has to take into account such a rise of a wave of triumphal radicalism that could destroy any compromises and which nobody would be able to contain. One cannot disregard the atmosphere of desperation and hatred, which are triggered off by both the crisis lasting already 10 years, and by the worsening economic situation.

5. The idea of selecting quite an odd ordinance to the senate (implementing in Poland the USA model and the treatment of administrative regions (Polish:*województwa*) as states /!/) was promulgated, most likely, because of the following aspirations: a/ the desire to give privileges to the agricultural regions in the hope that they would vote for the coalition's candidates; b/ counting on the fact, that in one-seat constituencies, in the process of voting for 'persons', many coalition candidates would camouflage 'their own' or 'crypto-own'. One cannot see any other reasons. These must be illusions. The support for the coalition is, indeed, better in the rural areas than in large cities, but this would not be enough to gain advantage over the opposition, even more so, that in the final count the voting in the majority of villages could be decided quite simply by the parish priest. The 'b' [option] is point-less to discuss, because the camouflage would be immediately removed and the appropriate candidate indicated, i.e. the political force would indicate its own candidate. One cannot be under the illusion of experiences of elections held until now, where we created the pretence of competition, however, the voters immediately recognized this and ignored our endeavours.

6. The only safe and somehow the most democratic ordinance to the senate seems to be, at present, the traditional Polish five-adjective ordinance (based on the March Constitution), providing for the proportional elections. Then one would have to form several seats' constituencies and vote for lists. It seems that the coalition would receive then not less than 30–35 per cent votes and the same number of seats. This would not be a catastrophe, and the sen-ate would be the reverse of the *Sejm*. Of course, if the atmosphere were to worsen to the level seen in 1980–81, it would be worse, but always better than in the majority elections. Furthermore, the proportional elections would not eliminate smaller groups, truly independent or intermediary; it would be worth while giving them access to the ballotage, when the dichotomous set-up contains the danger of the confrontation of two fundamentalists.

7. Technically, the proportional elections would require the setting up of 15 six-seat districts, joining several administrative regions into one district (regions), which would not rule out some kind of privileges for the agricul-tural districts (although this does not seem to be especially important). One could leave a small state list for the division of votes that were left unused in districts; there are in existence known and well developed models with the best tradition of parliamentary democracy. The list of candidates proposed in districts would compete with each other – as it used to be before the war. One could imagine that the coalition and some opposition groups would submit lists in all districts, which does not exclude the 'independent' lists in single districts. In such cases the campaigning is two-fold: for the candidates and for the political group as a whole. Despite superficial feelings, this situation would be more favourable (better arguments could be found) and more democratic.

Andrzej Werblan

Notes

1 Introduction

1 The Round Table Agreement signed on 5 April 1989 was the culmination of formal discussions between the communist government coalition and the Solidarity-led opposition which began on 6 February and informal contacts which had intensified in the summer of 1988. The Round Table discussion centred on three formal areas: union pluralism, political reform and social and economic reform. The main goal of Solidarność negotiators was the legalization of the union. This was conceded at an early stage of the negotiations. Essentially the agreement amounted to a power-sharing arrangement that would pave the way for a transition process. The political agreement provided for semi-free parliamentary elections in June 1989. Of the seats in the *Sejm*, 65 per cent was reserved for the government coalition, while 35 per cent of the seats could be contested by the opposition. It was agreed that the Senate would be elected in a free ballot and that a new presidential office would be established and that this position would be elected by an absolute majority of the National Assembly of both the *Sejm* and Senate.

2 D. M. Olson, 'Compartmentalized Competition: The Managed Transitional Election System of Poland', *The Journal of Politics*, 1993, vol. 55, no. 2, 415–41. 'No one in the political elite anticipated the replacement of a Communist government by a Solidarność government (Staniszkis 1990, 91; Rapaczyński 1991, 600; Kamiński 1991, 181–2; Gebethner 1992, 59). The purpose of this elaborate set of election procedures was to permit Solidarność to enter Parliament but to preserve the continuation of Communist rule. That effort of managed transition, however, failed'. p. 417. On the Round Table negotiations see also B. Geremek, *Geremek Opowiada Żakowski Pyta Rok 1989*, Warsaw: Plejada, 1990; K. Dubiński, *Magdalenka: Tranzakcja epoki. Notatki z poufnych spotkán kiszczak-Wałęsa*, Warsaw: Sylwa, 1990; W. Osiatyński, 'The Roundtable Talks in Poland', in J. Elster (ed.), *The Roundtable Talks and the Breakdown of Communism*, Chicago: The University of Chicago Press, 1996; F. Millard, *The Anatomy of the New Poland: Post-Communist Politics in Its First Phase*, Aldershot: Edward Elgar, 1994.

3 D. P. Green and I. Shapiro, *Pathologies of Rational Choice Theory*, New Haven, CT and London: Yale University Press, 1994, pp. 14–17. It is assumed within rational choice theory that human beings are utility-maximizers, that they are goal-seeking and that they can rank-order their preferences and that such preferences are transitive. Michael Laver explains that '[T]he basic premise of rational decision-making, however, is that rational people can be modelled, when they choose between the range of strategies that are open to them, as if they have made this choice on the basis of such a calculation'. M. Laver, *Private Desires, Political Action: An Invitation to the Politics of Rational Choice*, London: Sage, 1997, p. 22.

4 P. Lewis, 'Non-Competitive Elections and Regime Change: Poland 1989', *Parliamentary Affairs*, 1990, vol. 43, no. 1, 90–107; T. Garton-Ash, *The Polish*

Revolution, London: Jonathan Cape, 1983; G. Ekiert, *The State Against Society: Political Crises and Their Aftermath in East Central Europe*, Princeton, NJ: Princeton University Press, 1996; J. Staniszkis, 'Political Capitalism in Poland', *East European Politics and Societies*, 1991, vol. 5, no. 1, 127–41.

5 G. Sanford (ed.), *Democratization in Poland 1988–90. Polish Voices*, Basingstoke: Macmillan, 1992, p. 1.

6 Z. Brzeziński, *The Grand Failure: The Birth and Death of Communism in the Twentieth Century*, New York: Charles Scribner's Sons, 1989.

7 Ibid.

8 Ibid.

9 G. Ekiert, *The State Against Society*, p. 230; J. Hayden, *Poles Apart: Solidarity and the New Poland*, Dublin: Irish Academic Press, 1994, p. 142.

10 Sanford, *Democratization in Poland 1988–90*, p. 1.

11 Ibid. p. 2.

12 Ibid. p. 4.

13 A. Przeworski, *Democracy and the Market*, Cambridge: Cambridge University Press, 1991, p. 6.

14 Sanford, *Democratization in Poland 1988–90*, p. 3.

15 Przeworski, *Democracy and the Market*, p. 6.

16 J. Hayden, *Poles Apart*, p. 91.

17 Ekiert, *The State Against Society*, p. 320.

18 David Lane, *The Rise and Fall of State Socialism*, Cambridge, MA: Polity Press, 1996, p. 124.

19 Ibid.

20 Ibid.

21 Mikhail Gorbachev and Zdeněk Mlyná, *Conversations with Gorbachev*, New York: Columbia University Press, 2002, p. 84.

22 Lane, *The Rise and Fall of State Socialism*, p. 125.

23 Ibid., p. 133.

24 Ibid.

25 Gorbachev and Mlyná, *Conversations with Gorbachev*, p. 91.

26 While it is true that the Hungarian Socialist Workers' Party had agreed to a multi-party system in February 1989 and, therefore, was arguably ahead of the PZPR in the process of transformation, it is generally agreed that the Solidarity landslide in June following the Round Table decision to accept semi-free elections had an enormous psychological impact on both the public and party leaders throughout Eastern Europe. It was following the election of a Solidarność-led government in Poland in August that the Hungarian government and opposition agreed on constitutional changes to bring about a multi-party system. For more on the sequence of events in 1989, see Timothy, Garton Ash, *We the People: The Revolution of '89 Witnessed in Warsaw, Budapest, Berlin and Prague*, London: Penguin, 1999.

27 Przeworski, *Democracy and the Market*.

28 J. M. Colomer, *Strategic Transitions: Game Theory and Democratization*, Baltimore, MD and London: The Johns Hopkins University Press, 2000.

29 Przeworski, *Democracy and the Market*, p. 62.

30 Colomer, *Strategic Transitions*, p. 6.

31 S. J. Brams, *Negotiation Games: Applying Game Theory to Bargaining and Arbitration*, New York: Routledge, 1990.

32 Colomer, *Strategic Transitions*, p. 6.

33 Ibid., p. 65.

34 Ibid., p. 33.

35 Przeworski, *Democracy and the Market*, p. 54.

36 Colomer, *Strategic Transitions*, p. 64.

37 Ibid., p. 64.

38 Colomer, *Strategic Transitions*, p. 50.
39 R. H. Bates, A. Greif, M. Levi, J. Rosenthal and B. R. Weingast, *Analytic Narratives*, Princeton, NJ: Princeton University Press, 1998, p. 9.
40 Ibid., p. 16.
41 Ibid.
42 S. Gebethner, 'Political Reform in the Process of Round Table Negotiations', in G. Sanford (ed.), *Democratization in Poland*; Olson, 'Compartmentalized Competition'; J. Colomer and M. Pascual, 'The Polish Game of Transition', *Communist and Post-Communist Studies*, 1994, vol. 27, no. 3, 275–94.
43 For the details of the electoral results see Z. Pełczyński and S. Kowalski, 'Poland', *Electoral Studies*, 1990, vol. 9, no. 4, 346–54; Lewis, 'Non-Competitive Elections and Regime Change: Poland 1989', *Parliamentary Affairs*, 1990, vol. 43, no. 1, 90–107.
44 M. Kamiński, 'How Communism Could Have Been Saved: Formal Analysis of Electoral Bargaining in Poland in 1989', *Public Choice*, 1998, vol. 98, 83.
45 Lewis, 'Non-Competitive Elections and Regime Change', p. 94.
46 L. Vinton, 'Intricate Election Mechanisms, Simple Choices', *Radio Free Europe RFL/RL*, 2 June 1989, vol. 9, item 2.
47 Przeworski, *Democracy and the Market*, p. 56.
48 See Chapter 7.

2 Explaining change: the paucity of the agency–structure debate

1 J. M. Colomer, *Strategic Transitions: Game Theory and Democratization*, Baltimore, MD and London: The Johns Hopkins University Press, 2000.
2 Ibid., p. 137. See also J. Linz J. and A. Stepan (eds), *The Breakdown of Democratic Regimes*, Baltimore, MD: The Johns Hopkins University Press, 1978; J. Higley and R. Gunther (eds), *Elites and Democratic Consolidation in Latin America and Southern Europe*, New York: Cambridge University Press, 1992.
3 Colomer, *Strategic Transitions*, p. 137.
4 A. Przeworski, *Democracy and the Market*, Cambridge, New York, Melbourne: Cambridge University Press, 1991, p. 1.
5 Ibid.
6 Colomer, *Strategic Transitions*, p. 4.
7 Professor Jerzy Wiatr argues that neither category applies to regime change in Poland, which he describes as a case of negotiated reform (private correspondence with the author).
8 Przeworski, *Democracy and the Market*, p. 97.
9 M. Laver, *Private Desires, Political Actions: An Invitation to the Politics of Rational Choice*, London: Sage, 1997, p. 16.
10 See, in particular, Chapter 4.
11 Laver, *Private Desires, Political Actions*, p. 16.
12 D. A. Rustow 'Transitions to Democracy: Toward a Dynamic Model', *Comparative Politics*, 1970, vol. 2, 346.
13 L. Anderson, 'Transitions to Democracy: A Special Issue in Memory of Dankwart A. Rustow – Introduction', *Comparative Politics*, 1997, vol. 29, 346.
14 T. Skocpol, *States and Revolutions: A Comparative Analysis of France, Russia, and China*, Cambridge, New York: Cambridge University Press, 1979.
15 T. Skocpol, *Social Revolutions in the Modern World*, Cambridge, New York: Cambridge University Press, 1994, p. 8.
16 Ibid., p. 99.
17 Ibid., p. 100.
18 Ibid.

19 Przeworski, *Democracy and the Market*, p. 56.
20 Ibid., pp. 56–7.
21 J. A. Goldstone, 'Is Revolution Individually Rational? Groups and Individuals in Revolutionary Collective Action', *Rationality and Society*, 1994, vol. 6, 240. Also in A. J. Groth (ed.), *Revolution and Political Change*, Aldershot: Dartmouth, 1996.
22 P. Sztompka, *The Sociology of Social Change*, Oxford and Cambridge, MA: Blackwell, 1993, p. 315.
23 K. Poznański, 'An Interpretation of Communist Decay: The Role of Evolutionary Mechanisms', *Communist and Post-Communist Studies*, 1993, vol. 26, no. 1, 3–24. Also in Groth, *Revolution and Political Change*, p. 414.
24 Groth, *Revolution and Political Change*, p. 419.
25 Ibid.
26 Ibid., p. 425.
27 M. Burawoy, 'Reflections on the Class-Consciousness of Hungarian Steelworkers', *Politics and Society*, 1989, vol. 17, 1.
28 V. Tismaneanu, 'Reinvention of Politics: Eastern Europe after Communism'. Talk given at University of Washington, 12 November 1990.
29 S. Meuschel, *Revolution in the GDR*, Washington: University of Washington mimeo, 1991.
30 Poznański, 'An Interpretation of Communist Decay', p. 427.
31 Ibid., p. 429.
32 Ibid., p. 431.
33 Ibid., p. 432.
34 Ibid.
35 E. Szalai, 'Political and Social Conflicts Arising from the Transformation of Property Relations in Hungary', *The Journal of Communist Studies and Transition Politics*, 1994, vol. 10, no. 3, 56–81.
36 Poznański, 'An Interpretation of Communist Decay', p. 434.
37 In private correspondence with the author. I am indebted to Professor Wiatr for his comments on the evolutionary–revolutionary debate and more generally for his comments on this analysis.
38 W. Władyka, 'The Legacy of the Round Table', *Polityka*, no. 06/1999.
39 Ibid. I am indebted to Anna Gwiazda for her comments on the evolutionary–revolutionary debate and for alerting me to the relevant discussion in *Polityka*.
40 C. G. A. Bryant and E. Mokrzycki (eds), *The New Great Transformation? Change and Continuity in East Central Europe*, London: Routledge, 1994.
41 Stark as quoted in ibid., p. 34.
42 S. M. Lipset, *Political Man*, London: Heineman, 1959.
43 S. P. Huntington, *The Third Wave: Democratization in the Late Twentieth Century*, Norman and London: The University of Oklahoma Press, 1991.
44 Colomer, *Strategic Transitions*, p. 134.
45 G. A. Almond and S. Verba, *The Civic Culture*, Princeton, NJ: Princeton University Press, 1963.
46 Przeworski, *Democracy and the Market*, p. 96.
47 Ibid., p. 97.
48 Colomer, *Strategic Transitions*, p. 134.
49 Linz and Stepan, *The Breakdown of Democratic Regimes*, p. lx.
50 G. O'Donnell and P. C. Schmitter, 'Tentative Conclusions about Uncertain Democracies', in G. O'Donnell, P. C. Schmmitter and L. Whitehead (eds), *Transitions from Authoritarian Rule*, Baltimore, MD: The Johns Hopkins University Press, 1986.
51 T. L. Karl and P. C. Schmitter, 'Modes of Transition in Latin America, Southern and Eastern Europe', *International Social Science Journal*, vol. 43, no. 2, 269–84.
52 O'Donnell and Schmitter, 'Tentative Conclusions about Uncertain Democracies', p. 5.
53 Colomer, *Strategic Transitions*, p. 136.

154 *Notes*

54 D. Share and S. Mainwaring, 'Transitions through Transaction: Democratization in Brazil and Spain', in W. Selcher (ed.), *Political Liberalization in Brazil: Dilemmas and Future Prospects*, Boulder, CO: Westview Press, 1986, as quoted in S. Haggard and R. R. Kaufman, 'The Political Economy of Democratic Transitions', in L. Anderson (ed.), *Transitions to Democracy*, New York: Columbia University Press, 1999, p. 74.
55 S. P. Huntington, *The Third Wave*.
56 G. DiPalma, *To Craft Democracies: An Essay on Democratic Transitions*, Berkeley, CA: University of California Press, 1990.
57 Higley and Gunther, *Elites and Democratic Consolidation*, pp. 295–307.
58 T. L. Karl, 'Dilemmas of Democratization in Latin America', *Comparative Politics*, 1990, vol. 23, no. 1, 1–22.
59 Haggard and Kaufman, 'The Political Economy of Democratic Transitions', p. 74.
60 T. Vanhanen, *Prospects of Democracy: A Study of 172 Countries*, London and New York: Routledge, 1997.
61 O'Donnell and Schmitter, 'Tentative Conclusions about Uncertain Democracies', p. 3.
62 Przeworski, *Democracy and the Market*, p. 97.
63 U. Edvardsen, 'A Cultural Approach to Understanding Modes of Transition to Democracy', *Journal of Theoretical Politics*, 1997, vol. 9, no. 1.
64 Przeworski, *Democracy and the Market*, p. 54.
65 B. Geddes, 'A Game Theoretic Model of Reform in Latin American Democracies', *American Political Science Review*, 1991, vol. 85, no. 2, 371–92; B. Geddes, 'Initiation of New Democratic Institutions in Eastern Europe and Latin America', in A. Lijphart and C. H. Waisman (eds), *Institutional Design in New Democracies: Comparative Perspectives from Central-Eastern Europe and Latin America*, Boulder, CO: Westview Press, 1996.
66 Laver, *Private Desires, Political Actions*, p. 36.
67 E. Ostrom and J. Walker, 'Neither Markets Nor States: Linking Transformation Processes in Collective Action Arenas', in Denis C. Mueller (ed.), *Perspectives on Public Choice: A Handbook*, Cambridge: Cambridge University Press, 1997, pp. 35–73.
68 Ibid., p. 35.
69 Ibid., p. 36.
70 Ibid., pp. 36–7.
71 A. Oberschall, 'Opportunities and Framing in the Eastern European Revolts of 1989', in D. McAdam, John D. McCarthy and Mayer N. Zald (eds), *Comparative Perspectives on Social Movements: Political Opportunities, Mobilizing Structures, and Cultural Framings*, Cambridge: Cambridge University Press, 1996, pp. 94–7.
72 Ostrom and Walker, 'Neither Markets Nor States', p. 44.
73 Ibid.
74 Ibid.
75 Laver, *Private Desires, Political Actions*, pp. 70–1.
76 R. Hardin, 'Economic Theories of the State', in Denis C. Mueller (ed.), *Perspectives on Public Choice: A Handbook*, Cambridge: Cambridge University Press, 1997.
77 Ibid., p. 27.
78 F. Barth (ed.), *The Role of the Entrepreneur in Social Change in Northern Norway*, Oslo and Bergen: Universitet i Bergen, 1972.
79 Ibid., preface.
80 Ibid., p. 7.
81 Ibid., p. 81.
82 E. Hankiss, *East European Alternatives: Are There Any?* Oxford: Clarendon Press, 1990.
83 Ibid., p. 240.
84 Szelenyi, 1986–7, 132–41, as quoted in Hankiss, *East European Alternatives*, p. 242.

85 Hankiss, *East European Alternatives*, pp. 254–5.
86 Interview with Sławomir Wiatr, founder member of the post-communist SdRP, 13 December 1999.
87 Laver, *Private Desires, Political Actions*, p. 57.
88 D. C. North, *Institutions, Institutional Change and Economic Performance*, Cambridge: Cambridge University Press, 1990, p. 83.
89 Ibid., p. 86.
90 Ibid.
91 Oberschall, 'Opportunities and Framing', p. 97.
92 Przeworski, *Democracy and the Market*, p. 6.
93 G. Tullock, 'The Paradox of Revolution', *Public Choice*, 1971, vol. xi, 89–99. Also in Groth, *Revolution and Political Change*.
94 Groth, *Revolution and Political Change*, p. 204.
95 Ibid.
96 M. Silver, 'Political Revolution and Repression: An Economic Approach', *Public Choice*, 1974, vol. 17, 63–71. Also in Groth, *Revolution and Political Change*.
97 Groth, *Revolution and Political Change*, p. 213.
98 Hankiss, *East European Alternatives*, pp. 271–2.
99 K. Henderson and N. Robinson, *Post-Communist Politics: An Introduction*, London: Prentice Hall, 1997.
100 G. Tsebelis, *Nested Games: Rational Choice in Comparative Politics*, Berkeley, CA and Los Angeles, CA: University of California Press, 1990.
101 Ibid., p. 32.
102 Colomer, *Strategic Transitions*, p. 1.
103 Przeworski, *Democracy and the Market*, pp. 60–6.
104 Colomer, *Strategic Transitions*, p. 126.
105 Ibid., pp. 2–3.
106 Przeworski, *Democracy and the Market*, pp. 60–6.
107 Colomer, *Strategic Transitions*, pp. 63–4.
108 Ibid., p. 126.
109 Ibid., p. 106.
110 Ibid., p. 64.
111 Ibid., p. 106.
112 Ibid.

3 Explaining the collapse of communism in Poland

1 A. Kwaśniewski as quoted in W. Osiatyński, 'The Roundtable Talks in Poland', in J. Elster (ed.), *The Roundtable Talks and the Breakdown of Communism*, Chicago: The University of Chicago Press, 1996, p. 26.
2 M. Kamiński, 'How Communism Could Have Been Saved: Formal Analysis of Electoral Bargaining in Poland in 1989', *Public Choice*, 1998, vol. 98, 84.
3 For a more comprehensive discussion of the PZPR's bargaining over the electoral law see Chapter 6.
4 J. Colomer, *Strategic Transitions: Game Theory and Democratization*, Baltimore, MD and London: The Johns Hopkins University Press, 2000, p. 106.
5 J. Colomer and M. Pascual, 'The Polish Game of Transition', *Communist and Post-Communist Studies*, 1994, vol. 27, no. 3, 275–94.
6 This claim is substantiated in author interviews with Jerzy Wiatr, Sławomir Wiatr, Janusz Reykowski and Stanisław Gebethner. Wiktor Osiatyński ('The Roundtable Talks in Poland', p. 54) also supports the claim that Aleksander Kwaśniewski introduced the idea of a freely elected Senate without prior consultation with his PZPR colleagues. This move resolved the stalemate over the PZPR's preference for the introduction of the office of president. Kwaśniewski's idea was to legitimize the

presidential office by having it elected by the (contractual) *Sejm* and a freely elected Senate. However, the impact of the free elections to the Senate was not worked out in advance.

7 Colomer and Pascual, 'The Polish Game of Transition', pp. 275–94.

8 Kamiński, 'How Communism Could Have Been Saved', pp. 83–109.

9 Ibid., p. 83.

10 Ibid., p. 84.

11 A. Przeworski, *Democracy and the Market*, Cambridge: Cambridge University Press, 1991.

12 Colomer and Pascual, 'The Polish Game of Transition'.

13 Kamiński, 'How Communism Could Have Been Saved'.

14 Colomer, *Strategic Transitions*.

15 G. King, K. O. Keohane and S. Verba, *Designing Social Inquiry: Scientific Inference in Qualitative Research*, Princeton, NJ: Princeton University Press, 1994.

16 Colomer, *Strategic Transitions*, p. 106.

17 Ibid., p. 101.

18 Ibid., p. 52.

19 Przeworski, *Democracy and the Market*, p. 66.

20 Ibid.

21 Ibid., p. 62.

22 G. Tsebelis, *Nested Games: Rational Choice in Comparative Politics*, Berkeley, CA and Los Angeles, CA: University of California Press, 1990; R. H. Bates, J. P. Rui, D. E. Figueiredo Jr and B. Weingast, 'The Politics of Interpretation: Rationality, Culture and Transition', *Politics and Society*, 1998, vol. 26, no. 4, 603–24.

23 Przeworski, *Democracy and the Market*.

24 Bates *et al.*, 'The Politics of Interpretation', p. 613.

25 Ibid., p. 628.

26 R. H. Bates, A. Greif, M. Levi, J. Rosenthal and B. R. Weingast, *Analytic Narratives*, Princeton, NJ: Princeton University Press, 1998, p. 3.

27 J. Hayden, *Poles Apart: Solidarity and the New Poland*, Dublin: Irish Academic Press, 1994.

28 Professor A. Werblan and Professor S. Gebethner.

29 General W. Jaruzelski was interviewed on 16 March 1992 and on 5 May 1999; M. Rakowski was interviewed on 9 March 1992 and on 4 May 1999.

30 1 April 1992, 20 October 1993, 18 November 1995, 11 May 1999 and 13 December 1999.

31 24 June 1989.

32 I met the then trade unionist, Lech Wałęsa, on a number of occasions and spent several hours in his company on the eve of the Gdańsk Shipyard strike in August 1980. I was present during the meetings of the then founding committee of the Free Trades Unions of the Coast at the home of Anna Walentynowicz. I subsequently met and interviewed Wałęsa in Gdańsk in December 1989. This material is not tape-recorded. However, subsequent interviews on 22 June 1989, 21 November 1990 and 5 March 1992 were recorded.

33 Bates *et al.*, *Analytic Narratives*, p. 14.

34 The information for these biographical notes is mainly based on interview material gathered by the author as well as material published in connection with The Center for Russian and East European Studies' conference *Communism's Negotiated Collapse: The Polish Round Table, Ten Years Later*, at the University of Michigan at Ann Arbor, 7–10 April, 1999.

35 Former post-Solidarność minister for Foreign Affairs, Bronisław Geremek as quoted in J. Hayden, *Poles Apart*, p. 144.

36 Hayden, *Poles Apart*, pp. 131–46.

37 Ibid., p. 142.

38 W. Jaruzelski, *To Differ Wisely. How Did Marshal Law Come About?*, Warsaw: Książka i Wiedza, 1999.
39 Interview with Professor Janusz Reykowski, 10 May 1999.
40 http://www.warsawvoice.pl/v694/News01.html
41 Bates *et al.*, *Analytic Narratives*, p. 236.

4 PZPR strategic goals: expectation and outcome

1 Interview with Adam Michnik, 5 May 1999.
2 Z. Brzeziński, *The Grand Failure: The Birth and Death of Communism in the Twentieth Century*, New York: Charles Scribner's Sons, 1989.
3 A. Rychard, 'Politics and Society after the Breakthrough: The Sources and Threats to Political Legitimacy in Post-Communist Poland', in G. Sanford (ed.), *Democratization in Poland, 1989–90: Polish Voices*, New York: St Martin's Press, 1992.
4 For instance, General W. Jaruzelski and Prime Minister R. Rakowski both argued (in interviews with the author) that the need for dialogue with the Polish opposition arose out of the realization that the party could not carry the burden of economic reform alone.
5 A. Przeworski, *Democracy and the Market*, Cambridge, New York, Melbourne: Cambridge University Press, 1991, p. 6.
6 V. Zubek, 'The Threshold of Poland's Transition: 1989 Electoral Campaign as the Last Act of a United Solidarity', *Studies in Comparative Communism*, 1991, vol. 24, no. 4, 355–77.
7 Ibid., p. 360.
8 Interview with Adam Michnik, 5 May 1999.
9 W. Osiatyński, 'The Roundtable Talks in Poland', in J. Elster (ed.), *The Roundtable Talks and the Breakdown of Communism*, Chicago: The University of Chicago Press, 1996, p. 42.
10 PZPR negotiator and later president of Poland.
11 Osiatyński, 'The Roundtable Talks in Poland', p. 42.
12 Referendum on economic reform defeated in November 1987.
13 Interview with Professor Janusz Reykowski, 10 May 1999.
14 Ibid.
15 Ibid.
16 Ibid.
17 Interview with MP Professor Jerzy Wiatr, 11 May 1999.
18 Mieczysław Rakowski, the last PZPR prime minister of Poland.
19 Interview with MP Professor Jerzy Wiatr, 11 May 1999.
20 Ibid.
21 Strikes broke out in Poland in the spring and were followed by another round of strikes in the autumn of 1988.
22 Mieczysław Rakowski, the last PZPR prime minister of Poland.
23 Tadeusz Mazowiecki, elected as the first non-communist prime minister in the Solidarność-led coalition government on 24 August 1989.
24 PZPR trade union, the OPZZ (All Poland Trade Union Alliance), led by Alfred Miodowicz.
25 Interview with General Wojciech Jaruzelski, 5 May 1999.
26 Ibid.
27 Ibid.
28 Interview with General Czesław Kiszczak, 6 May 1999.
29 Ibid.
30 General Florian Siwicki, chief of the general staff.
31 Interview with General Czesław Kiszczak, 6 May 1999.
32 Bronisław Geremek, intellectual dissident and adviser to Lech Wałęsa throughout the 1980s.

33   Kiszczak is underestimating the level of support for the strikes.
34   Interview with General Czesław Kiszczak, 6 May 1999.
35   More radical and anti-Wałęsa wing of Solidarność.
36   *Armia Krajowa* (Home Army), the underground resistance formed in 1941 under the command of the Polish government in exile in London.
37   Interview with General Czesław Kiszczak, 6 May 1999.
38   Ibid.
39   Interview with author, 4 May 1999.
40   Interview with Stanisław Ciosek, 4 May 1999.
41   Ibid.
42   Ibid.
43   PZPR allied trade union.
44   Ryszard Bugaj, Solidarność activist and later leader of the UP, Labour Union in the early 1990s.
45   Interview with Mieczysław Rakowski, 4 May 1999.
46   Ibid.
47   Interview with Sławomir Wiatr, 13 December 1999.
48   ZSL, Peasant Party and SD, Democratic Party, former nominally independent allies of the PZPR.
49   Interview with Sławomir Wiatr, 13 December 1999.
50   Intellectuals, Bronisław Geremek and Adam Michnik were two senior Solidarność advisers and dissidents.
51   Interview with Sławomir Wiatr, 13 December 1999.
52   Interview with Adam Michnik, 5 May 1999.
53   Information on the visit of the first secretary of the KC PZPR and chairperson of the Council of State of the Polish Peoples Republic Com. Wojciech Jaruzelski to Prague (1 February 1989) in S. Perzkowski, *Tajne Dokumenty, Biura Politycznego I Sekretariatu KC: Ostatni rok władzy 1988–1989*, London: Aneks, 1989, pp. 259–62. Translated by Basia Bannister.
54   Ibid.
55   Ibid.
56   Ibid.
57   Ibid.
58   Ibid.
59   Ibid.
60   Interview with General Wojciech Jaruzelski, 5 May 1999.
61   Ibid.
62   K. Dubiński, 'Concept of Changes in the Political System of the Polish People's Republic in the Light of the Eighth Plenary Meeting of KC PZPR', in K. Dubiński (ed.), *Okrągły Stół*, Warsaw: KAP, 1999, pp. 62–4.
63   Ibid., p. 62.
64   P. Raina, *Droga do 'Okrągłego Stołu'*, Warsaw: Druk Drukarnia EFEKT, 1989. I am indebted to Anna Gwiazda for this translation.
65   Ibid., p. 202.
66   Ibid., p. 243. The meeting was held on 9 November 1988 in Warsaw.
67   Ibid.
68   Ibid., p. 280.
69   Ibid., p. 285.
70   Ibid.
71   Adam Michnik was speaking on the significance of the Round Table at 'Communism's Negotiated Collapse: The Polish Round Table Talks of 1989 – Ten Years Later'. A Conference at the University of Michigan, 7–10 April 1999.
72   Interview with Professor Janusz Reykowski, 10 May 1999.
73   Ibid.

74 Ibid.
75 Interview with General Jaruzelski, 5 May 1999.
76 Interview with General Czesław Kiszczak, 6 May 1999.
77 Interview with Mieczysław Rakowski, 4 May 1999.
78 Information on the visit of the first secretary of the KC PZPR and chairperson of the Council of State of the Polish Peoples Republic Com. Wojciech Jaruzelski to Prague (1 February 1989) in S. Perzkowski, *Tajne Dokumenty, Biura Politycznego I Sekretariatu KC: Ostatni rok władzy 1988–1989*, London: Aneks, 1989, pp. 259–62. Translated by Basia Bannister.
79 'Concept of Changes', in Dubiński, *Okrągły Stół*, pp. 60–88.
80 P. Raina, *A Path to the 'Round Table: Initial Talks behind the Scenes*, Warsaw: Druk Drukarnia EFEKT, 1999. This book is an edited volume of the contemporaneous notes of Bishop A. Orszulik.
81 Interview with MP Professor Jerzy Wiatr, 11 May 1999.
82 Interview with Sławomir Wiatr, 13 December 1999.
83 Interview with Stanisław Ciosek, 4 May 1999.
84 Ibid.
85 Ibid.
86 Ibid.
87 Ibid.

5 Strategies and outcomes: part 1 – institutional choices of the PZPR

1 D. M. Olson, 'Compartmentalized Competition: The Managed Transitional Election System of Poland', *The Journal of Politics*, 1993, vol. 55, no. 2, 415–41.
2 Ibid., p. 419. See also K. Dubiński, *Okrągły Stół*, Warsaw: KAP, 1999, p. 76; B. Geremek, *Geremek Opowiada Żakowski Pyta Rok 1989*, Warsaw: Plejada, 1990, pp. 89–90.
3 Olson, 'Compartmentalized Competition', p. 419. Interview with Bronisław Geremek, PAP in FBIS, 10 March 1989; *New York Times*, 10 and 11 March, 1989.
4 Interview with Professor Janusz Reykowski, 10 May 1999.
5 Stanisław Ciosek, senior member of the Politburo and the PZPR's chief contact with the Catholic Church; Aleksander Kwaśniewski was then a young member of the PZPR and later founder member of the post-communist SdRP and later president of Poland.
6 Interview with Professor Janusz Reykowski, 10 May 1999.
7 Dubiński, *Okrągły Stół*, pp. 83–9.
8 Ibid.
9 Ibid.
10 Ibid., p. 83.
11 Ibid., pp. 83–9.
12 Ibid.
13 Ibid.
14 Ibid., p. 89.
15 J. B. de Weydenthal, 'The Return of Wałęsa', *Radio Free Europe RFL/RL*, 2 September 1988, vol. 14, item 1, pp. 3–7.
16 Ibid., p. 4.
17 For details, see Jackson Diehl in *The Washington Post*, 1 September 1988.
18 F. Millard, *The Anatomy of the New Poland: Post-Communist Politics in Its First Phase*, Aldershot: Edward Elgar, 1994, p. 57.
19 See interviews with members of the Presidium of the Free Trades Unions of the Coast in J. Hayden, *Poles Apart: Solidarity and the New Poland*, Dublin: Irish Academic Press, 1994; see also Millard, *The Anatomy of the New Poland*, p. 58.

20 Millard, *The Anatomy of the New Poland*, p. 58.
21 Dubiński, *Okrągły Stół*, pp. 83–9.
22 General Florian Siwicki was a member of the Politburo.
23 Interview with General Czesław Kiszczak, 6 May 1999.
24 J. Colomer and M. Pascual, 'The Polish Game of Transition', *Communist and Post-Communist Studies*, 1994, vol. 27, no. 3, 284.
25 *Trybuna Ludu*, 19 January 1989, as quoted in L. Vinton, 'Polish Situation Report', *Radio Free Europe, RFL/RL*, 6 February 1988, vol. 3, item 2, 5–10.
26 Dubiński, *Okrągły Stół*, pp. 178–97.
27 Ibid.
28 Ibid.
29 Interview with Stanisław Ciosek, 4 May 1999.
30 Dubiński, *Okrągły Stół*, p. 194.
31 Ibid., pp. 196–7.
32 Interview with Janusz Reykowski, 10 May 1999.
33 Interview with Professor Jerzy Wiatr, 11 May 1999.
34 Ibid.
35 Ibid.
36 Patriotic Movement of National Revival.
37 Interview with Professor Jerzy Wiatr, 11 May 1999.
38 Interview with Stanisław Ciosek, 4 May 1999.
39 Interview with Grażyna Staniszewska, 6 May 1999.
40 Interview with Mieczysław Rakowski, 4 May 1999.
41 L. Vinton, 'The Approaching Round Table', *Radio Free Europe RFL/RL*, 6 February 1989, vol. 3, item 2, 5–10.
42 Ibid. Orzechowski was speaking on Radio Warsaw, 5.30 p.m. on 4 February 1989.
43 Colomer and Pascual, 'The Polish Game of Transition', p. 284.
44 'Concept of Changes in the Political System of the Polish People's Republic in the Light of the Eighth Plenary Meeting of KC PZPR', in Dubiński, *Okrągły Stół*.
45 Ibid.
46 Ibid.
47 The United Peasant Party (ZSL) and the SD were the two other parties in the government coalition.
48 'Concept of Changes', in Dubiński, *Okrągły Stół*.
49 Ibid., pp. 60–88.
50 Ibid.
51 Ibid.
52 S. Gebethner, 'Political Reform in the Process of Round Table Negotiations', in G. Sanford (ed.), *Democratization in Poland, 1980–90: Polish Voices*, New York: St Martin's Press, 1992, p. 60.
53 Ibid.
54 'Note from the Meeting of the Committee on Political Reforms, 18 February 1989', in Dubiński, *Okrągły Stół*, pp. 277–80.
55 Ibid. This note was prepared by the PZPR's Capt. Jerzy Kretkowski.
56 Gebethner, 'Political Reform in the Process of Round Table Negotiations', p. 60.
57 Interview with Piotr Winczorek, 20 March 2000.
58 Gebethner, 'Political Reform in the Process of Round Table Negotiations', p. 60.
59 'Concept of Changes', in Dubiński, *Okrągły Stół*.
60 Gebethner, 'Political Reform in the Process of Round Table Negotiations', p. 61.
61 Ibid.
62 PZPR negotiator, founder member of the SdRP and later president of Poland.
63 Interview with MP Professor Jerzy Wiatr, 11 May 1999.
64 Interview with Professor Janusz Reykowski, 10 May 1999.
65 Interview with MP Professor Jerzy Wiatr, 11 May 1999.

66 Gebethner, 'Political Reform in the Process of Round Table Negotiations', p. 61.
67 Interview with Stanisław Ciosek, 4 May 1999.
68 Aleksander Kwaśniewski, in an interview with Adam Michnik, Agnieszka Kublik, Piotr Pacewicz and Paweł Smoleński in *Gazeta Wyborcza*, 31 December 2001 (translation by Anna Gwiazda).
69 Interview with Professor Janusz Reykowski, 10 May 1999.
70 Ibid.
71 Interview with MP Professor Jerzy Wiatr, 11 May 1999.
72 Interview with Mieczysław Rakowski, 4 May 1999.
73 Interview with Stanisław Ciosek, 4 May 1999.
74 L. Vinton, 'The Approaching Round Table', *Radio Free Europe RFL/RL*, 6 February 1989, vol. 3, item 2, pp. 5–10.
75 'Concept of Changes', in Dubiński, *Okrągły Stół.*
76 Ibid.
77 Gebethner, 'Political Reform in the Process of Round Table Negotiations', p. 60.
78 Ibid., p. 61.

6 Strategies and outcomes: part 2 – the PZPR's choice of electoral system and voting formulae

1 D. M. Olson, 'Compartmentalized Competition: The Managed Transitional Election System of Poland', *The Journal of Politics*, 1993, vol. 55, no. 2, 420.
2 M. Kamiński, 'How Communism Could Have Been Saved: Formal Analysis of Electoral Bargaining', *Public Choice*, 1998, vol. 98, 83–109.
3 An evaluation of these claims follows later on in this chapter.
4 In interviews with the author, only Sławomir Wiatr, one of the young members of the PZPR, claimed to have anticipated that the party would not perform well in the 4 June election. Mr Wiatr claims that a group of younger party members, including future President Aleksander Kwaśniewski, took the view that the PZPR would have to lose power in order that a new social democratic party could be established from the remnants of the PZPR .
5 CBOS Opinion Poll BD/30/4/89. Centrum Badania Opinii Społecznej. Ul. Żurawia 4 skr.pt. 24, 00–955 Warszawa.
6 Ibid.
7 P. Kwiatowski, 'Opinion Research and the Fall of Communism: Poland 1981–1990', *International Journal of Public Opinion Research*, 1992, vol. 4, no. 4, 358–74.
8 Kamiński, 'How Communism Could Have Been Saved', pp. 9–100.
9 K. Lutyńska, 'Questionnaire Studies in Poland in the 1980s (Analysis of Refusals to Give an Interview)', *The Polish Sociological Bulletin*, 1987, vol. 3, 14–24.
10 Kwiatowski, 'Opinion Research and the Fall of Communism'.
11 Round Table negotiator Professor Janusz Reykowski was a member of PAN as well as being a senior party member as was Professor Jerzy Wiatr to name but two examples.
12 Kamiński, 'How Communism Could Have Been Saved', p. 98.
13 The author has interviewed Mieczysław Rakowski on a number of occasions between 1989 and 1999.
14 ZSL nominally independent Communist coalition partner.
15 J. Hayden, *Poles Apart: Solidarity and the New Poland*, Dublin: Irish Academic Press, 1994, pp. 93–4.
16 Interview with General Jaruzelski, 5 May 1999.
17 Interview with Lech Kaczyński, 7 May 1999.
18 Ibid.
19 Interview with Stanisław Ciosek, 4 May 1999.

20 Interview with MP Professor Jerzy Wiatr, 11 May 1999 and Sławomir Wiatr, 13 December 1999.
21 Interview with Lech Kaczyński, 7 May 1999.
22 Alfred Miodowicz, head of the PZPR's allied trade union movement, the All Poland Trade Union Alliance (OPZZ).
23 Interview with Professor Janusz Reykowski, 10 May 1999.
24 Interview with Stanisław Ciosek, 4 May 1999.
25 Ibid.
26 Ibid.
27 A discussion of the advice offered by Professor Werblan follows later in this chapter.
28 Interview with Professor Andrzej Werblan, 13 December 1999.
29 Ibid.
30 Kamiński, 'How Communism Could Have Been Saved', p. 83.
31 Ibid., p. 84.
32 S. Perzkowski, *Tajne dokumenty Biura Politycznego I Sekretariartu KC, 1988–1989*, London: Aneks, 1994, 'The concept of the system of election to Sejm, based on the formula of non-confrontational but competitive elections, held on the basis of agreed principles', pp. 289–92.
33 See Appendix 1.
34 Interview with General Jaruzelski, 5 May 1999.
35 Interview with General Czesław Kiszczak, 6 May 1999.
36 Interview with General Jaruzelski, 5 May 1999.
37 Ibid.
38 Olson, 'Compartmentalized Competition'. The seven compartments were the Senate, the national or country list for the *Sejm* and the five types of district seats for the *Sejm*.
39 Interview with Janusz Reykowski, 10 May 1999.
40 Interview with Stanisław Ciosek, 4 May 1999.
41 K. Dubiński, *Okrągły Stół*, Warsaw: KAP, 1999, pp. 394–7.
42 Interview with MP Professor Jerzy Wiatr, 11 May 1999.
43 S. Gebethner, 'Political Reform in the Process of Round Table Negotiations', in G. Sanford (ed.), *Democratization in Poland, 1988–1990: Polish Voices*, New York: St Martin's Press, 1992, p. 63. 'Under such circumstances I prepared in great detail a draft electoral system for the Senate based on the principle of proportional representation. In the draft I divided the country into 13 multi-member constituencies, each of which covered the territory of a number of provinces. Only the Warsaw and the Katowice provinces constituted an individually separate multi-member constituency. The number of seats in each constituency was proportional to the number of inhabitants. This would have ensured fair representation for each region in the Senate. The essence of this proposal was that candidates would have to be nominated on lists; the voter would have chosen between these lists while retaining the possibility of expressing personal preferences as well. I assumed that there might be several lists from the groups making up the then coalition just as there might be several opposition lists. This gave the coalition a chance of gaining some representation in the Senate according to the logic of the proportional principle. It was possible to forecast that the PZPR, and its allies of the time, by applying this principle might count on round about 15–25 per cent of the Senate seats. The results of the elections to the Senate confirmed this prognosis although it is not important at this juncture. Because, after all Solidarność candidates to the Senate received about 66 per cent. If a proportional system had been applied the remaining seats would have been allocated to other groups of non-party candidates. What is significant here is the reception accorded to my draft proposal for a proportional electoral system for the Senate... As far as I know my draft was considered carefully. A Politburo member declared, in conversation with me, that it was an interesting proposal based on academic knowledge. However he considered that political instinct went beyond academic knowledge. This political instinct was possessed by the

Provincial Party Secretary first secretaries; directed by this they assured the PZPR leadership that they could guarantee the election of their Senate candidates in the majority of provinces. Such was the state of consciousness of the provincial party bosses at the time. During the election campaign, these feelings about the certainty of their chances dominated many PZPR provincial administrations. This undoubtedly was a clear indication of the alienation of the authorities and their detachments from reality. The shock of defeat, which was almost a rout, was therefore all the greater.'

44 Ibid., p. 62.
45 PZPR member and co-chair of the Round Table.
46 Józef Czyrek was a member of the Politburo.
47 Interview with Professor Stanisław Gebethner, 13 December 1999.
48 Interview with Professor Janusz Reykowski, 10 May 1999.
49 See Appendix 2.
50 M. Rakowski, *Lata, Listy, Ludzie*, Warsaw: BGW, 1993, pp. 252–4. See Appendix 1.
51 Interview with Professor Andrzej Werblan, 13 December 1999.
52 Ibid.
53 Olson, 'Compartmentalized Competition', p. 427.
54 Interview with Professor Stanisław Gebethner, 13 December 1999.
55 Z. Barany and L. Vinton, 'Breakthrough to Democracy: Elections in Poland and Hungary', *Studies in Comparative Communism*, 1990, vol. 23, no. 2, 195.
56 Interview with Professor Andrzej Werblan, 13 December 1999.
57 Ibid.
58 Werblan regards Jaruzelski, Kiszczak, Barcikowski, Rakowski, Czyrek and Ciosek as the core of the reform wing of the PZPR.
59 Interview with Professor Andrzej Werblan, 13 December 1999.
60 The disaster of the national list created a constitutional problem, which was solved by agreement with Solidarity's leaders embodied in a decree of the retiring Council of State. The unfilled 33 *Sejm* seats were redistributed nationally by adding them to select constituencies reserved for the government coalition. The defeated candidates withdrew and the two new ones were nominated for every one of the 33 seats.
61 Interview with MP Professor Jerzy Wiatr, 11 May 1999.
62 M. Laver in private correspondence with the author.
63 Interview with Professor Andrzej Werblan, 13 December 1999.
64 F. Millard, *The Anatomy of the New Poland: Post-Communist Politics in Its First Phase*, Aldershot: Edward Elgar, 1994, p. 69.
65 Ibid.
66 Gebethner, 'Political Reform in the Process of Round Table Negotiations', pp. 62–3.
67 See Chapter 7 for a discussion of the PZPR's relationship with the Catholic Church.
68 Interview with Professor Andrzej Werblan, 13 December 1999.
69 B. Heyns and I. Białecki, 'Solidarność: Reluctant Vanguard or Makeshift Coalition?', *American Political Science Review*, 1991, vol. 85, no. 2, 351–70.
70 V. Zubek, 'The Threshold of Poland's Transition: 1989 Electoral Campaign as the Last Act of a United Solidarity', *Studies in Comparative Communism*, 1991, vol. 24, no. 4, 355–77.
71 Gebethner, 'Political Reform in the Process of Round Table Negotiations', p. 56.
72 Millard, *The Anatomy of the New Poland*, p. 70.
73 Ibid.
74 Interview with General Jaruzelski, 5 May 1999.
75 Kamiński, 'How Communism Could Have Been Saved', pp. 83–109.
76 Interview with Lech Kaczyński, 7 May 1999.
77 Gebethner, 'Political Reform in the Process of Round Table Negotiations', pp. 62–3.
78 Ibid.
79 A. Przeworski, *Democracy and the Market*, Cambridge: Cambridge University Press, 1991, p. 66.

7 The election campaign

1 P. Lewis, 'Non-Competitive Elections and Regime Change: Poland 1989', *Parliamentary Affairs*, 1990, vol. 43, no. 1, 90–107.
2 Ibid., p. 95.
3 Ibid.
4 This point was made by several PZPR interviewees, but, in particular, in my interview with Jerzy Wiatr, 11 May 1999.
5 D. M. Olson, 'Compartmentalized Competition: The Managed Transitional Election System of Poland', *The Journal of Politics*, 1993, vol. 55, no. 2, 415–41.
6 In particular, Stanisław Ciosek, General Jaruzelski, General Kiszczak.
7 Olson, 'Compartmentalized Competition', p. 426.
8 Ibid., quoted from an article in *Rzeczpospolita*, FBIS, 25 May 1989. The present author interviewed Jan Bisztyga on several occasions in June 1989 and later in 1992. Mr Bisztyga identified himself as being on the reformist wing of the party. He repeatedly pointed out that the PZPR was not prepared for the game it had to play during the campaign.
9 V. Zubek, 'The Threshold of Poland's Transition: 1989 Electoral Campaign as the Last Act of a United Solidarity', *Studies in Comparative Communism*, 1991, vol. 24, no. 4, 355–77.
10 It is a common theme running through the interview material gathered for this book that former PZPR reformers emphasize their reformist credentials and indicate their annoyance at not having received due recognition for their role in preparing the ground for democratic change.
11 F. Millard, *The Anatomy of the New Poland: Post-Communist Politics in Its First Phase*, Aldershot: Edward Elgar, 1994, p. 68.
12 Ibid.
13 Interview with General Czesław Kiszczak, 6 May 1999.
14 G. Sanford, *Democratization in Poland, 1988–90. Polish Voices*, Basingstoke: The Macmillan Press, 1992, p. 19.
15 See Chapter 3.
16 Zubek, 'The Threshold of Poland's Transition'.
17 Sanford, *Democratization in Poland*, p. 11.
18 M. Kamiński, 'How Communism Could Have Been Saved: Formal Analysis of Electoral Bargaining in Poland in 1989', *Public Choice*, 1998, vol. 98, 86.
19 B. Badora, L. Kolarska-Bobinska, K. Kosela, A. Paczkowski and A. Sulek (eds), *Społeczeństwo i władza lat osiemdziesiatych w badaniach CBOS (Society and Rulers of 1980s in the CBOS Reports)*, Warsaw: CBOS, 1994, p. 384 as quoted in Kamiński, 'How Communism Could Have Been Saved', p. 86.
20 Kamiński, 'How Communism Could Have Been Saved', p. 86.
21 S. Perzkowski, *Tajne Dokumenty Biura Politycznego I Sekretariatu KC: Ostani rok władzy 1988–1989*, London: Aneks, 1994, Document no. 34, minutes no. 57 of a Meeting of the Secretariat of the KC PZPR on 9 February 1989, pp. 265–78.
22 Z. Pełczyński and S. Kowalski, 'Poland', *Electoral Studies*, 1990, vol. 9, no. 4, 346–54.
23 Ibid., p. 349.
24 Ibid.
25 Ibid.
26 Ibid.
27 Lewis, 'Non-Competitive Elections and Regime Change', p. 93.
28 Pełczyński and Kowalski, 'Poland', pp. 346–54.
29 Sanford, *Democratization in Poland*, p. 19.
30 Ibid.
31 L. Vinton, 'Polish Situation Report', *Radio Free Europe RFL/RL*, 19 May 1989, vol. 8, item 3, 17–24.
32 Ibid., p. 17.

33 Ibid., p. 20.
34 Ibid., p. 1. Quoted from Radio Warsaw, 11 May 1989 at 6.05 p.m.
35 Olson, 'Compartmentalized Competition', p. 425.
36 Ibid., pp. 425–6. Stanisław Ciosek in *Trybuna Ludu*, FBIS, 7 June 1989.
37 Pełczyński and Kowalski, 'Poland', p. 349.
38 Interview with MP Professor Jerzy Wiatr, 11 May 1999.
39 'They Will Cross Us Out', *Gazeta Wyborcza*, 8 May 1989, as quoted in L. Vinton, 'Polish Situation Report', pp. 17–24.
40 Ibid., p. 22.
41 Ibid.
42 J. B. de Weydenthal, 'Polish Situation Report', *Radio Free Europe RFL/RL*, 2 June 1989, vol. 9, item 1, 3–6.
43 Ibid., p. 4.
44 L. Vinton, 'Intricate Election Mechanisms, Simple Choices', *Radio Free Europe RFL/RL*, 2 June 1989, vol. 9, item 2, 7.
45 Ibid.
46 The present author was in Poland in 1989 and witnessed this activity at numerous polling stations.
47 L. Vinton, 'Polish Situation Report', *Radio Free Europe RFL/RL*, 2 June 1989, vol. 9, item 2, 9.
48 Interview with Professor Andrzej Werblan, former Politburo member, 13 December 1999.
49 Interview with Stanisław Ciosek, 4 May 1999.
50 P. Raina, *A Path to the 'Round Table': Initial Talks behind the Scenes*, Warsaw: EFEKT, 1999, p. 5. This book is an edited volume of the contemporaneous notes of Bishop A. Orszulik. I am indebted to Anna Gwiazda for this translation.
51 Ibid., p. 78.
52 The meeting was held on 28 February 1985.
53 Ibid., pp. 78–81.
54 Ibid.
55 Ibid., pp. 214–18.
56 Ibid.
57 Interview with Andrzej Werblan, 13 December 1999.
58 Interview with Professor Janusz Reykowski, 10 May 1999.
59 Interview with MP Professor Jerzy Wiatr, 11 May 1999.
60 B. Heyns and I. Bialecki, 'Solidarność: Reluctant Vanguard or Makeshift Coalition?', *American Political Science Review*, 1991, vol. 82, no. 2, 351–70.
61 Ibid., p. 358.
62 Ibid., p. 359. Estimates of the relative voting strength of peasants and workers are based on ecological regressions that assume the probability of supporting Solidarność is constant for each group across voivodships.
63 Ibid., p. 361.
64 Ibid., p. 364.
65 Ibid.
66 Ibid.
67 Ibid.
68 PZPR spokesman Jan Bisztyga quoted from *Rzeczpospolita*, FBIS, 25 May 1989 in Olson, 'Compartmentalized Competition', p. 426.
69 Heyns and Białecki, 'Solidarność', pp. 351–70.

8 Discussion and conclusion

1 Colomer, *Strategic Transitions: Game Theory and Democratization*, Baltimore, MD and London: The John Hopkins University Press, 2000, p. 126.

2 A. Przeworski, *Democracy and the Market*, New York: Cambridge University Press, 1991, pp. 62–6.
3 Colomer, *Strategic Transitions*, p. 50.
4 R. H. Bates, J. P. Rui, D. E. Figueiredo Jr and B. Weingast, 'The Politics of Interpretation: Rationality, Culture and Transition', *Politics and Society*, 1998, vol. 26, no. 4, 603–24.
5 R. H. Bates, A. Greif, M. Levi, J. Rosenthal and B. R. Weingast, *Analytic Narratives*, Princeton, NJ: Princeton University Press, 1998, p. 9.
6 Ibid., p. 16.
7 See Chapter 3.
8 Ibid.
9 Information on the visit of the first secretary of the KC PZPR and chairperson of the Council of State of the Polish Peoples Republic Com. Wojciech Jaruzelski to Prague, 1 February 1989, in S. Perzkowski, *Tajne documenty: Biura Politycznego I Sekretariatu KC 1988–89*, Warsaw: Aneks, 1989, pp. 259–62. Translated by Basia Bannister.
10 Interview with General Czesław Kiszczak, 6 May 1999.
11 Interview with Stanisław Ciosek, 4 May 1999.
12 Ibid.
13 Interview with Professor Janusz Reykowski, 10 May 1999.
14 Information on the visit of the first secretary of the KC PZPR and chairperson of the Council of State of the Polish Peoples Republic Com. Wojciech Jaruzelski to Prague, 1 February 1989, in S. Perzkowski, *Tajne documenty,* pp. 259–62. Translated by Basia Bannister.
15 Interview with Professor Jerzy Wiatr, 11 May 1999.
16 Interview with Sławomir Wiatr, founder member of the post-communist SdRP, 13 December 1999.
17 Interview with Mieczysław Rakowski, 4 May 1999.
18 'Concept of Changes in the Political System of the Polish People's Republic in the Light of the Eighth Plenary Meeting of KC PZPR', in K. Dubiński, *Okrągły Stół*, Warsaw: KAP, 1999, pp. 62–4.
19 Ibid., pp. 60–88.
20 S. Gebethner, 'Political Reform in the Process of Round Table Negotiations', in G. Sanford (ed.), *Democratization in Poland, 1980–90: Polish Voices*, New York: St Martin's Press, 1992, p. 60.
21 Ibid., p. 61.
22 M. Kamiński, 'How Communism Could Have Been Saved: Formal Analysis of Electoral Bargaining', *Public Choice*, 1998, vol. 98, 83–109.
23 Ibid.
24 Interview with Professor Stanisław Gebethner, 13 December 1999.
25 B. Heyns and I. Białecki, 'Solidarność: Reluctant Vanguard or Makeshift Coalition?', *American Political Science Review*, 1991, vol. 85, no. 2, 351–70.
26 Ibid., p. 364.
27 See Chapter 4.
28 Przeworski, *Democracy and the Market*, p. 54.
29 G. O'Donnell, P. C. Schmitter and L. Whitehead, *Transitions from Authoritarian Rule*, Baltimore, MD: The Johns Hopkins University Press, 1986. See also D. North, *Institutions, Institutional Change and Economic Performance*, Cambridge: Cambridge University Press, 1990.
30 J. M. Colomer, *Game Theory and the Transition to Democracy: The Spanish Model*, Aldershot and Vermont: Edward Elgar, 1995.
31 Colomer, *Strategic Transitions*, p. 104.
32 Przeworski, *Democracy and the Market*, pp. 60–6.
33 Colomer, *Strategic Transitions*, p. 65.
34 Ibid., p. 126.

Bibliography

Acherson, Neil, *The Polish August*, London: Penguin Books, 1981
——*The Struggles for Poland*, London: Pan Books, 1987
Almond, G. A. and S. Verba, *The Civic Culture*, Princenton, NJ: Princeton University Press, 1963
Anderson, Lisa (Issue Editor), A Special Issue in Memory of Dankwart A. Rustow, *Comparative Politics*, 1997, vol. 29, no. 3
Anderson, L., 'Transitions to Democracy: A Special Issue in Memory of Dankwart A. Rustow – Introduction', *Comparative Politics*, 1997, vol. 29, no. 346
Andrain, Charles F. and David E. Apter, *Political Protest and Social Change*, Basingstoke: Macmillan, 1995
Axelrod, Robert, *The Evolution of Co-operation*, London: Penguin Books, 1984
Barany, Zoltan and Louisa Vinton, 'Breakthrough to Democracy: Elections in Poland and Hungary', *Studies in Comparative Communism*, 1990, vol. 23, no. 2
Barth, Frederik (ed.), *The Role of the Entrepreneur in Social Change in Northern Norway*, Bergen: Universitet i Bergen, 1963
Bates, Robert H., *Beyond the Miracle of the Market: The Political Economy of Agrarian Development in Rural Kenya*, Cambridge: Cambridge University Press, 1989
Bates, Robert H., Weingast, Barry and Rui de Figueiredo, 'The Politics of Interpretation: Rationality, Culture and Transition', *Politics and Society*, 1998, vol. 26, no. 4, 603–42
Bates, R. H., A. Grief, M. Levi, J. Rosenthal and B. R. Weingast *Analytic Narratives*, Princeton, NJ: Princeton University Press, 1998
Baylis, Thomas, 'Plus Ca Change? Transformation and Continuity Among East European Elites', *Communist and Post-Communist Studies*, 1994, vol. 27. no. 3, 315–28
Benoit, Kenneth, 'Models of Electoral System Change,' Trinity College manuscript, 22 February 2002
Benoit, Kenneth and Jacqueline Hayden, 'Institutional Change and Persistence: The Origins and Evolution of Polland's Electoral System 1989–2001', *The Journal of Politics*, 2004, vol. 66, no. 2, 396–427
Benoit, Kenneth and John W. Schiemann, 'Institutional Choice in New Democracies: Bargaining over Hungary's 1989 Electoral Law', *Journal of Theoretical Politics*, 2001, vol. 13, no. 2, 159–88
Brams, S. J., *Negotiation Games: Applying Game Theory to Bargaining and Arbitration*, New York: Routledge, 1990
Brams, Steven J., *Theory of Moves*, Cambridge: Cambridge University Press, 1994
Bryant, G. A. and Edmund Mokrzycki, *The New Great Transformation? Change and Continuity in East Central Europe*, London: Routledge, 1994

Brzeziński, Zbigniew, *The Grand Failure: The Birth and Death of Communism in the Twentieth Century*, New York: Charles Scribner's Sons, 1989

Burawoy, M., 'Reflections on the Class-Consciousness of Hungarian Steelworkers', *Politics and Society*, 1989, vol. 17, no. 1

Chong, Denis, *Collective Action and the Civil Rights Movement*, Chicago, IL and London: The University of Chicago Press, 1991

Chruściak, Ryszard, *System Wyborczy i Wybory w Polsce 1989–1998*, Warsaw: ELIPSA, 1999

Colomer, Josep M., 'Transitions By Agreement: Modelling the Spanish Way', *American Political Science Review*, 1991, vol. 85, no. 4, 1283–302

——*Game Theory and the Transition to Democracy: The Spanish Model*, Aldershot: Edward Elgar, 1995

—— 'Strategies and Outcomes in Eastern Europe', *Journal of Democracy*, 1995, vol. 6, no. 2, 74–85

——*Strategic Transitions: Game Theory and Democratization*, Baltimore, MD and London: The Johns Hopkins University Press, 2000

Colomer, Josep M. and Margot Pascual, 'The Polish Game of Transition', *Communist and Post-Communist Studies*, 1994, vol. 27, no. 3, 275–94

Cosmides, Lea and John Tooby, 'Better Than Rational: Evolutionary Psychology and the Invisible Hand', *American Economic Review*, 1994, vol. 84, 327–34

Cox, Terry and Andy Furlong (eds), *Hungary: The Politics of Transition*, London: Frank Cass, 1995

Davies, Norman, *God's Playground: A History of Poland, Volume II 1795 to the Present*, Oxford: Clarendon Press, 1981

Dawisha, Karen and Bruce Parrott (eds), *The Consolidation of Democracy in East Central Europe*, Cambridge: Cambridge University Press, 1997

——*Democratic Change and Authoritarian Reactions in Russia, Ukraine, Belarus and Moldova*, Cambridge: Cambridge University Press, 1997

DiPalma, G., *To Craft Democracies: An Essay on Democratic Transitions*, Berkeley, CA: University of California Press, 1990

Dubiński, Krzysztof, *Magdalenka: Tranzakcja epoki. Notatki z poufnych spotkań Kiszczak – Wałęsa*, Warsaw: Sylwa, 1990

——*Okrągły Stół*, Warsaw: KAP, 1999

Edvardsen, Unni, 'A Cultural Approach to Understanding Modes of Transition to Democracy', *Journal of Theoretical Politics*, 1997, vol. 9, no. 1, 211–34

Ekiert, Grzegorz, *The State Against Society: Political Crises and Their Aftermath in East Central Europe*, Princeton, NJ: Princeton University Press, 1996

Elster, Jon, 'Constitution-Making in Eastern Europe: Rebuilding the Boat in the Open Sea', *Public Administration*, 1993, vol. 71, 169–217

——*The Roundtable Talks and the Breakdown of Communism*, Chicago, IL and London: The University of Chicago Press, 1996

Finkel, Steven E. and Edward N. Muller, 'Rational Choice and the Dynamics of Political Action: Evaluating Alternative Models with Panel Data', *American Political Science Review*, 1998, vol. 92, no. 1, 37–50

Finkel, Steven N. and Edward N. Muller, 'Personal Influence, Collective Rationality, and Mass Political Action', *American Political Science Review*, 1989, vol. 83, no. 3, 885–903

Friedman, Jeffrey (ed.), *The Rational Choice Controversy*, New Haven, CT and London: Yale University Press, 1996

Garton Ash, Timothy, *The Polish Revolution*, London: Jonathan Cape, 1983

Gebethner, S., 'Political Reform in the Process of Round Table Negotiations', in G. Sanford (ed.), *Democratization in Poland, 1989–90: Polish Voices*, New York: St Martin's Press, 1992, p. 60

Gebethner, Stanisław, 'Free Elections and Political Parties in Transition to Democracy in Central and Southeastern Europe', *International Political Science Review*, 1997, vol. 18, no. 4, 381–99

Geddes, Barbara, 'A Game Theoretic Model of Reform in Latin American Democracies', *American Political Science Review*, 1991, vol. 85, no. 2, 371–92

Geremek, Bronisław and Jacek Żakowski, *Geremek Opowiada Żakowski Pyta Rok 1989*, Warsaw: Plejada, 1990

Goldstone, Jack A., 'Theories of Revolution and the Revolution of 1989 in USSR and Eastern Europe: The Past and the Future', in Alexander J. Groth (ed.), *Revolution and Political Change*, Aldershot: Dartmouth, 1993

——'Is Revolution Individually Rational? Groups and Individuals in Revolutionary Collective Action', *Rationality and Society*, 1994, vol. 6, 139–66

Gorbachev, Mikhail and Zdeněk Mlyná, *Conversations with Gorbachev*, New York: Columbia University Press, 2002

Gray, John, 'From Post-Communism to Civil Society', *Social Philosophy and Policy*, 1993, vol. 10, no. 2, 25–50

Green, Donald P. and Ian Shapiro, *Pathologies of Rational Choice Theory*, New Haven, CT and London: Yale University Press, 1994

Groth, Alexander J. (ed.), *Revolution and Political Change*, Aldershot: Dartmouth, 1997

Haggard S. and R. R. Kaufman, 'The Political Economy of Democratic Transitions', in L. Anderson (ed.), *Transitions to Democracy*, New York: Columbia University Press, 1999, p. 74

Hankiss, Elemér, *East European Alternatives: Are There Any?* Oxford: Clarendon Press, 1990

Hardin, Russell, 'Economic Theories of the State', in Denis C. Mueller (ed.), *Perspectives on Public Choice: A Handbook*, Cambridge: Cambridge University Press, 1997

Hayden, Jacqueline, *Poles Apart: Solidarity and the New Poland*, Dublin: Irish Academic Press, 1994

Heyns, Barbara and Ireneusz Białecki, 'Solidarność: Reluctant Vanguard or Makeshift Coalition?', *American Political Science Review*, 1991, vol. 85, no. 2, 351–70

Higley, John, 'The Persistence of Post-Communist Elites', *The Journal of Democracy*, 1996, vol. 7, no. 2

Higley, J. and Gunther, R. (eds), *Elites and Democratic Consolidation in Latin America and Southern Europe*, New York: Cambridge University Press, 1992

Higley, John, Jan Pakulski and Włodzimierz Wesołowski, *Postcommunist Elites and Democracy in Eastern Europe*, Basingstoke: Macmillan, 1998

Huntington, S. P., *The Third Wave: Democratization in the Late Twentieth Century*, Norman and London: The University of Oklahoma Press, 1991

Jaruzelski, W., *To Differ Wisely. How Did Marshal Law Come About?* Warsaw: Książka i Wiedza, 1999

Jones, Lynn, *States of Change: A Central European Diary*, London: The Merlin Press, 1990

Kamiński Bartłomiej, 'Systemic Underpinnings of the Transition in Poland: The Shadow of the Round Table Agreement', *Studies in Comparative Communism*, 1991, vol. 24, no. 2, 173–90

Kamiński, Marek, 'How Communism Could Have Been Saved: Formal Analysis of Electoral Bargaining in Poland in 1989', *Public Choice*, 1998, vol. 98, 83–109

Karl, T. L., 'Dilemmas of Democratization in Latin America', *Comparative Politics*, 1990, vol. 23, no. 1, 1–22

Kaufman, Michael T., *Mad Dreams, Saving Graces. Poland: A Nation in Conspiracy*, New York: Random House, 1989

King, G., K. O. Keohane and S. Verba, *Designing Social Inquiry: Scientific Inference in Qualitative Research*, Princeton, NJ: Princeton University Press, 1994

Kiszczak, Czesław, *Kiszczak mówi i prawie wszystko*, Warsaw: BGW, 1991

Konrad, George and Ivan Szelenyi, *The Intellectuals on the Road to Class Power*, Brighton: Harvester Press, 1979

Korboński, Andrzej, 'The Politics of Economic Reform in Eastern Europe: The Last Thirty Years', *Soviet Studies*, 1989, vol. XLI, no. 1, 1–19

Kubik, Jan and Grzegorz Ekiert, 'Civil Society and Democratization in Poland. Forms of Organization and Types of Foreign Assistance', draft of paper delivered at 'Democratic Consolidation: The International Dimension, Hungary, Poland, Spain' in Vienna 25–26 September 1998

Kuran, Timur, 'Sparks and Prairie Fires: A Theory of Unanticipated Political Revolution', *Public Choice*, 1989, vol. 61, 41–74

Kurski, Jarosław, *Lech Wałęsa: Democrat or Dictator*, Boulder, CO, San Francisco, CA, Oxford: Westview, 1993

Kwiatowski, Piotr, 'Opinion Research and the Fall of Communism: Poland 1981–1990', *International Journal of Public Opinion Research*, 1992, vol. 4, no. 4, 358–74

Lane, David, *The Rise and Fall of State Socialism*, Cambridge, MA: Polity Press, 1996

Laver, Michael, *Private Desires, Political Actions: An Invitation to the Politics of Rational Choice*, London: Sage, 1997

Lewis, Paul, 'Non-Competitive Elections and Regime Change: Poland 1989', *Parliamentary Affairs*, 1990, vol. 43, no. 1, 90–107

Lijphart, Arend, 'Democratization and Constituional Choices in Czecho-Slovakia, Hungary and Poland, 1989–91', *Journal of Theoretical Politics*, 1992, vol. 4, no. 2, 207–33

Linz, Juan J. and A. Stepan (eds), *The Breakdown of Democratic Regimes*, Baltimore, MD: The Johns Hopkins University Press, 1978

Linz, Juan J. and Alfred Stepan, *Problems of Democratic Transition and Consolidation: Southern Europe, South America and Post-Communist Eastern Europe*, Baltimore, MD and London: The Johns Hopkins University Press, 1996

Lipset, S. M., *Political Man*, London: Heineman, 1959

Lutyńska, Krystyna, 'Questionaire Studies in Poland in the 1980s (Analysis of Refusals to Give an Interview)', *The Polish Sociological Bulletin*, 1987, vol. 3, 14–24

McAdam, Doug, John D. McCarthy and Mayer N. Zald (eds), *Comparative Perspectives on Social Movements: Political Opportunities, Mobilizing Structures and Cultural Framing*, Cambridge: Cambridge University Press, 1996

McGregor, James P., 'Economic Reform and Polish Public Opinion', *Soviet Studies*, 1989, vol. XLI, no. 2, 215–27

McShane, Denis, *Solidarity: Poland's Independent Trade Union*, London: Spokesman, 1981

Margolis, Howard, *Selfishness, Altruism and Rationality: A Theory of Social Choice*, Cambridge: Cambridge University Press, 1982

Meuschel, S., *Revolution in the GDR*, Washington: University of Washington mimeo, 1991

Michnik, Adam, *Letters from Prison and Other Essays*, Berkeley, CA and Los Angeles, CA: University of California Press, 1987

——*The Church and the Left*, Chicago, IL and London: The University of Chicago Press, 1993

Millard, Frances, *The Anatomy of the New Poland: Post-Communist Politics in its First Phase*, Aldershot: Edward Elgar, 1994

Miłosz, Czesław, *The Captive Mind*, London: Penguin Books, 1981

Misztal, Bronisław and J. Craig Jenkins, 'Starting from Scratch is not always the Same: The Politics of Protest and Postcommunist Transitions in Poland and Hungary', in *Comparative Perspectives on States and Social Movements*, London: UCL Press, 1995

Moore, Barrington, *Social Origins of Dictatorship and Democracy*, London: Penguin Books, 1966

North, Douglass C., *Institutions, Institutional Change and Economic Performance*, Cambridge: Cambridge University Press, 1990

Oberschall, Anthony, 'Opportunities and Framing in the Eastern European Revolts of 1989', in Doug McAdam, John D. McCarthy and Mayer N. Zald (eds), *Comparative Perspectives on Social Movements: Political Opportunities, Mobilizing Structures, and Cultural Framings*, Cambridge: Cambridge University, 1996

O'Donnell, Guillermo, Philippe C. Schmitter and Laurence Whitehead (eds), *Transitions from Authoritarian Rule*, Baltimore, MD: The Johns Hopkins University Press, 1986

Olson, David M., 'Compartmentalized Competition: The Managed Transitional Election System of Poland', *The Journal of Politics*, 1993, vol. 55, no. 2, 415–41

Olson, Mancur, *The Logic of Collective Action*, Cambridge, MA: Harvard University Press, 1971

Osiatyński, W., 'The Roundtable Talks in Poland', in J. Elster (ed.), *The Roundtable Talks and the Breakdown of Communism*, Chicago: The University of Chicago Press, 1996

Ost, David, *Solidarity and the Politics of Anti-Politics*, Philadelphia, PA: Temple UP, 1990

——'A Behavioural Approach to the Rational Choice Theory of Collective Action', *American Political Science Review*, 1998, vol. 92, no. 1, 1–22

Ostrom, Elinor, *Governing the Commons: The Evolution of Institutions for Collective Action*, Cambridge: Cambridge University Press, 1990

Ostrom, Elinor and James Walker, 'Neither Markets nor Sates: Linking Transformation Processes in Collective Action Arenas', in Dennis C. Mueller (ed.), *Perspectives on Public Choice: A Handbook*, Cambridge: Cambridge University Press, 1997

Pełczyński, Zbigniew and Sergiusz Kowalski, Poland, *Electoral Studies*, 1990, vol. 9, no. 4, 346–54

Perzkowski, Stanisław, *Tajne Dokumenty Biura Politycznego I Sekretariatu KC: Ostatni rok władzy 1988–1989*, London: Aneks, 1994

——'Political Entrepreneurs and Peasant Movements in Vietnam', in Michael Taylor (ed.), *Rationality and Revolution*, Cambridge: Cambridge University Press, 1988

Popkin, Samuel L., *The Rational Peasant: The Political Economy of Rural Society in Vietnam*, Berkeley, CA: University of California Press, 1979

Porozumienia Okrągłego Stołu, Official Record of the Polish Round Table

Poznański, Kazimierz, 'An Interpretation of Communist Decay: The Role of Evolutionary Mechanisms', *Communist and Post-Communist Studies*, 1993, vol. 26, 3–24

Pridham, Geoffrey (ed.), *Transitions to Democracy: Comparative Perspectives from Southern Europe, Latin America and Eastern Europe*, Aldershot: Dartmouth, 1995

Przeworski, Adam, *Democracy and the Market*, Cambridge: Cambridge University Press, 1991

——(ed.), *Sustainable Democracy*, Cambridge: Cambridge University Press, 1995

Radio Free Europe, Polish Situation Report/14, 2 September 1988; SR/1, 11 January 1989; SR/2, 20 January 1989; SR/3, 6 February 1989; SR/5, 23 March 1989; SR/6 7 April 1989; SR/8, 19 May 1989; SR/9, 2 June 1989; SR/10, 16 June 1989; SR/11, 6 July 1989

Raina, Peter, *Droga do'Okrągłego Stołu': Zakulisowe rozmowy przygotowawcze*, Warsaw: EFEKT, 1999

Rakowski, Mieczysław, *Lata, listy, ludzie*, Warsaw: BGW, 1993

Rapaczyński, Andrzej, 'Constitutional Politics in Poland: A Report on the Constitutional Committee of the Polish Parliament', *University of Chicago Law Review*, 1991, vol. 58, 595–631

Rostowski, Jacek, 'The Decay of Socialism and the Growth of Private Enterprise in Poland', *Soviet Studies*, 1989, vol. XLI, no. 2, 194–214

Ruane, Kevin, *The Polish Challenge*, London: BBC, 1982

Rustow, Dankwart, 'Transitions to Democracy: Toward a Dynamic Model', *Comparative Politics*, 1970, vol. 2, 337–63

Rychard, A., 'Politics and Society after the Breakthrough: The Sources and Threats to Political Legitimacy in Post-Communist Poland', in G. Sanford (ed.), *Democratization in Poland, 1989–90: Polish Voices*, New York: St Martin's Press, 1992

Sabat-Świdlicka, Anna, *Poland: Towards the Rule of Law*, Radio Free Europe, RFL/RL Research Report, 1992, vol. 1, no. 27, 25–33

Sanford, George, *Democratization in Poland 1988–90. Polish Voices*, Basingstoke: Macmillan, 1992

Shepsle, Kenneth, 'Studying Institutions: Some Lessons from the Rational Choice Approach', *Journal of Theoretical Politics*, 1989, vol. 1, no. 2, 131–47

Silver, Morris, 'Political Revolution and Repression: An Economic Approach', *Public Choice*, 1974, vol. 17, 63–71

Singer, Daniel, *The Road to Gdansk: Poland and the USSR*, New York and London: Monthly Review Press, 1981

Skocpol, T., *States and Revolutions: A Comparative Analysis of France, Russia, and China*, Cambridge: Cambridge University Press, 1979

Skocpol, Theda, *Social Revolutions in the Modern World*, Cambridge: Cambridge University Press, 1994

Skyrms, Brian, 'The Dynamics of a Breakthrough in the Socialist System: An Outline of Problems', *Soviet Studies*, 1989, vol. XLI, no. 4, 560–73

——*Evolution of the Social Contract*, Cambridge: Cambridge University Press, 1996

Staniszkis, Jadwiga, *Poland's Self-Limiting Revolution*, Princeton, NJ: Princeton University Press, 1984

Sulek, Antoni, 'Systemic Transformation and the Reliability of Survey Research: Evidence from Poland', *Polish Sociological Review*, 1994, vol. 2, 85–100

Szalai, Erzsebet, 'Political and Social Conflicts Arising from the Transformation of Property Relations in Hungary', *The Journal of Communist Studies and Transition Politics*, 1994, vol. 10, no. 3, 56–77

Szelenyi, Ivan, *Socialist Entrepreneurs*, Wisconsin: University of Wisconsin Press, 1988

Szelenyi, Ivan, E. Wnuk-Lipinski and D. Trelman, Special Issue on Circulation v. Reproduction of Elites during the Postcommunist Transformation of Eastern Europe, *Theory and Society*, 1995, vol. 24, no. 5

Sztompka, Piotr, 'The Intangibles and Imponderables of the Transition to Democracy', *Studies in Comparative Communism*, 1991, vol. XXIV, 295–311

——*The Sociology of Social Change*, Oxford and Cambridge, MA: Blackwell, 1993

Taylor, Michael, *Anarchy and Cooperation*, New York: Wiley, 1976

——*The Possibility of Cooperation*, Cambridge: Cambridge Univeristy Press, 1987

——(ed.), *Rationality and Revolution*, Cambridge: Cambridge University Press, 1988

Tismaneanu, V., 'Reinvention of Politics: Eastern Europe after Communism'. Talk given at University of Washington, 12 November 1990

Tokes, Rudolf L., *Hungary's Negotiated Revolution: Economic Reform, Social Change and Political Succession*, Cambridge: Cambridge University Press, 1996

Torańska, Teresa, *Oni: Stalin's Polish Puppets*, London: Collins-Harvill, 1987

Tsebelis, George, *Nested Games: Rational Choice in Comparative Politics*, Berkeley, CA and Los Angeles, CA: University of California Press, 1990

Tullock, Gordon, 'The Paradox of Revolution', *Public Choice*, 1971, vol. XI, 89–99

Vanhanen, Tatu, *Prospects of Democracy: A Study of 172 Countries*, London and New York: Routledge, 1997

Vinton, L., 'Intricate Election Mechanisms, Simple Choices', *Radio Free Europe RFL/RL*, 2 June 1989, vol. 9, item 2

Wałęsa, Lech, *A Path of Hope: An Autobiography of Lech Wałęsa*, London: Pan Books, 1987

'Wałęsa's Leadership and Poland's Transition', *Problems of Communism*, 1991, vol. XL (January–April), 69–83

Weschler, Lawrence, *The Passion of Poland*, New York: Pantheon Books, 1982

Weydenthal, Jan B. de, *Politics in Poland after the Round-Table Agreement, Radio Free Europe*, RAD Background Report/67, 26 April 1989

Yeltsin, Boris, *Against the Grain*, New York: Summit, 1990

Zieliński, Jakub, 'The Polish Transition to Democracy: a Game-Theoretic Approach', *Archive European de Sociologie*, 1995, vol. 36, 135–58

Zubek, Voytek, 'The Threshold of Poland's Transition: 1989 Electoral Campaign as the Last Act of a United Solidarity', *Studies in Comparative Communism*, 1991, vol. 24, no. 4, 355–76

Index